DICTIONARY OF COMPUTER TERMS

A
Sunrise Financial Series
Book

Charles E. Puffenbarger

Sunrise
Publishers, Inc.
Murfreesboro, TN

Copyright © 1993 by Charles E. Puffenbarger
All rights reserved.
No part of this book may be reproduced in any form, or incorporated into any information retrieval system without the written permission of the publisher.

Address inquiries to:
Sunrise Publishers, Inc.
1807 Florence Rd.
Murfreesboro, TN 37129

ISBN 1-882912-00-4

Printed and bound in the United States of America

M 9 8 7 6 5 4 3 2 1

CONTENTS

Introduction 5

Terms 7

Symbols 288

Abbreviations 293

INTRODUCTION

Computers are very much a part of our lives, and most of us deal with them on a day-to-day basis. Yet for anyone who is not a technician, computer terminology and the vocabulary that has evolved from computer usage can often be confusing. This dictionary is designed for the average, non-technical computer user as well as the beginner who needs a quick and handy reference guide to computer terminology. Whether you're checking the meaning of instructions and advertisements, or utilizing new computer-oriented words in a business environment, the <u>Dictionary of Computer Terms</u> will help you understand and communicate more effectively in the remarkable world of computers.

A

A: Identifier used to specify the first or primary floppy disk drive that the system checks for a boot disk upon bootup.

Abend An abnormal ending of a computer program due to a program or system error. Used more widely in the mainframe environment than with microcomputers.

ABIOS Acronym for Advanced Basic Input/Output System—routines built into microcomputers that use Micro Channel Architecture. Stated routines allow for multitasking and running a computer in a protected mode, which means to reserve a part of memory for a particular program so that no other computer programs can interfere with its operation by trying to access the same memory allocations.

Abort Ability to cancel or terminate a program, command, or software procedure while it is in progress.

Absolute Address Designation of a certain portion of memory by using the actual system address location of the memory. Also known as **direct address**.

Absolute Coding Ability to access a portion of memory by using the direct address location or the absolute address.

Absolute Coordinates Placements defined in reference to their distance from an intersection of axes that run in right angles to each other. An absolute coordinate may be used in computer graphs and graphics to determine locations of points on charts or a grids.

Absolute Pointing Device Pointing device whose location is equal to a similar location on the computer screen. If a graphics tablet pointing device is placed in the lower left corner of the tablet, then the cursor will take the same location on the computer screen.

Absolute Value Magnitude of a number without recognition of whether it is a positive or a negative number. The number 5 and the number -5 both have an absolute value of 5.

Accelerator Card Circuit board card that replaces the main microprocessor or enhances it to enable more speed in processing. With an accelerator card, a user can upgrade to a faster system without having to replace most of the equipment.

Acceptance Test

Acceptance Test Test performed by the user that checks a device for its proper function as specified by the manufacturer.

Access Code A special coded password or identification name or number used to obtain access to a computer system.

Access Arm Arm of a disk drive to which the drive heads are attached that moves the read-write heads over the surface of a disk.

Access Code Special formation of letters or numbers that make up a code or password needed for a user to access either a network or a BBS. Each user has a unique code; the code identifies them with the system they are attempting to gain access to. Users can thus be monitored by the personal accounts set up for them on a system. If misuse of a system is detected, this code will identify the person responsible so necessary action can be taken to remedy the situation.

Access Mechanism Disk drive parts that move and position the read-write heads over the tracks on a disk. Also used to describe a part of the computer that allows one part of the computer to be able to send signals to another part of the computer.

Access Number Telephone number that allows a user to gain access to another system through telephone lines and a modem or direct link.

Accessory Any peripheral or add-on device for a computer that is not part of the original system, such as a mouse or modem. These are extras and are not needed for the operation of the system.

Access Path The path that the system follows when seeking a particular file. The access path must define the location of the file from the root of the drive through the proper directories leading to the actual file. An access path must be defined in the autoexec.bat file to point to the most-used directories; this allows the user to be able to access and run a program from any location on a disk.

Access Time The amount of time required from the instant the computer asks for data until the data is transferred to the computer for processing.

Account An arrangement by a on-line service through which the user establishs an understanding and agreement with the service to have access to the service and be billed by the service for the use.

Account

Some systems have user accounts without a billing process just to keep a record of the users and their activities on the system. A user account is a privilege that allows the person to have access to another computer for his or her benefit, such as communicating with other users or accessing files for download, or for entertainment, such as playing on-line games.

Accuracy The degree of correct information in data recording. Refers to the degree of correctness of a result.

ACK Short for acknowledgment, which is used widely in communication programs to send acknowledgment of system readiness or the error-free reception of data.

Acoustic Coupler Communication device that enables a telephone receiver handset to be placed into rubber acoustical cups to communicate through the phone lines by transmitting signals through the receiver to the other computer. This was the earliest type of transmission method, which has been replaced by the direct phone-line connection modem.

Active Program that is currently being used in a window or on the system that is ready for processing.

Active Cell The cell that is currently selected for receiving data in a spreadsheet program.

Active File The file that is currently open and being used by a program.

Activity Light A small yellow, red, or green light on the front of the computer face panel that lights during disk drive writing or reading.

Active Program The program currently running that has control of the microprocessor in the computer.

Active Window The window currently in use on a Macintosh or on an IBM with Microsoft.

Activity Ratio In database program, the number of records actually being used in relation to the total number of records contained in the database file.

Actuator A portion of the disk drive that causes movement of the read-write heads over the surface of a disk to the track location on which the information being accessed is found. There are two type of

Actuator

actuators. One is the stepper motor, which works with small incrementing rotating movements that translate to linear motion to position the heads correctly over the desired location of the disk. The other type is the much faster voice coil, in which a magnetic coil either pulls the spring-mounted heads from the outer edge of a disk toward the center for locating data, or releases the heads back toward the edge.

Adapter Circuit board plugged into a computer's expansion bus slot that gives the computer extra capabilities, such as a video card adapter.

Adder Unit within the central processing unit that gives a sum of two numbers. Also refers to any circuit that can add binary numbers.

Add-on An added device, such as an external hard drive or an expansion card, that enhances or increases system capabilities.

Address Each section of the computer memory has a specific address designation that allows the computer to locate specific information when needed.

Addressable Cursor A cursor with the ability to move to any location on the computer screen instead of being limited to sequential positions on the same line or on successive lines of a display. Because of its freedom of movement, most software programs use an addressable cursor.

Address Bus The hardware pathway that handles signals that designate locations in the computer memory. This allows the processor to select a memory location for transferring data by way of the data bus.

Addressing Process of assigning or making reference to an address location in memory.

Address Mode A defined method that an instruction uses to designate a memory address.

ADP Acronym for Automatic Data Processing.

Alarm An audible sound made by the computer to signal that an error has occurred or that a critical condition has arisen that needs attention.

Alert

Alert An audible or visual alarm sent by the system to signify that an error has occurred or that the system is giving a warning of some type.

Alert Box In many graphics-based programs, this box displays a warning of some type and usually requires operator intervention before processing can continue.

Algorithm A special set of simple mathematical and logical procedures used to solve a problem in a finite number of steps.

Aliasing The effect of stair-stepping—the jagged, irregular appearance of diagonal lines in computer graphic images.

Align To place the paper so that the margins and paper start line are in the appropriate position to start the print job.

Allocate To reserve memory to be used by a program. Programs require a designated amount of memory to operate and this memory is usually allocated by the program for the program to run efficiently.

Alphabetic Anything having to do with the use of the letters of the alphabet.

Alphanumeric Use of both alphabetic and numeric characters, and sometimes including control characters, spaces, and other special characters.

Alternate Key Any key in a program that is not the primary key. An alternate key may be designated to perform the same or similar function of a different key.

Alt Key A special-effect key used in conjunction with another key. Holding down the Alt key while pressing an associate key enables a special function in the software to be performed.

Ampere Unit of measurement for electric current, which is the amount of an electrical charge that flows through a conductor.

Amplitude Refers either to peaks and troughs in waveforms, such as a sound waveform, or to the size and the strength of an electrical signal.

Analog Electronic device that represents values by a continuously varying physical property; for example, the voltage of an electrical circuit.

Analog Computer

Analog Computer Computer designed to process continuously variable data rather than processing digital coded information such as binary numbers. Used mainly for scientific or industrial applications.

Analytical Graphics Charts and graphs that aid in a professional presentation of data.

Anchored Graphics A fixed graphic or picture in a locked in position on a page allowing text to flow around it.

Animation Representation of movement through a series of successive images displayed in rapid motion.

Annotation Note of explanation or a comment placed in a document that provides additional information for the reader. Some high-end programs allow the user to place annotations in a document electronically.

ANSI Acronym for American National Standards Institute, an organization devoted to development of voluntary standards to enhance productivity and international competition of American industrial enterprises.

ANSI Graphics Terminal control codes combined with IBM PC special character set; used on BBSs (Bulletin Board Systems).

ANSI.SYS Device driver in DOS and OS/2 that contains instructions to display information using the recommendations of the American National Standards Institute and allows ANSI colors and characters to be displayed to the monitor. A line must be included in the Config.sys file to load this driver upon boot up of the computer; for example, DEVICE=ANSI.SYS.

Answer Mode Setting at which a modem is ready to answer incoming calls.

Answer-Only Mode Setting at which a system is only able to answer incoming calls and is unable to place any outgoing calls.

Antialiasing An automatic means of removing or reducing the stair-step effect of diagonal lines in computer graphic images.

Anti-Static Devices Devices used to prevent the discharge of static electricity onto computer components. There are several types of these devices, such as wrist straps, floormats, sprays, and lotions.

Anti-Static Mat A special pad or mat placed near or under the computer to absorb static electricity. This static removal is vital to the life span of the semiconductor devices if they are not properly grounded.

Append To add to a file such as a data file. New records are added following the last previous record, becoming part of the original master file.

Application Developer Someone who does research and designs and specifies the appearance and function of an application program. This person may also do the programming, but in most cases the programming is done by a second party.

Application Development Language Computer language used in the writing of application programs.

Application Generator Program used for the design and layout of an application so that once the creation is finished, the software will automatically generate the program application necessary to carry out the task.

Application Program Program that performs specific useful work not directly related to the computer itself, such as spreadsheets, word processors, and graphics-developing programs.

Arcade Game Coin-operated computer game with high-quality graphics and sounds and smooth, fluid motion, controlled by one or more players. Some computer-oriented games are of arcade-game quality.

Architecture Main overall design in which each individual hardware component of the computer system is interrelated. The most common uses of this term are 8-bit, 16-bit, or 32-bit architectural design systems.

Archival Storage Refers to the storing of data that is seldom used but needs to be kept for a long time, such as backups of the system drives. The most popular means of archival storage are floppy disks and magnetic tape drives.

Archive A means to file information that needs to be kept for a long time. An archive file can be a compressed file containing several other files that can be uncompressed for use at a later date. This compression of archived files allows more information to be stored on a given disk.

Archive Attribute

Archive Attribute A hidden code in DOS and OS/2 stored along with the file's directory entry, indicating whether the file has been changed since the last backup of the file. This attribute code may be used when backing up just the files that have been changed since the previous backup.

Area Search A search done over a wide span of information seeking out a particular piece of data designated by the user.

Argument Refers to a value or expression that is used with an operator or is passed to a subroutine program procedure. The program being run can then use the argument to perform operations.

Arithmetic Logic Unit Circuitry used to perform arithmetic and the comparative and logical functions. This circuit is built into the microprocessor in the computer system.

Arithmetic Operator Symbol designating to a program what specific arithmetic operation to perform, such as addition, subtraction, multiplication, or division, represented by the following symbols: addition, (+) plus sign; subtraction, (-)minus sign; multiplication, (*) asterisk; division, (/) forward slash.

Array Listing of data values that are all of the same type.

Arrow Keys Found on most computer keyboards and used to move the cursor up, down, left, and right on the screen. The use and effect of the keys are determined by the software employed. Some software cannot recognize the arrow keys, and using them with improper software could be disastrous and cause a system lockup.

Artificial Intelligence A field of science that has attempted to improve computers by trying to incorporate characteristics of human intelligence, such as the ability to understand natural language and to perform reasoning under certain conditions of uncertainty.

Ascending Order Sorting items in order from smallest to largest or from first position to last. This order of sorting is the default method used by most sorting programs.

ASCII Acronym for American Standard Code for Information Interchange, a standard set of characters devised in 1968 to enable efficient data exchange and compatibility among different computer devices and peripherals.

ASCII Character Set

ASCII Character Set Set of characters composed of only those characters included in the original 128-character ASCII standard.

ASCII File File containing only characters from the ASCII character set.

Aspect Ratio In computer graphics, the ratio of the horizontal dimension to the vertical dimension of an image. Maintaining the height-to-width ratio is a very important factor in avoiding distortions.

Assembly Language Programming language in which each line of code corresponds directly with a single system instruction or command. This type of programming gives the programmer precise control over the computer system.

Asterisk (*) Character used in most computer software applications to signify multiplication. Also used as a wildcard character that represents one or more other characters. The command *.* would refer to all files in a given area.

Asynchronous Device Device that is not synchronized in internal operations with any other part of the computer system.

AT Acronym for Advanced Technology, a class of computers introduced in 1984 that used the 80286 microprocessor and a 16-bit bus. Most IBM PCs from the 286 up are referred to as AT-class machines.

AT Bus Electronic pathway used by an IBM AT and a similar compatible computer to connect add-on cards with the motherboard. The AT bus supports 16 bits of data transmission, while the older IBM PC only supported 8-bit data structure. The 16-bit structure allows for the moving of twice as much data in the same amount of time. The newer high-end 386 and 486 machines now support a 32-bit path, which increases the data speed by double again.

Attached Processor Second processor that can be added to a computer system. Some of the newer 486 systems have the ability to accept a second processor that will double the speed of the system by letting each processor perform different tasks instead of one processor performing all the tasks.

ATTRIB External DOS command to set, display, or clear a file read-only attribute or its archive attribute.

Audio

Audio Any sound or noise heard by the human ear.

Audio Output Connection through which the computer can send audio signals to an outside source. Sound cards that have become popular recently have a audio output in which to connect a set of speakers to take the place of the internal computer speaker.

Authorization Special permission given to access a computer system. Most systems require a special access code as well as a password to ensure only authorized use of the system.

Authorization Code Special code or password that allows access to a restricted area.

Auto Answer Modem able to answer incoming calls automatically without operator intervention.

Autocad Popular CAD program (computer-aided drawing, widely used by designers and architects) produced by Autodesk, Inc., of Sausalito, California.

Auto Dial Ability of a modem to access phone lines and start a call by sending a telephone number as a series of pulses and tones.

Autoexec.bat One of the startup files on a DOS system that contains commands that are executed when the computer boots up. This is a normal batch file with the exception that DOS looks for this particular file upon bootup, and upon finding it, will run it automatically.

Automated Office Office environment making full use of computers and other electronic devices.

Automatic Backup Special application feature that saves a document to disk automatically at a user-designated period of time (such as every two or three minutes) to prevent the loss of data already typed if the system loses power or locks up.

Automatic Error Correction Feature that checks for errors in processing or data transmission; when it detects a problem it will either try to correct it or have the information sent over again.

Automatic Font Downloading Automatic transmission of printer fonts located on a disk to the printer as the fonts are needed by the application program for the print job.

Automation

Automation Using machines to do work that was once done manually by people. Automation is usually speedier and more reliable.

Auto Repeat Key Key that enables automatic repetition when it is held in the depressed position.

Autosave Feature incorporated in many programs that when activated will automatically save the job in progress at designated intervals while work continues.

Autostart Routine Instructions stored in ROM (read-only memory) that tell the computer the necessary procedures to perform when the system is turned on.

Autotrace Process that traces lines along the edges of a bitmapped image to convert it to an object-oriented image.

AUX Abbreviation for an auxiliary device. Most commonly this refers to the system's first serial port, also known as COM1.

Auxiliary Storage Sstorage device such as a tape or disk not directly accessible by the microprocessor. This type of media today refers to either storage or permanent storage and also to the RAM chips in the system that can be used for temporary storage as memory.

B Abbreviation for **byte**.

B: Identifier referring to the second floppy-disk drive on a system.

Back Up Procedure used to make an exact duplicate copy of original data files and program files onto either floppy disks or other portable media to be stored in a safe location.

Background Capacity of computers to do more than one task at a time. The background area is for the low-priority jobs such as downloading files or doing a print job, which are run unseen in the background while the operator is working on another project in the foreground. Also known as **multitasking**.

Background Noise Noise occurring sometimes during communications that does not pertain to data transmission. Most times this causes unintelligible graphical characters to display on the screen.

Back Panel Panel at the back of a computer where most connections for external cables are located.

Background Processing Capacity to run certain programs at the same time as another program that has priority to the system; when a break period develops in the main running program, such as waiting for key input, the background program resumes its operation until the main program takes the system again. A good example of background processing is the printing of a document while working in another program. The printing is done in the slack times of the main running program, which allows two chores to be accomplished at once, although the background chore is completed somewhat slowly.

Backplane Back of a computer where receptacles are located for peripheral devices and power cords.

Backspace Key usually marked with a left-pointing arrow. Pressing this key deletes the character immediately to the left of it. The left arrow key will allow cursor movement to the left without deleting the typing.

BACKUP External DOS or OS/2 command that creates a backup copy of information contained on the hard drive and preserves a record of the directory locations of each file.

Backup

Backup To copy master disks that come with software when bought in order to preserve the originals from possible destruction and to make a usable copy of the master.

Backup and Restore Procedure in which files are backed up to another storage device and are available to be restored for use if the need arises.

Backup Copy Extra copy of a disk that is copied from the original and is generally used for working with in place of the original to keep the integrity of the original intact.

Backup Utility A program that performs the backup procedure more easily by copying designated files and programs from the hard disk to floppy disks or other means of alternate storage.

Backward Search Ability to search either a database or word processing document from the cursor location back to the beginning of the document.

Bad Sector Area of a hard disk or a floppy disk that is unable to record data reliably due to damage to the sector.

Bad Track Table A listing, usually attached to the hard drive or packaged with the drive, to designate the locations of the bad sectors and other bad areas on the disk.

BAK File extension generally used for a backup of a file that has been changed by another program. Most good programs make an automatic backup copy of the files changed by the user so the the original file can be retrieved if the changes are not suitable.

Bandwidth Measurement in cycles per second (hertz) or in bits per second (bps) of the quantity of information that is able to flow through a channel.

Bank A group of like electronic devices joined together to be used as a single device; for example, the connecting of several memory chips onto a small circuit board to form a memory module, such as the very popular SIMM.module.

Bank Switching A means to expand the system memory beyond the operating system's or the microprocessor's limitations. This method switches very rapidly between two banks of memory chips in the computer.

Bar Codes

Bar Codes A pattern of different-sized vertical bars used for representing numerical codes in machine-readable form. Bar codes are placed on products and scanned by a bar code reader to streamline inventory control and sales.

Bar Code Reader Device that scans the bar codes on an object by means of a stylus and converts this bar code into a number relayed to the screen.

Bare Board Circuit board that has not yet had any type of memory chips mounted on it.

Bar Graph Horizontal display of bars used in a presentation to show the values of individual items and give an overall view of the items being discussed.

Base Font Font that a word processor program uses as default for documents unless otherwise specified.

Base Memory The first 640K of installed memory that is used for DOS. Also referred to as **conventional memory**.

Baseline An imaginary line in a program that is used to align the base or bottom of a group of letters or a graphic to help keep the entire line of information aligned.

BASIC Programming language for writing computer programs on personal computers that is easy to learn and use.

Basic Input-Output System (BIOS) A section of read-only memory (ROM) containing encoded programs that regulate the transfer of data between the computer and the attached peripherals such as disk drives.

BAT Extension designated for batch files.

Batch File A file that contains a group of DOS that are to be executed in sequence as if typed from the keyboard. These files are useful for easing the use of repetitious command entries. The most familiar of batch files is the Autoexec.bat, which DOS loads at starting of every operating session.

Batch Job Program or set of commands that can be run without any kind of user intervention.

Battery Backup

Battery Backup Battery-operated power source that supplies power to a circuit in the event that the main power source is disrupted. In computers, a battery backup is used for the internal clock and ROM to allow both to retain the information in case the main electric power to the computer system is disconnected. Another form of battery backup is Uninterrupted Power Supply (UPS),which powers the computer from a battery pack that is continuously recharged by electricity. This backup system is convenient because if electric power goes out completely, the system can still be powered down safely by turning off the system power and using the electricity stored in the batteries to back up the files, thus preventing loss of data that had not been recently saved.

Baud Measurement of the number of times per second that switching occurs in a communication channel.

Baud Rate Speed of transmission of an asynchronous communication channel. Rate of transfer between two modems.

Bay Opening or box used for mounting electronic devices in a computer, such as disk drives and tape drives.

BBS Acronym for Bulletin Board System, a computer accessible by other computers for the exchange of information and files. Most are set up by individuals in their homes and allow access to the general computer public.

Beginning-of-File Special code generated by a program to designate the start of a file on a disk or other storage device.

Bell-Compatible Modem Any modem using AT&T standards for the transmission of data.

Bells and Whistles Advanced added features of computers or computer programs that may a program more usable and more appealing.

Benchmark Measurement standard used when testing the performance of different brand names of equipment to rate them.

Benchmark Program Program utility used to measure the processing speed of a computer so that it can be compared to that of another computer running the same program.

Bernoulli Box

Bernoulli Box Mass storage system similar to removable floppy disks only on a larger storage scale; developed by Iomega Corporation for IBM compatibles and Macintosh computers.

Beta Software Stage of software testing before it is released to the public. These tests are usually conducted at sites other than the premises of the company manufacturing the software.

Bezier Curve Curve created in a computer graphic that is mathematically calculated to connect separate points into smooth, free-flowing curves and surfaces, which is a strict requirement of illustration and CAD programs.

Bi-directional Capacity to operate in both directions. In printers, it is the ability to print from left to right as well as from right to left. In a modem it is the ability to transmit data to another modem while receiving data from that modem at the same time. This allows for uploading and downloading files at the same time.

Binary File Computer file or program stored in computer-related format. The contents of binary files cannot be viewed by the DOS-type command or a word processing program.

Binary Numbers Numbering system that uses a base of 2 instead of the usual base of 10. This system allows for two possible choices, either a high-current reading or a low-current reading.

Example:

Binary	Decimal
0000	0
0001	1
0010	2
0011	3
0100	4
0101	5
0110	6
0111	7
1000	8
1001	9

Binary Conversion Changing a number to and from the binary numbering system.

Binary Device

Binary Device Term is used to identify any device that can process information as a series of on-and-off or high-and-low electrical states.

Binary Digit One of the two digits or numbers in the binary system, either 0 or 1.

Binary File Executable file consisting of 8-bit data or code that is only readable by a program because of the way the file is structured or compressed .

BIOS Built-in set of routines and commands that work with the system hardware to support the transfer of data between the different devices of a system, such as disk drives, memory, and monitor. The BIOS is located on a ROM chip inside the system and is mostly invisible to the general computer user, though it can be accessed by programmers.

Bit Shortened term for binary digit. There are only two digits: 0 and 1.

Bit Density Measurement of the amount of information per linear distance or by surface area in a storage device.

Bit Image Sequential grouping of bits stored in memory that when displayed as a unit form an image on a computer screen. Each bit in a bit image is equal to a pixel or dot on the computer screen when generating the image.

Bit Map Displaying a video image from the computer memory. The picture is split into elements or pixels, which contains the information for displaying the colors needed to create the picture on the monitor. These picture files can be very memory-intensive.

Bit-mapped Graphics Picture image or graphic created in paint programs by a pattern of pixels, limited to the maximum screen resolution of the monitor and video card being used.

Bits Per Inch Either the amount of data that can be placed on one inch of tape on a tape backup, or the inches of circumference of a given track on a disk.

Bit Rate Speed at which binary digits can be transmitted.

Bits Per Inch Measurement of data-storage capacity—the number of bits that can fit into an inch of storage space on a disk or tape system.

Bleed

Bleed In printed output, the running of the print out to the edge of the page or into the page or column gutter. Also refers to the effect caused when the type point size is so small that the centers of many letters—such as an "e" or "o"—are connected solidly because of print bleeding into the open area.

Block A grouping of information in packets to enable the transfer or processing of same. The size of the packets can vary. On a disk drive a block of information is 512 bytes. Used for marking and moving a related group of information in word processing programs.

Block Device Any computer device able to move data in blocks instead of by single characters.

Block Gap Very minute space allocated for the separation of data blocks or records on a disk drive. Also refers to the unused space between formatted sectors of a disk.

Block Header Specific information that defines the beginning of a block of data and contains such pertinent information as block identification, error-checking information, description of characteristics such as block length, and the type of data contained in the block.

Blocking Process of splitting a file into fixed-size blocks. When used in respect to communications, it refers to the process of stopping a signal from transmission.

Block Length Size of a block in bytes. The block size varies according to the purpose for which the block information is being used.

Block Move Process of marking off a block or specific amount of data that, once marked, can be moved to a new location as a whole grouping of information.

Block Transfer Process in which a designated block of information can be transferred to a new location.

Blowup Computer slang term meaning irregular termination of a program, which usually occurs when a program tries to perform a routine that is beyond its capabilities, causing it to terminate itself or lock up due to inability to proceed.

BNC Connector

BNC Connector Coaxial type of connector that locks itself when one end of the connector is placed within the other matching end. Most common in a closed television environment.

Board Short for computer-printed circuit boards; also called add-on cards. These boards are placed in the computer by means of the expansion slots on the motherboard.

Body Type Font used in the setting of paragraphs in the main body text of a document, distinct from headings and footers.

Boilerplate Section of data or a program code that can be used many times in several different documents. The boilerplate size can vary from a paragraph up to several pages of text.

Boldface Darker type used to make certain words stand out from the rest of the document.

Boolean Algebra Developed by George Boole in the 1850s, this system of mathematical calculations is carried out on variables having only two values, either 1 (true) or 0 (false).

BOOT To start or turn on the computer. The term originated from the concept that the computer has to "pull itself up by bootstraps" to load a program that enables the system to run larger programs. There are two types of booting—the cold boot, which completely starts the system, and the warm boot, which is a type of restart that retains parts of the startup program in memory.

Boot Block Portion on a disk that stores the operating system loader file and other basic information to enable the computer to start up when turned on or rebooted.

Boot Sector Special reserved part of a disk used to store the bootup machine coded program that starts up the computer.

Border The area around the edge of the actual workspace. Some users set up a colored border for aesthetic effect.

BPS The short abbreviation for Bits Per Second. Used in referring to the transfer speed of data.

Breadboard Plastic board that contains hundreds of small, regularly spaced holes interconnected by metal strips, in which electronic components can be connected. These boards are used by electronic circuit designers to build experimental circuits and prototypes.

Break

Break Signal sent by the user to tell the system to discontinue its processing and stop the running program, usually initiated by the Control-C entry from the keyboard. Some programs have other breaks built in, such as pressing the ESC key.

Bring-to-Front Procedure for putting graphic objects in front of other created objects, regardless of the order in which they were created. Used to overlay objects for different effects.

Brownout Insufficient power-line voltage for an extended period of time that can be very damaging to the computer.

Browse To look view the contents of a file without doing anything to the data. This allows searching for particular information quickly.

Brush Tool—contained in all paint programs—that functions like a paintbrush, allowing the user to paint on the screen. Most good programs allow for the selection of many different varieties of brush.

Bubble Sort A sorting method in which information is sorted beginning with the end of a list of data and moving all the way through the data, testing the value of adjacent pairs of data and reversing them if they are not in the proper order. This process is repeated throughout the entire set of data until it reaches the end, which will place the data in sorted order with the largest item being the last item in the list. This is one of the older methods of sorting. It compares two adjacent sets of numbers or words and places the one of lesser value ahead of the one of greater value causing them to be in sequence. This procedure is repeated until all data is in a specified sequence.

Buffer Area used for holding data. There are several type of data buffers. The printer buffer acts as a secondary memory for the printer to store the data to be printed. The disk buffer stores data being read from or written to a disk by use of system memory. The keyboard buffer records a set number of keystrokes in memory while waiting for the keystrokes to be interpreted by the computer.

Bug An error in a computer program, usually a problem with the program code.

Bundled Software Software distributed with hardware when the hardware is purchased. In most cases this software cannot be bought separately.

Built-in Font

Built-in Font Font permanently coded in the printer's memory; prints more quickly than other fonts.

Bulk Eraser Mechanism that uses a strong magnetic force to erase the information on tapes and disks; it scrambles the material on the magnetic media storage devices, thus destroying the information they contain.

Bulk Storage Storage device, such as tape drive, that has the ability to store unusually large amounts of data.

Bullet Dot generally used to set off a block of text or an item in a group. Other graphic characters may be used in the place of a dot.

Bundled Software Generally refers to software sold with a new computer system. Also refers to smaller programs included with the purchase of larger software packages to enhance the package.

Burn-in Complete test of a newly assembled computer system with the power on and running a continuous program for a set amount of time. This ensures that all parts are working together properly with no immediate errors.

Bus Main communication path in a computer, consisting of a set of parallel wires connecting the CPU, memory, and input-output devices.

Bus Extender Device added to the system to extend the capacity of the bus. On some older machines only capable of using 8-bit cards, a bus extender enables the system to use 16-bit expansion cards.

Bus System Interface circuit that controls the operations of the bus and connects it to the rest of the computer system.

Button Graphical rectangle or circle within a window that allows a decision to be made. The user activates the chosen button by pointing to it with a mouse and clicking on it.

Byte Size of memory space needed to store a single character, which is usually 8 bits. The computer's memory size is measured in kilobytes; 1 kilobyte = 1,024 bytes.

C Very powerful and efficient programming language comparable to assembly language. C language was used to write the code for most of the UNIX operating system.

Cable Collection of wires used to connect devices such as a mouse, keyboard, and printer to a computer.

Cable Connector Device located on each end of a cable to allow it to be attached to a device or another cable.

Cable Matcher Device that allows for the connecting of mismatched connector ends.

Cache A special designated part of memory used to store information that is read from the disk drive so that the information can be retrieved quickly from cache memory the next time it is needed instead of the slower disk drive. The drive is read once and the information is stored in the cache and when that same information is asked for again by the system, it searches the cache memory first, therefore speeding up the search process.

Cache Controller A controller card that has memory built on the card for the storing of disk information that is often read. Caches are used to speed up the read and writes of the disk system.

CAD Acronym for Computer-Aided Design, a graphics-oriented design program used by architects and engineers to draw plans for projects or design new machinery. CAD enables the design to be manipulated much more easily on screen than could be done on paper by hand.

Calculator Any device that performs arithmetic operations.

Calendar Program Application program used to produce output that resembles the look of a calendar. These programs come in various types; some allow for more manipulation of the calendar layout and design.

Call Waiting Special service offered by most phone companies that sends a signal to a line already engaged, informing it of another incoming call without giving a busy signal to the second caller. This is a problem in data transmission between computers because the call-waiting signal causes an interference in the data transmission,

Call Waiting

usually corrupting the data sent and sometimes causing loss of intelligible communications.

Camera-Ready Completed printed page or graphic design ready to for final printing or copying. Camera-ready copy can be taken to any printing firm to be transferred to final multiple-copy output.

Cancel Control character that stops information from being sent to a device; used in communication with printers and other computers.

Canned Routine Previously written set of commands that can be copied into another program and used as it is without making any modifications.

Caps Displaying and printing of alphabetic letters in the upper-case mode.

Caps Lock Key Key that, when depressed, will lock the keyboard in capital mode to type all letters in upper case.

Capture Process of transferring received data into a file for archiving and later use. Also refers to the process of copying information contained on the monitor to a file on the disk for later use.

Carrier Detect Signal sent and received by modems designating that a carrier or transmitting signal has been detected and that the systems are in communication with each other.

Carriage Return When the return or enter key on the keypad is pressed, the cursor returns to the beginning of the next line, as with the return key on a typewriter. Most carriage returns are linked with a line feed that advances the line being printed as it returns to the beginning of the line. Often abbreviated as CR.

Cartridge Most cartridges are made of a mechanism or device enclosed in a plastic case; they can be removed and replaced by a fresh cartridge. There are several types of cartridges. Toner cartridges contain the toner needed for printing on laser printers. Font cartridges can be added on to some printers. Tape cartridges are inserted into the tape drive for backup purposes.

Cascade Windows Method that overlays several windows on each other, keeping just the top edge of each window exposed to show the name of the window.

Case Sensitive

Case-Sensitive Ability to distinguish between upper and lower case letters; very useful for exact text searches in word processing. DOS is not case-sensitive since a search will work regardless of the upper and lower case letters used.

Catalog Complete listing of contents on a disk or of all files contained on all disks, enabling a particular file to be located more rapidly.

CD-ROM Abbreviation for compact disk read-only memory, which means the user can only read the information from the disk and cannot write to it. This media stores hundreds of megabytes of information on compact disks very similar to audio disks.

Cell Area in a spreadsheet—the intersection of a row and a column—where information can be entered.

Central Processing Unit Main brain of the computer—a large chip mounted on the computer main or motherboard—that does all the processing and handling of computer functions, as well as the arithmetic and logic operations. Generally referred to as CPU.

CGA Acronym for Color Graphics Adapter, the most popular video display because it made use of colors on the screen. The basic CGA allowed the use of four basic colors that greatly changed the screen from the dull monochrome displays.

Channel An internal or external passageway or link through which information passes between two devices.

Character Any type of symbol recognizable by the computer.

Character Definition Table Internal table set up in the system containing the arrangement of dots that are used in creation and display of bit-mapped characters.

Character Density Measurement of the number of characters per unit of area in printing or screen display.

Character Recognition Process of matching patterns to character shapes that are read into a computer (usually by means of a scanner) to determine which characters or punctuation marks are represented. The patterns are then transposed to the characters determined. Character recognition is not 100 percent accurate but is a quicker method of placing large amounts of data into the computer without having to type it all in.

Character Set

Character Set Grouping of alphabetic, numeric, and other various characters that have some relationship in common.

Characters Per Inch Measurement of the number of characters at a particular size and font that can be placed in a one-inch line.

Character String Grouping of letters with a cohesive meaning, such as a name or address. This entire string of letters is a character string.

Chart Diagram that displays data, or relationships between a set of data, in pictorial form instead of numeric form.

CHDIR (CD) Internal DOS command that allows the operator to change to other directories. By typing "CD\" on the DOS command line, the system will change to the root directory of the present drive.

Check Box Control found in graphical interfaces that displays a box allowing the user to enable or disable one or more features or options from a set of options.

Checksum Method of verification used by the computer to ensure that transmitted data is free of errors. The computer sending the information sends a checksum on the unit of data sent; the receiving computer verifies the checksum against the data received to see if it arrives at the same figure. If so, the data has transmitted properly.

Chip Tiny, mass-produced silicon wafer containing a miniaturized electronic circuit.

Circuit Any path able to carry electrical current. Refers to a combination of electrical components interconnected to perform a particular purpose.

Circuit Board Flat piece of insulating material on which electronic components are mounted and interconnected to form a circuit.

Clean Room Room specially designed to prevent contamination of electronic components and other delicate equipment. Personnel wear protective clothing, and dust and small particles are filtered out of the air. Hard disk drives are assembled in such contaminant-free rooms to greatly extend the life of the drives.

Click To press a mouse button to perform a task. Some operations require a double-click, which means pressing the mouse button rapidly twice.

Client

Client The computer in a computer link accessing the **server**, which is the main computer supplying a service to other computers.

Clip Art Drawings or designs that can be used freely in publications. Numerous types of clip art can be obtained for use in various computer publishing and drawing programs.

Clipboard Designated notepad area of memory where information can be copied from one program and stored for later retrieval by another program.

Clipping Computer graphics term referring to the trimming of a picture to fit into a specified area of space.

Clock The computer clock consists of a circuit that generates series of equally spaced pulse signals. The machine's functions are carried out by the rate of the clock pulses. Also refers to the real-time clock, a special circuit that tracks the date and time and can be battery-backed to keep the date and time current even when the electric power to the computer is turned off.

Clock/Calendar Separate timekeeping circuit within a computer that maintains the correct date and time, which are used by the operating system and can be accessed by software programs. The circuit is battery-powered so it can retain the information even when the system is powered down or turned off.

Clone An exact imitation of something else. An IBM clone computer is identical to an IBM model in looks and function.

Closed File File on the disk drive that is not being used presently by an application program. Applications must open files to read them and when finished must close the files for later use.

Cloth Ribbon Inked ribbon used primarily on dot-matrix printers and typewriters. The ribbon material is rolled onto a spool that is inserted directly into the printing device or is enclosed into a cartridge and then inserted into the printing device. The ribbon advances slightly with each character printed.

Cluster A group of disk sectors or areas treated as a whole unit in which the operating system is able to read or write information.

CLS Internal DOS command that will clear the screen.when entered on the command line and the enter key is pressed; abbreviated form of "Clear Screen."

CMOS

CMOS Low-energy memory in the computer that saves and stores the information about the configuration of the computer. Most systems allow for the changing of some CMOS settings to conform to the particular setup needed for different system configurations, such as when more memory or another disk drive is added.

Coding Process of writing the actual instructions in program code that tells the machine what to do.

Cold Boot Turning on the power switch to start the computer, which will perform some system testing before loading the operating system.

Color Monitor Display screen capable of showing numerous different colors instead of the monochrome screen that shows only one color on either a white or black background. Color monitors are popular because offer more variety and produce less eye strain.

Color Printer Generic term for any printer with the capability to print output in full color.

Color Saturation Amount of hue contained in a color. The more saturation, the more intense the color.

COM File Executable file with the extension .COM. These types of executable files are usually rather small compared to most .EXE files. To run these files you merely type the name of the file without the .COM extension.

Command Instruction given to the computer to perform an operation in a certain manner.

COMMAND.COM Command interpreter for Microsoft DOS.

Command Line String of text written in the command language and then passed to the command interpreter to be executed.

Command-Line Operating System Command-line-based operating system such as DOS that requires the operator to enter commands from the keyboard to perform an operation.

Comment Line of information ignored by the computer but which documents for the user the purpose of the procedure being carried out. Used in batch files with REM preceding the text so that the computer will ignore it.

Communications Program

Communications Program Computer program that enables two computers to communicate through the phone line to transmit and receive data.

COMP External DOS command with which a user can compare two files to see if they are identical.

Compact Disc (CD) Nonmagnetic polished metal disk (sometimes called an optical disk) used for storing digital data. A special optical scanning device uses high-intensity light, such as lasers, and mirrors to read the information on the disc.

Compact Disc Player Specially designed device that reads the contents of a compact disc.

Compatible Capable of running the same programs. Hardware compatibility refers to the ability of various components of hardware to work together as one unit.

Composite Video Televisions receive and use composite video signals, which are transmitted over a single wire. **RGB** monitors, on the other hand, receive signals for red, green, and blue levels over separate lines.

Compressed File File that has been run through a file compression program, which makes the file smaller by changing the formatting without altering the integrity of the file contents. File compression is widely used on a BBS so that large files can be stored in as small a space as possible.

Compuserve Large computer-operated consumer information service located in Columbus, Ohio. Users can access information from this service by communicating through a modem from anywhere in the United States. Compuserve allows users to exchange electronic mail as well as to access numerous file and information areas.

Computer Complex electronic machine capable of manipulating data by carrying out and storing instructions, as well as performing multiple operations without human intervention. High-end computers are able to carry out thousands of instructions per second.

Computer Science Study of computers that entails the design, operation, and use in processing information. There are several

Computer Science

aspects of computer science, such as programming, computer architecture, artificial intelligence, and robotics.

Computer Security With computers being used for highly valued information such as payroll records or company finance statements, there is strong need for computer security and protection. There may be several levels of security related to different levels of information access. The most common form of computer security requires users to employ passwords to access particular areas; the password only allows access to a certain level of information.

CON Logical device name used for the **console**.

Condition Term referring to a result being either true or false, or equal or not equal.

Conditional Process or action that takes place based on the determination of whether or not a condition is true.

Config.sys Special file, read only when the computer is started up or warm booted, that contains information on the configuration layout of the system such as device drivers and some memory allocations, like buffers.

Configure To set up the computer to make the different devices function as one unit, or to set up or fine tune software to run more efficiently on a particular machine.

Configuration Makeup of a computer system, including all internal and external components such as memory, disk drives, keyboard, video, and add-on hardware such as a mouse, or printer. Some configurations are monitor type, amount of memory, type of memory to use, and which disk drive to use. Also refers to a specific setup of a software program to make the best and most efficient use of the system resources.

Console A console consists of a computer display terminal, or monitor (an output-only device), and a keyboard (an input-only device).

Constant Item that remains the same and is not changed during program execution.

Contents Directory Series of queues containing the descriptors and addresses of routines located in a particular region of memory.

Context-Sensitive Help

Context-Sensitive Help Special, very useful type of built-in help screen in some of the newer software packages. When a certain key is pressed, specific help is displayed pertaining to the procedure in progress. If a user is about to start a spell checker, for example, and hits the help key, the help file gives information on using the spell checker.

Contiguous Refers to having things right next to each other. Several files placed on a disk one right after another are said to be contiguous. If the disk contains gaps in some tracks and the disk writes one file to several different areas, thus splitting the file, this is not contiguous. Noncontiguous files take longer to read when retrieving later, since the system must jump to several areas for all the pieces. This leads to **fragmentation**.

Control Break Process of interrupting the processor to gain control either through the keyboard or through software.

Control Key One of the special function keys. When this key is used in conjunction with another key, it gives the second key new meaning, usually causing some machine reaction depending on the key combination and the software in use. Holding down the Control key and pressing the "C" key will cancel most DOS operations.

Controller Card Add-on card that controls the floppy and hard disk drives in the computer system.

Conventional Memory The first 640K of memory that is reserved for use to run programs by DOS. DOS itself is only capable of recognizing this 640K of memory for use. Any memory on the system above this 640K needs a memory management program to make use of it.

Coprocessor Totally separate computer circuit that extends extra functions to the system CPU and can handle some of the extra work while the processor continues something else. Math coprocessors take over the mathematical functions from the processor and allow the system to function much more rapidly because the software makes full use of the coprocessor and allows the processor to continue with the rest of the program functions.

Copy To transfer something from one place to another, such as data on a disk to a tape drive for backup purposes. Also refers to moving information from one program into another, used for

Copy

making working copies of software disks so that the originals can be stored to prevent damage.

Copy Protection Copy protection prevents illegal copies of a program, since a disk with copy protection on it cannot be copied. The practice is slowly being done away because it prevents users from having duplicate disks in case the originals get worn out or destroyed. There are means to copy these copy protected disks, but they require either a special software package or a special add-on board for the computer.

Copyright Laws that prohibit the copying of writings, computer programs, books, songs, and various other types of materials, to protect the ownership rights of the author of said item.

Corrupted File Unusable file due to data contained in the file being damaged to the point that the system is unable to read or decipher it.

CPU Acronym for **Central Processing Unit**.

Crash Event occurring when the computer develops a software or hardware problem that makes the computer completely inoperative and in most cases requires a warm or sometimes a cold boot up to recover.

Cropping Procedure used to trim the edges of a graphic image to size it for fitting into a given space.

CRT Acronym for Cathode Ray Tube, a tubular-shaped glass with a screen that displays images by means of being struck by electrons. Two examples of a CRT are a television set and a computer monitor.

CTRL Short form for **Control Key**.

CTRL-ALT-DEL Keyed command used to perform a warm reboot of the computer system. The Control and Alt keys are held down and the Delete key is pressed at the same time, a combination that was developed so that the operator would not reboot the system accidentally.

Cursor Symbol that displays on a computer screen to designate the type position for the next entered character. Cursor movement is widely used in word processing programs. Most cursors are either a

Cursor

blinking line or a square box. The cursor keys—the arrow keys on the keyboard—are so called because they allow the operator to move the cursor on the screen; a mouse is also capable of moving the cursor on the screen.

Cut To remove something from a document. The information that is cut is normally kept in a temporary storage area and can be accessed again until something else is cut, which deletes the previously stored item.

DAC Acronym for Digital-to-Analog Conversion.

Daisy Chain Linking of several peripherals, such as disk drives, into a chain in which first device is connected to the computer, the second is connected to the first, the third to the second, and so on. They all use the same communication link to the computer and can detect when the line is available for their use.

Daisy Wheel Circular, removable part of a printing device that contains all available characters, each on its own separate bar extending from the central hub. The device functions in a way similar to a typewriter, in that the letters on the extended arms strike the paper through a ribbon to leave a letter imprinted on the paper.

Daisy-Wheel Printers Printer that uses a daisy wheel element to print characters on paper. The daisy wheel gives output of the same quality as a typewriter, so this type of printer was very popular until laser printers were developed.

Damping Technique used to prevent overshoot—reaching the desired limit—of a circuit or device.

DASD Acronym for Direct Access Storage Device, which contains data that can be accessed directly, instead of having to start at the beginning of a data source to read every record until the one needed is found. A disk drive is a DASD unit, whereas a tape drive is not.

Data Any items of information that have been gathered to be used in some type of process.

Data Aquisition Gathering of data from an outside source that is not part of the immediate system.

Data attribute Term relating to the structure information that establishes the context of the data and gives it meaning. Also used to refer to the descriptive structure information of a field in a data record.

Data Bank Any collection of data.

Database Collection of related records containing information to be used for processing. The records are broken down into individual fields that allow for various means of manipulating the data to produce specific, individualized reports. Data bases are used widely for record keeping and data tracking.

Database Administrator

Database Administrator Individual or groups of individuals responsible for the database. They mainly determine the information content of a database, internal storage structuring and access strategy, and a means of checking security and integrity and of monitoring database performance and upgrading to stay with the requirements of the environment.

Database Designer Individual responsible for designing and implementing functions required in a database management system. This person lays out a database structure similar in setup and writing code to that used by a programmer for a new program.

Data Bit Generally, a group of bits—typically 5,6,7, or 8—that represents a single character of data for transmission. Both the sending and receiving systems must be in agreement on the same number set for the data-bit size.

Data Buffer Area of memory designated to hold data temporarily as it is transferred from one place to another.

Data Capture Collection of information that usually occurs during the time of the transaction that creates the data, such as the automatic tracking of withdrawals from a cash machine.

Data Chaining Process of placing files onto a storage device, breaking the files into two or more noncontinuous areas on the device, but with the ability to read the data and use it on the machine again as a single file.

Data Collecting Assembling data from a source and manipulating that data into an organizational structure.

Data Compression Process by which the contents of a data file are changed to enable the information to take up less disk space. This procedure eliminates repeating items in the data and has a code to show different lengths for certain character sequences. Data compression can make a regular text file about half its original size.

Data Control Process of managing data through the tracking of how and by whom the data is being used, accessed, owned, altered, or reported on.

Data Element Single unit of data used for processing purposes. It may have a specific size, type, and range.

Data Entry

Data Entry Process of entering new data information into the system, mainly by way of a keyboard.

Data Field Designated area for a specific piece of information to be stored in a data record. It can be a space allocated for a name, address, and so on.

Data Flow Process by which data information moves through a computer system from an entry point to a destination point. It can be as simple as reading records and printing the record as it is read, or it can very complex to include a performing mathmatical calculations on portions of the data and setting them up in a report format before the final product is printed.

Data Format Layout of structure that an application will apply to data. The application stores the data in a format from which it can access the data again when needed.

Data Integrity Accuracy of file data. The importance of data integrity is to ensure that the data is pure and not corrupted.

Data Library Catalog collection of data files on a disk or other storage device that can be accessed to locate a particular piece of data or a file.

Data Link Actual connection through which data can be transferred from one computer device to another. This type of link is used to connect any two or more devices that have the capability to send or receive data.

Data Management Orderly and accurate control of data from the time it is acquired until the time it reaches its final point of use.

Data Processing Preparation, manipulation, and storage of data through the use of a computer.

Data Protection Process used to ensure the preservation, integrity, and reliability of data.

Data Rate Speed at which a system or device can transmit information, measured in bits per second.

Data Server Station on a computer network that is designated as the system dedicated to storing a shared database and processing database requests sent by users on the other systems in the network.

Data Sharing

Data Sharing Use of the same file by more than one person at a time or by more than one computer system at a time. This can be done by copying the file for use by all persons or systems needing it, or it can be done by accessing the file from a main server and using the file directly from that source.

Data Structure Organization of data in a recognizable format so that the data can be used for specific operations.

Data Transfer Process of moving data from one physical location to another either through internal means in a computer by transferring data from memory to disk, disk to tape, or hard disk to floppy, or through external means by transferring data between computers on a network or through a communications link.

DATE DOS command that displays the system date and allows the user to change the date if necessary.

Daughterboard Printed circuit board that attaches to another circuit board; for example, add-on cards connected to the main motherboard.

DB Connector One of the many different types of connectors used to attach input and output devices to serial and parallel ports. The different styles are named by the number of wires that are contained in each. A nine-wire connector, for example, is referred to as a DB-9 connector.

DDE Acroynym for **Dynamic Data Exchange**, a function incorporated in Windows that allows programs to exchange data among themselves while they are running. This enables the user to update a spreadsheet by merely updating a database linked to the spreadsheet.

Dead Halt Circumstance in which a system stops processing due to some malfunction or error with no hope of recovery by either the program or the operating system. The only possible solution to regaining the system from this circumstance is to reboot the system.

Deallocate To free up memory that had been previously allocated but is now available.

Debug To remove errors from computer programs. This usually requires more time than the actual writing of the original code.

DEBUG

DEBUG DOS command that allows the user to alter memory contents and to modify disk sectors. Thorough knowledge of computer machine language programming is recommended before using this DEBUG feature.

Decimal Base-10 number system used for normal calculations.

Decision Box Box displayed to the screen when an operator must intervene to make a choice between two or more options

Decoder System device or program routine able to translate coded data back into its original form to make the information usable by the system and operator.

Decollate To separate the different sections of a multipart form, which can be done either manually or with a machine called a decollator that does it automatically.

Decrement Process of decreasing a number by a given amount. Also refers to the amount by which the number is reduced.

Decryption Decoding of encrypted or specially coded information to allow use of the data in a normal manner. This is a form of guarding information to help ensure limited access.

Dedicated Term referring to the use of an item for one main function. If a phone line is used for the computer and nothing else, it is considered a dedicated phone line.

Dedicated Channel Communications line totally reserved for a particular use; also referred to as dedicated line.

Default Assumption that a computer makes if no other options have been selected for a particular function. Most programs have default settings to allow them to run even if the user has no knowledge to set the advanced options. The default options are usually adequate for the average user.

Default Directory Directory that DOS searches for or places files in if no specific directory is indicated.

Default Drive Drive that DOS looks to when it needs to access a disk drive for information. This can be changed to any of the drives available. If a hard disk drive is installed, it is labeled the "C" drive and in most cases is the default drive.

Degausser

Degausser Device used to demagnetize objects such as the heads of tape recorders. This device is also used to quickly erase the information contained on magnetic tapes or other magnetic media storage devices.

Degradation Term referring to the deterioration in the transmission signal caused by interference in the line; used mainly in communications.

Defragmentation Process by which all the files on a disk are rewritten into a contiguous form, removing any empty gaps between files. Disks get fragmented when files are written and deleted over a period of time. After a time the open areas on a disk are spread out over the disk and when a new file is written it may be broken into several different areas on the disk because of these fragmented openings. Fragmentation causes a slowdown in system operation because it takes longer to write and read fragmented files.

DELETE or DEL Delete key on the keyboard, used to eliminate the character located immediately to the left of the cursor on the screen. This key is also programmable in an application to be used to carry out a special task, such as ending an operation that is presently active.

Delimiter Special character used to set off or separate individual items of data in a program or in a set of data. Commas are commonly used as delimiters in programs to separate each field of the record.

Demonstration Program Usually a sample disk showing the screen appearance and possibly some very basic functions of an application either under development or recently on the software market. It is in no way a complete working model of the actual program application; instead it may be a scaled-down version with many features disabled or it may be just an on-screen slide show to demonstrate the uses and advantages of the software. Also known as a demo program.

Derived Font Font created by altering and scaling another font.

Descender The part of a lower case letter that extends below the regular baseline of a line of text.

Deselect Opposite of selecting an object. By deselecting an object, the object is cannot be manipulated in any way as a single object.

Desk Accessory

Desk Accessory Small but convenient accessory programs—such as a calculator or a card file—that can be popped up on the screen by a single keypress to perform some specific chore.

Desktop Main screen of a window-based system that is empty and resembles a desktop in that objects (programs) can be placed on it for use. This environment is intended to make using the computer a much simpler task than having to do everything manually by commands.

Desktop Computer Computer small enough to be placed on a office desk without taking up too much room. Most personal computers and some workstations are considered to be in the desktop-computer catagory.

Desktop Publishing Process of setting up professional typeset documents with the use of the computer. A desktop publishing program such as Pagemaker enables the user to flow text and manipulate layout on the screen before doing the final print. Desktop publishing incorporates several types of applications to create text, graphics, and actual publication layout and printing.

Detection Finding a specific condition that can affect a computer or the data with which it works. The processor can detect when a device is interrupting the system to gain access for attention. Another form of detection is the error detection and correction of modem data transmissions to ensure that the information that was sent was received properly by another system.

Device One of the components of a computer system, such as a printer, disk drive, or tape drive. These devices generally require separate software called a **device driver** in order to operate.

Device Driver Special short program installed in the computer to extend its operating system to recognize added features such as a special video card, a tape drive, a scanner, and so on. Device drivers are usually loaded into the system upon bootup by the config.sys file.

Dialog Box Box that appears on the screen requiring operator intervention before any other operations can be carried out.

Dial-Up Service Service relying on telephones to place station-to-station calls throughout a switched network.

Digital Communications

Digital Communications Transmission of binary-coded data through a communications channel.

Digital Computer The type of of electronic device that most people refer to as a computer. It performs operations based on two or more discrete states. A binary digital computer is based on two states, either logical ON or OFF, which are used to represent all types of data.

Digital Display Computer monitor capable of displaying only a set number of colors or gray scales.

Digitize To transfer an image into computer-readable data by use of a scanner.

Digitizing Tablet Graphics drawing tablet that works in a way similar to a mouse, but with built-in graphic design features that make it more useful in drawing programs.

DIN Connector Connector with multiple pins that conforms to the specifications of Deutsch Industrie Norm, the German national standard organization. On most desktop computers, a DIN connector is used to connect the keyboard to the computer.

Dingbat Small graphical symbol used to add decoration to a document.

Diode Electronic device that allows current to flow through in one direction but not the other.

DIP Acronym for Dual In-Line package.

Dip Switch Small switch or series of switches used frequently on computer circuit boards to allow different options to be set, such as the amount of memory on the motherboard, type of display adapter used, and so on.

DIR Internal DOS command that displays a listing of all the files in a particular **directory**. By using command line parameters, the command can be used to list directories of any disk drive on the system.

Direct Access Ability to locate and proceed straight to a specific storage location in memory or a location on a disk in order to read or store an item of information. Also called **random access**.

Direct-Connect Modem Type of modem that allows a phone cord to be attached directly into the modem rather than having to use accoustic couplers as in the older models.

Directory Area on a disk where all file names and disk locations for those files are stored. The main directory is called the root directory and all other directories branch off from the root. Each directory acts as a separate folder or holding area distinct from all other directories, so that related files may be kept in one area to make it easier to keep track of them.

Disk Storage device for computers that uses magnetic media for writing, much like a cassette tape recorder. The information is written to the disk in a circular form onto a **track**. A magnetic head moves across the disk, writing information to the disk with magnetic impulses. During a read procedure, this magnetic head moves across the disk to read magnetic signals and translates them to the computer.

There are two main types of disks. One is the hard disk, which remains inside the computer case and is not designed to be portable, and the floppy disk, which can be of several formats depending on the amount of information that it can hold. Floppy disks are convenient because they are easily transported.

Disk Access Time Time from which the system requests information from a device until the time that the information is supplied or read.

Disk Buffer Small area of memory used to store data that is read from or about to be written to a disk.

Disk Cache Designated portion of **RAM** used to hold information that is read from a disk. The information requested from the disk is read and stored in this area along with some additional information that the computer read, possibly following the requested information. When the information is actually needed, it is read into the system from this cache area. If new information is asked for, the system will first check to see if it is contained in the extra information read into the cache before going to the disk to retrieve the information. The computer tries to make a guess as to the next chunk of information that may be asked for and places that information into the cache area. **DISKCOPY** DOS command used to make a complete copy of a particular disk. The two disks must be of the same format for the copy procedure to work.

Disk Capacity

Disk Capacity Amount of data that can be stored on a disk; expressed either as K (kilobytes) or M (megabytes).

Disk Drive Device attached to the computer that allows for the reading of computer disks.

Diskette Another term used for removable computer disks, which are made of a flexible inner circular piece of flat plastic with a magnetic coating that is then enclosed in a harder, square plastic case.

Disk Jacket Protective covering of a floppy disk.

Disk Operating System (DOS) System dependent on the disk drive to get itself started upon bootup.

Disk Unit Either the disk drive itself or the drive and the case it is contained in.

Disperse To break up and place in different locations; for example, to place data in such a way that it appears in several locations in a printed document.

Display Generally refers to the computer monitor screen. The type of display depends on the type of monitor used and the video card that drives the monitor.

Dithering Method using black and white dots to represent a gray-scale image on a screen or a printer not capable of producing true gray-scale output.

DLL Acronym for Dynamic Link Library, popular in the windows environment. This is a library of procedures, written in machine language, used by a program at run time when needed. This allows the program code to be smaller, and making changes requires only a change to the DLL file instead of to the program itself.

Document File that contains text that has been made ready for printing.**Documentation** Text file or book that comes with software describing the computer program. It tells the uses of the program as well as how to operate it. Reading the documentation is important for developing knowledge to use the software to its fullest advantage.

DOS Acronym for **Disk Operating System**, a term used by various manufacturers for different types of operating systems.

DOS Prompt

DOS prompt Prompt displayed on the screen when a computer is ready for operation input. The prompt normally consists of a letter and the "greater than" sign; "C>" is perhaps the most common.

Dot Period used to separate a file name and extension. Also refers to the **dithering** process of converting gray-scale images into images for printing.

Dot-Matrix Printer Most popular and least expensive type of printer, which forms characters with patterns of small dots placed on the paper by print pins. The quality of the print depends on the number of pins in the printer. The main two types are a 9-pin and a 24-pin printer. The 24-pin produces far better output because of the greater number of pins.

Dot Pitch Smallest dot size that a computer monitor is capable of displaying. The smaller the dot pitch, the higher the resolution.

Double-Click Procedure required by many programs in the user presses a mouse button twice in rapid succession. The most common double-click button is the left mouse button.

Double Density Disk capable of storing double the amount of information as the older single-density formatted disk.

Down Term applied to computers that are inoperable due to testing or need for repairs.

Download Process of transmitting a program from a host or main computer to another computer at a remote site.

DPI Acronym for Dots Per Inch.

Draft Quality High-speed but low-quality printing mode offered by most dot matrix printers. This mode is used mostly to examine a document for typographical errors to make changes before printing the final document.

Drag Process of holding the mouse button down to select an item and bring it to a new location.

DRAM Acronym for **Dynamic Random Access Memory**.

Drop-Down Menus Command options in a program that don't appear until selected. When selected, the drop-down menu appears on the screen, allowing the operator to chose from various options.

Drop Out

Drop Out A quick temporary loss of a signal during a read or write operation that produces errors in the data being transmitted.

Drum Rotating cylinder used in some printers or plotters as a magnetic medium for data storage. A drum in a laser printer is used to create a photocopy image of a page.

Dual Density Ability of a disk drive to read and write more than one designated type of disk format.

Dual Disk Drive Computer system with two floppy disk drives installed.

Dual Processors Use of two processors on a system speeds operation since one processor can be used to control the system memory and bus while the other processor manages input and output.

Dynamic Data Exchange Process in which two programs with **DDE** capability can exchange information and commands with each other when running together. When one program updates its information, the other program is automatically updated.

Dynamic Random Access Memory Widely used form of computer memory that requires the computer to send a refresh signal frequently to keep the information stored in the DRAM fresh.

Echo Sending of information to the place from which it came. The echo command allows characters to be displayed on the screen as well as to be sent over a modem when interlinked with another computer. It also enables the user to see certain instructions displayed on the screen for system information.

Edge Connector Set of wide flat metallic contacts located along the edge of a printed circuit board that slides into an expansion slot on the motherboard of a computer system or into a ribbon cable connector.

Edit To view and change the contents of a computer file.

Editor Program that allows a user to view the contents of a file on the monitor and either make changes or add to the file. There are basically two types of editors. One is a full screen editor, which displays the file on a full screen view and thus shows more of the file for editing purposes. The other is a line editor, which allows the file to be displayed and edited one line at a time.

EDLIN Text editor that comes with DOS. It can be used to do an editing job but it is not very easy to use.

EEPROM Acronym for Electrically Erasable Programmable Read-Only Memory, a chip that can be written to or read from by electronic signals. The contents of this chip remain in the chip even when power is removed from it.

Efficiency Ability to accomplish a task with the least amount of time and work involved but still retain accuracy and intactness.

EGA Acronym for **Enhanced Graphics Adapter**.

EISA Acronym for Extended Industry-Standard Architecture, a system using a 32-bit bus that allows data to be transferred between peripherals in 32-bit chunks instead of the 16-bit or 8-bit that most systems use. With the transfer of larger bits of information, the machine is able to perform much faster than the standard ISA systems.

Electronic Bulletin Board Bulletin board system that can be accessed with a modem for the purpose of exchanging information and acquiring files by downloading.

Electronic Mail

Electronic Mail Process of exchanging mail messages by way of a computer system. The messages are stored on a mutually shared system and users can send and receive messages at their own convenience. Generally referred to as EMAIL.

Electronic Music Music generated with a computer and an electronic device such as a MIDI setup.

Electronic Office Office environment that relies solely on computers for communicating within the office to produce reports and other office-related material.

Electronic Publishing Distributing information by means of electronic media such as disks, CD-ROMs, or telecommunication services.

Electronics Branch of physics that deals with the characteristics of electrons and electronic devices such as tubes, semiconductors, and the circuits that make use of them.

Embedded Items built into a part of the system instead of being called up by the system when needed. Embedded printing codes are codes inserted into a document by an application that controls the printer and changes print formats.

EMM386.EXE Device driver found in DOS from versions 5.0 up that simulates expanded memory on a system from a 386 up equipped with extended memory. This also allows the user to load device drivers and some programs into the upper memory areas, saving the lower 640K for program execution.

Emulation Ability of the machine to take on the features and functions of a similar part that is being emulated or imitated. If a printer has the Laserjet III emulation, for example, it operates and prints just like the Laserjet III.

Enable To make something available for use by the system when it is needed.

Encapsulated PostScript (EPS) Set of PostScript commands incorporated in an image to allow the image to take on PostScript-quality output in a desktop publishing program.

Encryption Using a special coding process to make files inaccessible to nonpermissive users. A password or secret keyword is needed to decrypt the file for use.

END KEY

END KEY Key on the keyboard that can be programmed for a specific task by the software being used. The most common use of this key is to advance to the end of a file.

End-of-File Mark Character used to designate the ending of a computer file, because the computer needs a means of keeping track of file beginnings and ends.

End User Person who will actually be using a program after it is placed in the open market.

Enhanced Graphics Adapter (EGA) Type of video display adapter capable of emulating **CGA** and **MDA**, as well as adding several additional video modes. This video display adapter allows for more colors and higher resolution than the standard CGA.

Enhanced Keyboard 101- or 102-key keyboard used on most newer computers today. This keyboard incorporates twelve function keys instead of the ten used on earlier keyboards, and provides extra Control and ALT keys. It also includes a set of cursor-movement and editing keys on the main part of the keyboard as well as on the numeric keyboard. Some of the keys—such as the pause and print-screen keys—are placed in different locations.

Enhanced Small Device Interface (ESDI) A standard that can be used on high-capacity hard disk drives, floppy drives, and tape drives to allow these devices to communicate with the system at high rates of speed. A typical ESDI drive can transfer data at the rate of ten megabytes per second or faster. This drive was introduced by Maxtor as another interface for hard drives comparable to the ST-506 standard.

Enter Key Key that is depressed after each section of information to allow that information to be processed by the computer or to create a new paragraph. The key is usually the largest one on the keyboard and is sometimes called the **return key**.

Entry Processing of information for a computer program to use.

Environment Different uses for a particular computer designate separate environments. Operating systems, word processing, and databases are all different environments. The DOS environment is a specific area of memory where data can be stored by the DOS SET command.

EOF

EOF Acronym for End of File.

EOL Acronym for End of Line.

EPROM Acronym for Erasable Programmable Read-Only Memory. PROMS can only be written to once, whereas an EPROM is a special PROM that can be erased by exposure to ultraviolet light and can then be reprogrammed.

EPSON Japanese firm that produces one of the most popular printers in the computer environment and that has set many printer standards that other manufacturers use in printer development.

Erasable Optical Disk Drive Storage device that can read and write by means of a laser light for storing data on an optical disk.

ERASE DOS command that deletes or erases a file from a disk.

Error Checking Testing of transmitted data with received data to ensure the integrity of the data.

Error Message Message displayed to inform the user of the inability to perform a task or function. Some error messages designate the cause of the problem and some give possible solutions to the problem.

Escape Key Key on the keyboard that usually has a specific use according to the software being run. Its usual function is to exit from one point to a previous point in a procedure.

Escape Sequence Special character code sequences that send particular commands to a printer or monitor. These codes can change the print type styles to display ANSI characters to the screen in a colorful display.

ESC Character One of the control codes in the ASCII character set used to send instructions to the printer. Escape codes sequences are used extensively in Hewlett-Packard's PCL printer language to control the operation of the Laserjet line of printers.

ESDI Acronym for **Enhanced Small Device Interface**.

EXCEL Microsoft program that contains a spreadsheet, database manager, and graphics.

EXE File

EXE File Compiled computer program executable from DOS by typing the name of this file on the command line and pressing the enter key.

Executable Program Computer program that has been written, compiled, and tested and is ready to run and be used as received without any user alterations to the code.

Execute To carry out an instruction. The computer executes in two processes—the fetch process, in which it fetches the information, and the process that actually executes the information.

Exit Normal termination of a program, which returns it to a designated position or state.

Expandability Ability to add more devices or memory to a computer system, thus allowing for future upgrades.

Expanded Memory Memory over the normal 1 Meg recognized in most DOS systems. The memory employs bank switching to allow the system to use the higher memory blocks by swapping them in and out of the normal 640K range. This process requires a special memory-management program called LIM-EMS to do the switching process.

Expanded Memory Manager Program that can manage and make use of the memory located in the expanded memory area in the computer. This also makes use of expanded memory cards than can be installed into computers.

Expansion Ability to increase the capabilities of a computer by adding hardware that allows the user to perform a task that the basic system cannot perform on its own. Expansion usually refers to the printed circuit boards placed on the motherboard by use of the expansion slots.

Expansion Board Printed circuit board containing special chips and electronics, such as high-resolution video or disk controllers, that can be added to a system by way of the expansion slots to enable the system to perform tasks it could not do without the boards.

Expansion Bus Area on the computer motherboard with slots to install expansion cards into the system, allowing for the installation of internal modems, video cards, sound boards, and so on.

Expansion Slot

Expansion Slot Slot on the motherboard designed to hold add-on expansion cards to increase the performance of the system. Expansion slots can be used to add memory, disk drive controllers, video graphics cards, I/O cards for input and output devices, and an internal modem, among other things..

Export To transfer information from one program to another or from one system to another. The two programs that are dealing with the transferred file must be able to recognize the format of the data being transferred. Several programs are compatible in the exchange of data, while others are totally proprietary.

Extended ASCII ASCII characters with values between decimal 128 and 255. Most of these characters are graphical characters that can be used in drawing procedures.

Extended Memory Memory located at address higher than 1 Meg in the computer system but accessed through memory addresses the same as the first meg of memory.

Extension Last three letters of a file name, following a period. There are some standardized extensions that are easily recognized, such as .EXE, .COM, .BAT, .TXT, .DOC, and .BAS.

External Command DOS command that is a separate file that must be accessible by the system upon its execution.

External Drive Self-contained drive device that is not mounted inside the computer but is attached to the system by means of a cable and is fully accessible by the system.

External Modem Self-contained modem connected to the computer by means of a serial port. External modems are popular because they do not use up a valuable expansion slot in the system.

F Keys Special function keys located along the top of the keyboard and sometimes also available on the left side of the keyboard. They are programmable keys used by the operator or by the software for specific tasks.

Facing Pages Displaying two pages of a document that would face each other if bound in a book form.

Fail-Safe System Computer designed to continue to function without losing data or damaging programs if part of the system malfunctions.

Fallout Failure of any of the components of a computer system during the burn-in or testing period.

Fan Cooling mechanism built into the computer case or mostly located in the power supply that circulates air throughout the internal part of the computer to keep the system cool.

Fanfold Paper Computer paper connected as a continuous sheet with pin-feed holes along the edges, enabling the printer tractor-feed mechanism to feed the paper through the printer without stopping.

Fastback Popular hard-disk utility used for backing up data. It is very dependable and fast, thus the origin of the name.

FASTOPEN External DOS command that stores directory information in the computer memory to allow DOS to access the most-used programs more readily.

FAT Acronym for **File Allocation Table**.

Fatal Error Problem that develops on a system causing the system or the running program to totally stop operation. This error normally is unrecoverable.

Fault Problem preventing a computer or computer device from operating in a normal manner. Faults can be of permanent nature, such as a broken piece, or they can be irregular, such as a situation that occurs periodically.

FAX Short for facsimile, a machine used to transmit a copy of a paper document or a graphic file over the telephone lines by

FAX

converting the document on paper into an electronic signal. This signal is intercepted at the other end by another FAX machine, which converts it back to its original form and prints it back to paper.

FCC Acronym for Federal Communications Commission, which regulates any equipment that produces radio frequency signals, such as two-way radios and computers. There are two FCC classifications—class A pertains to industrial regulation; class B regulates equipment for home use.

F Connector Cable connector used mostly in video applications that has a screw-on device to make the connection.

Feathering Placing even amounts of space between each line of a document, forcing it to vertical justification and giving a neater appearance.

Feature Special added abilities incorporated into a program or computer to make them more attractive, such as multiple columns in a word processor or front-and-back printing of pages in documents. Most software companies keep adding more features in an attempt to make their products more appealing and useful than their competitors'.

Female Connector Receptacle able to accept the pins of a male connector. Computer cables are made of a male and a female connector.

Fiber Optics Special cable made from a thin fiber of glass that carries light instead of electrical energy. Huge chunks of data can be transferred through a single fiber-optic cable.

Field Individual pieces of information that make up a record. A name can be one field, while the address is another field. The designation of individual fields allows more-useful manipulation of data.

Field Name User-designated name for a specific piece of data in a record to identify that data, such as name, address, or city. Field names are more useful if they coincide with the information they pertain to.

Field Separator Character used to separate one data field from another.

Field Template

Field Template Particular setting given to a specific field to allow it to accept only one type of data entry. A field template designated as a number-only field will not accept any alphabetic character input. This is used to eliminate a large amount of improper data entry.

File Grouping of related information stored on disks, tapes, or other storage device. A file may be documents, groups of related data, or even entire programs.

File Allocation Table (FAT) Hidden file on each disk that contains the information about the size of each file and which sectors on the disk it occupies. This is how DOS keeps track of file locations so it can access the files easily when needed.

File Attribute Hidden code imbedded in the description of a file on the disk designating the status of the file, such as whether it is a hidden, read-only, system, or archive file.

File Backup Copying of all important files on a system to be used in case of accidental destruction or deletion. The backup files are usually stored on floppy disks or tapes for later reference.

File Compression Utility Program or add-on card that compresses and decompresses files on the hard drive to make more storage room available. Most of the good programs of this type function without even being noticed; a file is decompressed when accessed and then recompressed when the system is through with it. All files on a bulletin board system are in compressed format to allow them to store enormous amounts information. Once a file is downloaded to the system, it must be run through a compression utility to decompress it for use. The most widely used BBS compression program is called PKZIP. Many times this compression reduces the file to nearly 50 percent of its original size.

File Control Block (FCB) Area of memory designated by a computer system to store information about a file that has been previously opened for use. This control block contains file information such as file identification, location on the disk, and a pointer to mark the user's current position in the file.

File Conversion Utility Program that can convert file formats from one type to another so the file can be used with other programs. A well-written word processor has this capacity, so they

File Conversion Utility

can read files created by different word processing systems. Many programs call this feature importing and exporting files, and allow the user to designate which file formats are being used.

File Deletion Procedure for removing a file from a disk directory without physically removing it from the disk itself. By removing the filename from the directory, the file space on the disk becomes available for other files. On the other hand, by not actually removing the file itself, the file can still be undeleted in case it turns out to be needed again. But if another file has already been written to the disk since the deletion, chances are it has overwritten the space occupied by the deleted file, which then can no longer be recovered.

File Extension Three-letter addition to the actual file name that normally designates the type of file it is, such as EXE, COM, BAT, DOC, TXT, PCX, GIF, and so on.

File Format Particular file structure that a program uses to store files on a disk. Most programs have their own proprietary formats for storing their data files.

File Handle Number given to an open file by the system. May also reference a device as well.

File Handling Routine Creation, accessing, and opening and closing of files. Most programs have built-in file handling procedures.

File Layout Structure of records that make up a file.

File Librarian Person in charge of maintaining and providing access to a collection of computer data.

File Locking Method to allow a file to be locked so it can be accessed by one person at a time on a networking system; used to retain file integrity.

File Maintenance Procedure of altering or updating information contained in files to keep information current and to ensure that the files are always without errors.

File Manager Section of either an operating system or operating environment that controls the actual access and manipulation of files and manages the files for the system using it.

File Name

File Name Name given to a file allowing it to be located by the operating system. Upon creation, each file must be given a unique name, which can contain eight characters (with a few restrictions) and a three-character extension.

File Protection Ability to prevent a file from being destroyed. One such protection is to set the file attribute to a read-only status, making it impossible to overwrite the file. Another form of protection is to cover the write protection notch on the floppy disk to prevent the drive from writing to the disk. Passwords are another widely used form of protection, allowing only those knowing the password to have access to the file.

File Recovery Ability to undelete or recover a file already deleted, providing no files have been written to the disk since deletion time.

File Server Master computer used to store files that may be accessed by other computers connected to it by networking or direct cabling. This saves disk space on the individual systems since the main server stores the bulk of the information.

File Sharing On a network system, all files are stored on a master system or server and are accessible by more than one user at the same time, thus allowing many users access to the same file on different systems at the same time.

File Size Amount of space that a file requires to be stored on a disk. The file actually has two file sizes—the actual size of the file, and the amount of file space allocated to the file by DOS. DOS allows a set number of blocks to suit the file size, though the file may not actually take up the entire space allocated. This could give two different readings for a file's size.

Filespec Specific location of a file that includes the drive letter, path to the file, filename, and extension; for example, C:\UTILITY\QEDIT.EXE.

File Structure Basic setup of a file or group of files that are to be used for a specific purpose.

File System Structure to store, name, and organize files composed of the files, the directories listed their locations, and other information needed for the proper access and use of these files.

File Transfer

File Transfer Ability to move files from one place to another or to transmit them from one computer to another.

File Type Specific designation to let the user identify a file easily. In DOS the most common form of identification is the three-letter extension.

Fill In drawing and paint programs, process by which an entire designated area can be filled or painted in one operation.

Filter Passing data through a special command before processing the command. A widely used type is the MORE filter used in DOS to display one screen of data and then pausing before showing more.

FIND Command that will search and find the exact location of a particular file on the disk as designated by the user.

Firmware Software that is stored on a fixed system, such as the read-only memory (ROM) of the system.

Fixed Disk Another term for the hard disk drive, so called because the disk is fixed in the system and is not removable.

Flatbed Scanner Device able to read pictures or text from a document and transpose them into a digitized image that can be used with other computer programs. Flatbed scanners can scan in a full-page letter-sized document (8 1/2 by 11 inches), and are very useful for incorporating pictures and graphics from printed material into desktop publishing programs. The scanner can also be used to scan text to be converted to usable text by the use of **optical character recognition** programs (OCR), saving much time over typing the text by hand.

Flicker Quick, fluttering motion caused when a screen is updated too slowly. The refresh rate of the screen determines the ability to notice any flicker. A refresh rate of 60 times per second is adequate enough to eliminate any noticeable flicker.

Floating Graphic Graphic placed on a page with no absolute designated position so it can float as text is rearranged in the document.

Floppy Disk Removable disk used on computers. The two most popular sizes are the 3 1/2-inch floppy, which is encased in hard

Floppy Disk

plastic, and the 5 1/4-inch floppy, which is encased in a floppy soft plastic jacket, hence the name.

Floppy Disk Controller Card mounted on the motherboard inside the computer that regulates the operation of the floppy disks installed on a computer system. When the disk is accessed, the controller actually sends the message to the drive and then retrieves the information from the drive for the program being run.

Floppy Disk Drive Mechanical device used to read and write data to and from floppy disks.

Flow Placing text into a particular place in a document with the ability for the text to flow around graphics and continue to other columns or pages as needed.

Flowchart Process of creating a chart with the use of special symbols and written instructions to show the setup and function of a procedure. Flow charts are used to show the procedures for solving a problem and the different possibilities that may arise in the solving process.

Flush Left Typed or printed text lined up along the left margin, though the end of each line may vary in length.

Flush Right Text aligned along the right margin. This gives the left margin a rugged look.

Folder Holding device for files in a graphical user environment. The folder can be represented on a computer screen either by a graphical icon or image of a file folder.

Font Grouping or set of characters of the same size and style. Most desktop publishing systems allow the use of more than one font per file.

Font Cartridge Add-on card that can be inserted into a printer to give it the capability to print more fonts. These fonts are stored on the cards in ROM memory chips.

Font Editor Program that allows a user to change the look of existing fonts or to create new fonts. A font for display and one for the printer is usually created.

Font Size Actual size of the characters used in a particular font. Some fonts only allow a set number of font sizes, but with a type

Font Size

manager program or by using true type fonts, the sizes are greatly enhanced.

Font Smoothing Removing any distortion in printed text by high-resolution printers, making the document much neater and more presentable.

Font Substitution Replacing bit-mapped fonts with an outline font for printing.

Footer Short copy of a document's title or other pertinent text that is located at the bottom of every page in a created document.

Footprint Space of a hard disk drive that is used by a program. Small footprint software is preferred to save on disk space.

FOR Batch command that allows for placing a procedure into a loop to process the same operation numerous times. This is used with the NEXT command, creating the FOR\NEXT loop.

Foreground Foremost text on the screen or the top layer in a color display. In a black background with white letters, the letters are the foreground. In the multitasking environment, foreground refers to the program that is executing in a current window or an operation on the screen while other lower-priority programs may be running unseen in the background.

Forced Page Break Page break inserted by the user, causing the break to occur at this position throughout the document.

Format Systematic method of setting up information for storing or displaying. Formatting disks or tapes designates how the information is to be stored on them through the use of the block addresses. Another use of format is the structure of data used in a program. The data layout is such that each record contains the same information in the same layout or format.

FOR\NEXT Loop Structure sequence to carry out the same procedure a designated number of times.

Form Letter Letter to be sent to a group of people; the names and addresses for insertion into the letters are retrieved from a database file and inserted into each letter.

Fragmentation Splitting of files due to successive deleting and creating new files on a disk drive. This occurs mainly on a hard

Fragmentation

drive since most of these drives are rather large. Files are stored on the disk in a continuous one-piece manner so when several megabytes of data are stored on a drive and then some are deleted in random order, the disk starts having blank or open areas in different places. When a new file is created and saved, DOS writes this file to the first available space on the disk. If the file is larger than the first open area, DOS will place the remainder of the file into the next open area. After doing this continuously with hundreds of files, the files become fragmented. Since they are no longer in one continuous area, the system takes longer to access the file. There are utility programs that will successfully defragment a disk, which in turn speeds up the system by making file access more rapid.

Frame Buffer Small area of memory used to store the contents of the monitor into a screen image.

Frame Grabber Add-on card that enabling the user to capture an image from a video camera or VCR and transpose it into a bitmap image to use in computer programs. The frame grabber is able to capture a frame at a time, hence the name.

Frame Rate Speed at which individual frames are transmitted and displayed to the monitor, measured by the numbers of times per second the electron beam refreshes the screen; 60 times per second is a basic rating.

Free Software There are a few different types of free software.
1. Public Domain software is written and placed into public use without any copyrights. There are still a few pieces of software of this type, but this term is usually misused to describe other forms of software.
2. A certain type of copyrighted software is placed into public use with the owner's permission. The owner still retains the copyright to the software and may change the status of it if he so desires.
3. Shareware is the most popular type of freeware. This software is placed into public use and is usually a full-featured program to be used and evaluated. If the software is satisfactory, the user is requested to pay a registration fee to the author to continue using it. In some shareware, certain features are disabled until registration; this is not a popular type of shareware and has been nicknamed crippleware.

Friction Feed Printer

Friction Feed Printer Printer that relies on the pressure of the platen to feed the paper through—like a typewriter—instead of the perforated holes used in a pin-feed printer.

Friendliness Ability to use hardware or software easily without needing a great amount of tutoring or reading. User friendliness is a goal that most companies are leaning toward to entice more people to become computer buyers.

Front Panel Front face plate of a computer or monitor on which the controls or buttons are placed for access by the user.

Front End A computer or a piece of software that is accessed to enable access to another computer or another program. Many bulletin board systems have a front end that enables the user a choice of special features to access or to go straight to the BBS.

FTP Acronym for File Transfer Protocol, a program that enables files to be transferred from another computer. Both systems must have the same protocol software available to transfer properly. There are many good protocols available and most are incorporated into the communication programs. The most popular protocol used on a BBS is Zmodem because of its error correction and speed.

Full Duplex Ability to transmit data in two directions at the same time.

Full-Height Drive A 5 1/4 inch drive that is about 3 1/4 inches in height. These were popular in the older systems and still exist in some of the larger-capacity drives. The most popular drive is called the half-height, which is about half the height of the older full height. The half height drives allow for more room in the PC to add more drives to the system.

Full Justification Aligning text along both the left and right margins.

Full-Motion Video Adapter Video adapter able to show moving television images on the computer monitor. Most of these adapters allow images to be captured and saved.

Full-Page Display Computer monitor that can display a full page of text on the screen at one time.

Full Pathname

Full Pathname Entire listing of a location of a file on a disk including the path needed to get to the file from the root directory of the disk.

Full-Screen Editor Word processor created for application developing. It allows for editing or creating a file being viewed on the screen and gives the user the ability to move to any area on the screen to edit. Most even allow for automatic indenting.

Full-Screen Terminal Terminal screen that allows the user to type anywhere on the display screen, as opposed to the kind of terminal that allows only one line to be typed at a time (usually the last line on the screen).

Full Text Search Ability to search through every word in multiple or single documents to find a particular designated word or phrase, enabling the user to access only those documents containing information pertaining to the point of interest and to ignore all others.

Fully Populated Board Board in which all the available spaces for memory chips have been filled.

Function Reason or action taken by a computer to achieve a specific task.

Function Keys Keys on the keyboard labeled F1 through F12; also referred to as "F" keys. These keys can usually be programmed by the software to perform different features while in that particular program.

G Abbreviation for gigabyte.

Game Control Adapter Special I/O port on an IBM compatible system that allows for the use of a joystick with computer games and simulators.

Gamut Range of colors a color monitor can display in computer graphics.

Gantt Chart Special type of chart that displays a schedule for a series of operations.

Garbage Any unintelligible data, mostly noticeable on the monitor.

Gas Plasma Display Screen used on many laptop-type computers. It works on the same principle as neon light and is easier to read on laptops than LCD, but does consume more power.

Gate Logic or decision-making circuit, such as the **AND** gate or the **OR** gate.

Gateway Link made between several computers in a network setup.

GB Abbreviation for gigabyte, which is equal to approximately one billion bytes. Many of the high-end systems now on the market are being equipped with gigabyte drives for massive storage.

Gender Bender Adapter that allows for two adapters of the same gender to be joined. One type enabling two female plugs to be connected to each other; the other type can be used to join two male plugs together.

General Purpose Computer Computer with an instruction set that is simple in structure and general enough that numerous algorithms can be developed for it.

Genie On-line information service that computer owners with modems can access to receive files as well as up-to-date stock quotes, news updates, and other features such as home-shopping services.

Germanium Second most popular material used in making semiconductors; the most popular is silicon.

GIF

GIF Acronym for Graphics Interchange Format, a format developed by the Compuserve company to be used for saving bitmap images on a disk. This is a very popular format with BBSs because it reduces files to reasonable sizes for storage and easy downloading by users.

Gigabyte Approximately one billion bytes of space.

Glare Filter Special filter that fits over the front of a monitor to reduce user eyestrain caused by glare.

Glitch Internal response in a computer caused when signals that are supposed to be simultaneous arrive at a designation at slightly different times. Errors in software programs are also referred to as glitches.

Global Relationship to a complete document, a file, or any other such source.

Global Backup Procedure in which all programs and files on the entire hard drive are backed up to another media such as floppy disks.

Global Operation Operation performed throughout an entire document or file.

Global Variable Piece of data that can be recognized in any part of a program.

Grabber Hand Graphical mouse pointer—often shaped like a hand—used to move text or graphics by dragging them to their new location.

Graceful Exit Program that terminates in a normal manner and does not cause any conflicts with the operating system.

Graphical User Interface Means of operating a computer by manipulating picture icons and windows with the use of a mouse.

Graphics Pictures produced with computer devices. There are many ways of creating graphics on a computer, including the use of a specific drawing or design program or a scanner. Graphics are widely used to make newsletters and advertising media more appealing to the eye. There are several different aspects graphics use.

1. The use of plotters to draw charts and graphs of mathematical data.

Graphics

2. The use of CAD (**computer-aided design**) for designing with the help of the computer. The computer enhances the drawing by straightening the lines and making the curves more precise.
3. The ability to manipulate and change typesetting and graphical arts images by rearranging and greatly enhancing the components of the original design.
4. The use of graphic pictures for education and entertainment by incorporating them in learning programs and computer games.

Graphics Card Card connected internally to the computer to control the video display on the monitor. The card is capable of displaying graphics as well as text. There are many different types of graphics cards, the most popular being the VGA card.

Graphic Character Special character that when combined with one or more other special characters of the same or similar shape can be used to form graphical figures such as a box.

Graphics Coprocessor Special computer chip on a graphics card that allows the card to do most of the graphical layout and manipulation, freeing the system CPU to do other functions, thus speeding up the graphical display.

Graphics File Format Format used in placing a graphical file into storage on a disk.

Graphics Mode Graphic adapter that allows the system to display bitmap graphics onto the monitor.

Graphics Printer Printer that can print graphical as well as text characters. Most printers are changed to the graphical mode through software, though some must be adjusted manually by setting switches on the printer itself.

Graphics Scanner Add-on device that allows the user to scan a printed object and transform it into a computer-usable graphic.

Graphics Tablet Device that allows the user to draw on a special pad and transposes the pad drawing to the monitor; the graphic thus drawn can also be used in other programs.

Graphics View Feature available in many programs that offers a much more appealing screen display by showing a graphical environment instead of plain text.

Gray Scale

Gray Scale Use of various shades from white to black to represent an image similar to a black-and-white photograph.

Gray-Scale Monitor Monitor equipped with a matching video adapter that can display the various shades from black to white, creating the different levels of gray.

Greeking Using symbols to represent text on a page when the page is displayed too small for the presentation of legible text.

Group Most commonly used in the Windows environment, group refers to the set of program icons that exist in the same main group icon. When the group icon is expanded, the individual icons for all the programs are then made visible.

Group Icon Icon in Windows representing a particular group of files that when activated will expose the files contained in the group.

Guide Dotted line in a program showing page layout, such as margins, gutters, and various other layout elements.

Gutter Additional margin added to the left and right pages respectively in a word processing document to allow room for binding the pages into book format.

Grid Special feature of drawing and paint programs that when activated will make sure that lines drawn are drawn only in certain locations coinciding with the lines of the grid. This is helpful in lining up text and graphics in documents.

Grid System Used when laying out numerous related pages to keep the basic layout structure the same. The user designs and draws a grid to define columns and picture positions .

Grounding The third prong of the electrical plug is used to ground the system to prevent possible damage from lightning and also to reduce radio frequency interference and line noise.

GUI Acronym for Graphical User Interface, which presents the user with graphic symbols or pictures that can be activated by clicking with a mouse to perform a certain functions.

Gun Part of a computer monitor that fires electrons to the inside of the monitor to produce the display.

GW-BASIC

GW-BASIC Form of **BASIC** but without the need for an IBM ROM chip.

H

Hack To change a portion of a program by altering the code of the program instead of through the normal running of the program. Many programmers have illegally broken the code of certain copy-protected software and bypassed the copyright by rewriting the code at that point.

Hacker Extremely skilled computer programmer, or a person who programs computers as a recreation or hobby, or a person who illegally breaks into a computer system.

Half Card Shorter add-on card, in comparison to a full-length card.

Half Duplex Transmission of data in one direction only.

Half-Height Drive Drive that is about 1 5/8 inches high, compared to the full-height drive, which is double this size.

Halftone Process of representing a graphic picture by replacing the gray tone with different patterns and darkness of dots. Darker shades are represented by dense, dark dots while lighter shades are represented by less dense patterns of smaller dots.

Hammer Part of a printer that either strikes the ribbon to make characters or is the mechanism that strikes another parts that strike the ribbon. In dot-matrix printers, the hammers are the pins.

Handle In numerous graphics programs, a set of black squares or handles are placed around an object when an object is selected. These handles can be selected and dragged to alter the appearance of the selected object.

Handshaking Connecting two computers successfully to sent and receive data properly.

Hands On Learning by actually working on a computer.

Hanging Indent Situation in which the first word of a paragraph is flush along the left column and all lines following are indented.

Hard Card Hard drive built onto an expansion card that fits into an expansion slot on the motherboard instead of in a drive space.

Hard Copy Material printed out by a printer onto paper.

Hard Disk

Hard Disk Device made of aluminum disks coated with iron oxide permanently mounted in the computer to store data and programs. Hard disks have much larger storage capacities than floppy disks.

Hard Disk Backup Utility Program that aids in backing up files located on the hard disk onto either floppy disks or a tape backup unit. This program will generally guess at the number of disks that will be needed for the backup procedure and will also let the user randomly select the areas for backup if the entire drive does not need backing up.

Hard Disk Interface Standard in electronics for the connection of a hard drive to the computer.

Hard Disk Management Following are some guidelines for maintaining a hard drive.

1. Make frequent backups of the drive.
2. Organize the drive by creating subdirectories that contain related files. This makes it easier to locate a file when needed and also keeps the drive organized in a fashion similar to a file cabinet.
3. Always have a PATH command set up in the Autoexec.bat file so that commonly used utilities can be accessed regardless of your location on the hard drive.
4. The command PROMPT PG, in the Autoexec.bat file, will show at the DOS prompt the current directory.
5. Always keep disks fresh by deleting any unwanted or outdated files.
6. After numerous deletions, run CHKDSK to check for disk integrity and to locate any lost clusters that have occurred due to deletions.
7. A defragmentation program should be run on a monthly basis on the hard drive to optimize the disk by putting all the fragmented files back together in one continuous area.

Hardware All the elements and devices that make up a computer system, such as the integrated circuit boards, monitor, printer, drives, and so on.

Hardware Interrupt Interrupt generated internally by the microprocessor or externally by the hardware. External interrupts are generated to signal the attention of the microprocessor. Internal interrupts are used to control events such as a program trying to divide by zero.

Hardware Platform

Hardware Platform Standard related to computer hardware, such as IBM PC compatible or Macintosh.

Hardware Reset Pressing a reset button on the computer to warm boot it once it has been initially turned on.

Hayes Compatibility Ability of a modem to respond to commands that have been designed for the Hayes Smartmodem. Modems do not have to be Hayes-compatible to be able to communicate. These commands are only the means by which the computer communicates with the modem.

Head Part of a disk drive that reads and writes to a disk. A double-density disk and a hard drive have a head for each side of the disk.

Head Cleaning Device Device that removes any debris from the drive head usually with the application of a cleaning liquid.

Head Crash Circumstance that occurs when the read-write head on a disk collides with the disk surface, usually causing damaged areas to the disk.

Header Portion of text that appears at the top of every page of a printed document, such as a report title or page numbers.

Heat Sink Specially shaped device used in many electronic projects to direct the heat from delicate electronic components. Heat sinks have fins that help to absorb heat and allow more area for the heat to dissipate into the atmosphere.

Help Most newer software programs have a built-in help feature that can be accessed for helpful tips on how to perform a certain task. In many programs, pressing the F1 key will bring up a help screen.

Helvetica Typeface generally used in display applications and occasionly for body type in a letter.

Hercules Graphics Card Card providing the same functions as an IBM monochrome card, but able to display higher-resolution graphics.

Hertz Unit of measurement of electrical vibrations. One single Hz is equal to one cycle per second.

Hewlett-Packard Company well known in the computer industry for its Laserjet printers.

Hewlett-Packard Control Language

Hewlett-Packard Control Language (HPPCL) Printer-control language, developed by Hewlett-Packard for the first Laserjet printer in 1984, that has become a standard in the field of laser printers.

Hexadecimal Number written in base 16, which contains 16 possible digits—0, 1, 2, 3, 4, 5, 6, 7, 8, 9, A (10), B (11), C (12), D (13), E (14), and F (15).

Hidden Codes Hidden instructions in a document that the computer uses to format a document to the screen or printer.

Hidden Files Files that exist on a disk but do not appear when a directory listing is done. There are two hidden system files on a boot disk that are needed when booting the system; these two files are also read-only. They are hidden for the sole purpose of preventing the operator from deleting them. The DOS commands COPY and XCOPY will not copy hidden files from one disk to another.

High Density Disk capable of storing more data than double-density disks. High-density disks were created to make backups a little more tolerable.

High-End Top-of-the-line products produced by any one company. In most cases, high-end computers are used by professional users.

High-Level Format Formatting process that sets up area on a disk for certain files such as the boot record, file allocation table, number of tracks free, and the areas in use on a disk system.

High-Level Programming Language Very powerful programming language, such as Basic or Pascal, similar to human language.

High Memory Usually refers to the amount of memory above the standard 640K DOS memory.

High Memory Area (HMA) Generally the first 64K of memory located above the one-megabyte area of memory. Programs that conform to the extended-memory specification can make use of this extended memory the same as conventional memory.

High Resolution Ability of a monitor or printer to produce smooth-looking characters at large as well as small type sizes. It

High Resolution

also allows for the display and printing of smooth, well-defined curves in graphical images.

Highlight Selecting a block of text or other object, which is generally shown in reverse video on the screen when selected. Once highlighted, that specific portion of the object or text may be manipulated.

HIMEM.SYS DOS driver included with Microsoft Windows and DOS that configures the upper memory on a computer along with any extended and high memory to allow programs with the capacity to use these areas to do so. Such programs must conform to the XMS or extended memory standard.

Home Computer Computer designed and marketed for the home user. Uses range from game playing to checkbook record keeping all the way to private home businesses like desktop publishing. Home computers started out as low-memory, limited systems but gradually business computers were introduced to the home market; now the systems in most homes are more than capable of handling the work of a major business.

Homegrown Software Software that an individual writes at home and not in a professional type of environment. Many of the shareware programs are homegrown software.

Home Key Key on the keyboard usually programmed to do a particular function according to the program being used. In several programs it is used to return either to the beginning of a page or document or to the beginning of a line.

Host Computer Main computer in charge of all operations in a series of computers linked in a network. Also refers to the system that runs a BBS.

Hot Key One- or two-key command used as a shortcut in many programs. It can be used to access different features in a program or it to switch the user to a completely different program. Hot key are popular in most well-written programs to make features less troublesome.

Hourglass Icon Icon that appears in Microsoft Windows to indicate that an operator needs to wait for processing to be completed.

Hung system

Hung system Situation in which a terminal error occurs in a program that is running. The system completely freezes up, becoming inoperable and causing all data to this point to be lost.

Hypertext Means in which topics can be viewed by selecting any of the options highlighted. Keywords are highlighted in the text file, and the user can select any of these highlighted words to jump to the area describing the word selected. Most good hypertext files give the option to return to the previous screen or advance ahead in steps of a screen at a time. Hypertext is used for program tutors as well as for help files to make it easier for the user to obtain help on any particular area of the program.

Hyphenation Option in most word processors that allows the program to split and hyphenate words at the end of lines to enhance the spacing on a page. Some programs allow the user to select a grade of hyphenation.

Hz Abbreviation for Hertz.

I-Beam Pointer Cursor used in most word processing programs to indicate that the user is editing the text.

IBM Acronym for International Business Machines, the computer industry's biggest manufacturer.

IBM PC-Compatible Computer Clone or copy of an IBM computer designed to run all or most of the software designed to run on an IBM system. IBM Compatibles are very popular now because their price is generally far less than that of a true IBM system.

IC Acronym for **Integrated Circuit**.

Icon Small picture that represents either a program or a function in a graphical approach to computer systems. The trash can on a Macintosh screen, for example, is used for deleting files by dragging the icon of a file or to the trash can with a mouse and releasing the mouse button.

Iconic Interface User interface that employs icons for manipulations instead of typed-in commands. Most newer programs are being designed with this type of environment.

IDE Acronym for Integrated Device Electronics, a type of drive with the largest part of the disk controller built right into the drive to save space on the motherboard. These drives are popular because they are fast and affordable.

Idle Time during which a device or computer is available for processing but has no task to perform. Also refers to the time of waiting for a device while it waits for command execution.

IF Condition used in programming that allows a decision to be made, such as IF balance = 0 then go to stop. The IF designates that a condition must be met for the process to continue.

Image Can refer to a copy or duplication of something. In graphics programs an image is a stored description of a picture. There are several formats in existence for computer images, the most popular of which is probably the GIF format.

Image Compression Program that enables the user to compress graphics files to reserve disk space.

Image Processing

Image Processing Use of the computer to enhance and modify a graphic image. There are many good image-processing software programs on the market that enable the computer work with graphic files the same as a photographer would with a portrait in a photo lab.

Imaging Process of capturing, storing, displaying, and printing graphical images. Capturing can be done with a scanner or a capture program. Storing can be done on the hard drive or on floppy disks. Displaying the files usually requires the presence of a graphics presentation program or viewer. Printing can be done using various programs.

Impact Printer Printer—such as a dot-matrix printer—that creates images by striking against a printer ribbon to form characters or images on paper.

Import Ability to load a file created with one program into a totally different program retaining its integrity and formatting.

Increment Set amount by which a number is increased.

Incremental Backup Backup procedure that copies only newer files that had not already been backed up previously.

Indicator Visual method to display the status of a device to the user. On disk drives, a light comes on to show that the drive is being accessed.

Industry Standard Architecture (ISA) Architecture design of computer circuit boards that have become a standard.

Infection Existence of a virus or a "Trojan Horse" in a computer system. These infections may not be visible until a certain time or date is reached. There are many types of viruses, and there are programs that can scan the system and locate the virus before it does any harm.

Infinite Loop Loop in a program code that because of logical errors can never finish by normal means, since it processes a set of instructions continuously without any provision for a way to exit.

Information Management Gathering, evaluating, safeguarding, and distributing data for an organization or a computer system.

Information Processing Acquiring, storing, manipulating, and displaying data by electronic means.

Inhibit

Inhibit Disabling a function. To inhibit an interrupt on a device prevents that device from using that particular interrupt.

Initialize Preparing a device to be put into use. A disk must be initialized before it is able to store data. A modem needs to be initialized for it to know the settings to communicate with another computer.

Initial Program Load Procedure of loading the operating system into the computer upon bootup.

Ink Cartridge Disposable cartridge containing ink, most commonly used in inkjet printers.

Inkjet Printer Type of printer that prints by firing small dots of ink onto the paper. This printer is a cheaper alternative to a laser printer. It is faster and quieter than a dot matrix printer and offers higher resolution.

Input Any data entered into the computer to be processed. Some input devices for getting the information into the computer are a keyboard, floppy disk, or a hard disk drive.

Input Buffer Memory area reserved for storing information entering the system awaiting processing.

Input Device Any device that enables the user to input data into the computer system. Some sources for input are the keyboard, modem, mouse, trackball, and graphics tablet.

Input/Output (I/O) System Main part of the computer that governs the smooth flow of data into and out of the central processing unit.

INS Key Short for insertion key, primarily used to toggle from insert mode to typeover mode in word processing programs.

Insert Mode Mode in a word processor that allows a user to insert text at a certain point and in doing so all letters to the right of the inserted letter will be moved farther to the right making room for the newly inserted text.

Insertion Point Point designated, usually by the cursor, to show where the next character typed will appear in a document.

Install To set up and prepare for operation. Most software

Install

packages include a special program that installs the software onto the drive.

Installable Device Driver Special device driver or control program loaded into memory to be used by the operation system to enable data transfer to and from a device such as a printer, monitor, disk drive, scanner, or mouse. Most device drivers are loaded into the system at bootup. On high-end systems, these drivers can be loaded into upper memory so they do not take up valuable DOS memory.

Installation Program Utility program that comes with much of the purchased software that installs the program to the hard drive with very little effort on the user's part. Most installation programs will query the user for some minor input or to verify that any changes being made to the system setup are satisfactory with the user.

Instruction Set Set of keywords of all actions and operations that a central processing unit can perform.

Integrated Circuit Any electronic device made of several small transistors and various other circuit elements located on a single silicon computer chip. Integrated circuits were first developed in the 1950s and have been vastly improved since.

Integrity Accuracy and pure contents of data stored on a computer system, particularly after it has been modified.

INTEL Corporation that makes most of the microprocessors used in PCs today. They make processors for the 8088, 80286, 80386, and 80486 computers.

Interactive Back-and-forth response of operations, such as when a user enters a question to the computer and the computer responds immediately.

Interface Electronic circuit that monitors the connection between two pieces of hardware to ensure they exchange data properly.

Interference Any noise or a signal that inhibits the proper operation of a computer's communication channel. Many phone lines have a high noise level, which makes communicating through the use of a modem intolerable.

Interlacing Refreshing a video monitor first on all odd-numbered lines and then on all even-numbered lines on the screen or vice

Interlacing

versa. This is supposed to eliminate any flicker seen because of the screen being scanned twice as often as it would if all lines were refreshed in a single pass. This process is fine for television viewing but is not very appealing in computer monitors.

Interleave Factor Ratio of physical disk sectors of a hard drive that are skipped between each sector that is written. The most favorable interleave is 1:1; anything other than that will slow down the system.

Interleaved Memory Process of increasing system speed by having two banks of memory chips; while the system is accessing one of the banks, the other bank can be refreshed, thus giving better system performance.

Intermittent Errors Errors that occur infrequently but are nevertheless annoying. Many occur because of a program glitch or a system malfunction and are hard to trace because of their irregularity.

Internal Bus Data and control connections from a microprocessor to its other circuits and the memory on the system. Also referred to as local bus.

Internal Clock Chip in the system that keeps track of the date and time, which can be accessed from this chip to be used in various software packages.

Internal Fonts Fonts that are permanently stored inside the computer on ROM chips.

Internal Modem Modem on an add-on card that is placed inside the system in one of the expansion slots.

Internal Storage Amount of memory built into a computer.

International Business machines (IBM) The computer industry's largest manufacturer.

Interpret To decode and execute a statement or an instruction to the computer.

Interpreter Program that can read the code of a programming language one line at a time and execute the program in this manner.

Interrupt Message sent to a microprocessor telling it to drop its present project and carry out a special instruction that needs

Interrupt

performed at this time. When the processor finishes with the instructions for the interrupt, it continues where it left off when interrupted.

I/O Abbreviation for Input/Output.

IO.SYS One of the hidden system files installed onto the hard drive. This file contains the drivers that run the keyboard, display, floppy and hard drives, serial port, and real-time clock, and is needed during bootup.

ISA (Industry Standard Architecture) Refers to the IBM PC (8-bit system) and the IBM PC AT (16-bit system).

J

Jack Connector with the ability to receive some type of plug. One type of jack is the connector jack in a modem for connecting a phone line plug to the modem. In most cases a jack is wired to a circuit board, most commonly for video and audio connections to the computer.

Jacket Plastic covering on a disk that has openings to allow for a disk drive to read the actual disk inside. This jacket is a part of the casing and should never be removed from the disk.

Jaggies Jagged effect of a line drawn at an angle, which will also print jagged. Programs such as Adobe Type Manager will eliminate this jagged effect and give a neater appearance to a project

Jargon Specialized type of speech. Computer jargon refers to terms related to use computers. Many people refer to this jargon as computereeze because they consider it a foreign language.

JCL Acronym for Job Control Language, a batch file type language that gives specific instructions to the computer about the process it must follow to perform a task.

Jitter Fluttering effect seen on a television or a computer monitor when a weak or irregular display signal is received.

Job Specific task that needs to be completed that is mostly done by a computer, usually without human intervention. This term originated in the mainframe environment in which the programmer did not actually run the computer but instead submitted programs as a job to the operator, who in turn ran the job on the system and returned the end product to the programmer.

Job Processing Method of computing by which a series of jobs—each containing one or more tasks grouped together as a whole task—is processed in order.

Job Queue Listing of jobs that are automatically executed on a computer system one after the other.

Join Connecting two or more compatible data files. In DOS the term means being able to connect a disk drive to a directory on a second drive, giving the appearance that the directory is stored on the second drive.

Julian Date

Julian Date Method in computer programming and computing in general in which the date is represented as the number of days elapsed since the first of the year; for example, 92.24, which would be day 24 of 1992.

Jumper Electrical connector that can be moved to different settings to alter the function of a circuit board. The jumper consists of a small block of plastic with two or three metal receptacles that can be inserted over pins located on the circuit board.

Jump Instruction Instruction that when reached sends the flow of execution of a program from one program instruction to another instruction, such as the GOTO statement used in some programming languages.

Joystick Input device found on many computers that is a great aid in game playing or simulators. The joystick is maneuverable by hand to control the movement on the computer screen.

Junction Place where two or more electronic parts are connected.

Justification Spacing of text to fill out a column so that the right and left margins are even and smooth. Many of the good word processors have a text justification feature.

K Short for kilobyte, the measurement of memory in a computer. A memory storage of 1K is equal to 1024 characters of information. The maximum memory size without using bank switching is 640K. Many of the newer high-end systems have several megabytes of memory far surpassing the kilobyte range.

Kbps Abbreviation for kilobyte per second, to describe speed.

KAYPRO Corporation in Solona Beach, California, that manufactures microcomputers containing the 80286 and 80386 microprocessors, which were usually were bundled with a word processing package along with a few other selections of software.

Kermit One of the numerous protocols for transferring files from one computer to another. The Kermit protocol makes an exact copy of a file even if the phone line is extremely noisy. All chunks of transmitted data are checked for transmission errors. If errors are detected, then that chunk of information is resent.

Kernel Main part of an operating system that has control over disk input and output as well as managing the system memory.

Kerning Spacing of certain combinations of letters of proportional type size, allowing certain letters to have less space between them while others will be given wider spaces. The spacing of the letters "Th," for example, would be less than the letter "Ty" because of the width of the overall double letter structure.

Key Key has several different meanings in the computer field.
1. The buttons on the keyboards.
2. An item identifier preassigned by a user to locate that item quickly.
3. A password or another secret entry used to gain access to an encrypted file.

Key Disk Special disk included with software from some companies that must be inserted into a drive and be recognized by the system and the program before the program can run.

Key Status Indicator Displaying of special keys that can be toggled in a program. The keys are usually displayed along the top or bottom of the screen and show whether they are off or on.

Keyboard

Keyboard The most-used part of the computer for input. There are several different styles and sizes of keyboards on the market, the most popular of which is the 101 keyboard. The keyboard's resemblance to a typewriter makes it easy for typists to acquaint themselves with it.

Keyboard Buffer Small memory storage area that stores the keystrokes that entered on the keyboard. This buffer can vary in size and can store numerous keystrokes while waiting for the system to respond to them.

Keyboard Template Paper or plastic insert that fits over the keyboard keys (mostly the function keys), with hints and tips printed on them to show different key combinations of the software that can be used for shortcuts while working in the program.

Keycap Plastic cap with letter printed on it that is attached to the actual key striker bars.

Key code Code assigned to the keys of a keyboard that can be used in accessing that key. Each key has its own special code or identifier, which can be used in programming to change the function of certain keys on the keyboard.

Key Field Field of a record that serves a special purpose, such as having an identifying number that can be used for finding a particular record. Using this number for the finding process makes that field a key field.

Key In To enter information into the computer by means of the keyboard.

Keypad Usually refers to the numeric keypad located to the right side of a keyboard on a 101-type of keyboard.

Keypunch Machine that was used for entering data onto computer cards by punching holes in certain combinations that are defined by the computer as characters. Through new technology, the keypunch has become a thing of the past. Most data is now entered through keyboard input or through floppy disk or tape.

Keystroke Action of pressing the keys on the keyboard to enter characters into the computer.

Keyword

Keyword Special identifier words in programs. In Basic the word GOSUB is referred to as a keyword because it has a special meaning to the Basic compiler.

kHz Abbreviation for kilohertz.

Kill To stop or abort a process in action on a computer. Also used to mean erasing a file without the possibility of recovering it by any means.

Kilobyte Equal to 1024 characters of information.

Kilocycle Unit of measurement of 1000 cycles per second.

Kilohertz Unit of measurement of frequency equivalent to 1000 Hertz or 1000 cycles per second.

L

Label Name of a statement in the program code used in programming. Files stored on tapes have a file identifier label that precedes the file when written to the tape that contains pertinent information about the file. In a spreadsheet program, label refers to text or a heading that is placed in a cell. Label also refers to the stick-on labels that come in a package of floppy disks and are used to identify the disk and its files.

Label Printer Printer able to print names and addresses on continuous feed labels that can be peeled from their backing and placed on envelopes for mailing or used for identification purposes.

Lag Time difference between two events. Also refers to the time difference between a change of input and a change of output.

LAN Acronym for **Local Area Network**, a grouping of computers connected to a main unit called the server.

Lan Backup Program Program designed to back all pertinent files on a Lan network file server to be stored for safety purposes.

Lan Ignorant Program Stand-alone program that is written with no previsions for use on a Lan network and is run on a single system at a time.

Lan Memory Management Program Program that manages the memory on each system connected on a Lan network to create the most available conventional memory to allow users to run applications on the network. Each workstation must have its own memory management program to move items around in memory to make the best use of the system resources.

Lan Server Main computer to which all other systems in a Lan network are connected, containing all the files and programs needed to be used on all other systems. Servers usually are fast, high-end systems with large amounts of memory and disk storage space.

Landscape Type of page layout in which the page is wider than it is tall (derived from the horizontal orientations of landscape painting). The printer prints to the paper in a sideways manner to make the printout appear in the landscape format. Many of the high-end programs that print allow the option to print either in landscape or portrait.

Laptop

Laptop Compact computer with a flip-up screen, generally weighing under eight pounds. These computers can be powered by batteries, making them ideal for people who need to use a computer while traveling. Laptops have advanced to the stage that they now offer many of the same features as large systems, such as color VGA displays, large-capacity hard disk drives, modems, floppy disk drives, and the ability to add expansion cards.

Large-Scale Integration In integrated-circuit technology, refers to the fabrication of up to 100,000 transistor devices on a single computer chip.

Laser Printer Printer that employs a laser beam to produce an image that is then transferred to paper through a special process. Instead of using a ribbon process to place print on a page, the laser printer uses toner and a drum to print, much like a copy machine. Laser printers—though more expensive than standard dot-matrix printers—are preferred by desktop publishers because of their exceptionally high-quality output. They are much faster and quieter than dot-matrix printers, making them even more admired in an office environment.

Laser Storage Storage of data onto metallic discs—such as compact disks—by use of optical read and write technology, allowing for extremely large storage onto a relatively small space.

Laserjet Popular brand of laser printer produced by Hewlett-Packard. There are several types of Laserjet: Laserjet Plus, Laserjet II, and Laserjet III. Each model was enhanced with improved commands that control the printer operation, as well as more and improved built-in fonts. Laserjet printers have openings into which extra font cartridges may be plugged to allow for more built-in fonts.

Laserwriter Laser printer widely used with the Macintosh computer. It uses the Postscript command language.

Latency Delay incurred in disk drives when the rotating disk is locating desired data under the read-write heads.

Launch To start a program.

Layer In some applications this term refers to the ability to have multiple screens independent of other generated screens. Several

Layer

layers of text and graphics can be utilitzed to create the illusion of special effects in documents.

Layout Arrangement of text and graphics on a page for printing or presentation. Also refers to the manual design of a project to determine the results to be achieved by use of the computer.

LCD Acronym for **Liquid Crystal Display**.

Leader Dots or dashes used in some word processing to make it easier for the eye to follow a path across a line on a page.

Leading Inserting space between lines of type to improve the appearance of the page. In the old printing-press days, this process was done with strips of lead, hence the origin of the word.

Leading Zero Zeros placed in front of numbers to take up the entire allocated space for the numeric field. Much of the newly written software either does not require the leading zeros or automatically eliminates the leading zeros when printing the file.

Leapfrog Test Diagnostic test performed on a disk or tape in which a routine repeatedly copies itself onto the storage device.

LED Acronym for **Light Emitting Diode**.

Left Justification Alignment of text along the left margin, which gives the right margin a jagged appearance.

Legend Area that explains the meaning of the different colors or patterns used in a graph or chart.

Length Amount of disk storage space occupied by a file. Also refers to the actual size allocated to a field in a data record or to the size of a record.

Letter Quality Printed text equal in quality to that produced by the best typewriters. All laser printers and daisy-wheel printers are of letter quality, as are some brands of inkjet and dot-matrix printers.

Library Collection of computer programs, files, or programming subroutines or procedures.

Library Routine Previously written and tested subroutines, procedures, or functions in a particular programming language that can be incorporated into future programs as modules. These are

Library Routine

used to eliminate the need for writing codes over again for tasks that almost all programs use, such as reading data from a disk.

Light-Emitting Diode (LED) Form of display used in some laptop computers—as well as many digital clocks—that functions by passing current through diodes, much like a light bulb.

Light Pen Light-sensitive, pen-shaped device used to control pictures on a computer screen. Light pens perform in a way similar to a mouse, except that the light pen is placed directly on the screen to activate functions.

Limit Check Check used in programming to verify that information is within a set acceptable limit.

Line Single statement or line of code in programming. In communications the term refers to the circuit that connects two or more electronic devices.

Line Adapter Electronic device able to convert signals from one form to another to enable the signals to be transmitted in a data communications program.

Line Analyzer Device used to monitor and test the transmission characteristics of a communications line.

Linear Addressing Architecture Design that enables the microprocessor to access any specific memory location by the use of a single-address value.

Linear Search Simple algorithm reading data sequentially by each item until either the target element is located or the end of the list of data has been reached. Also known as a sequential search.

Line Art Computer-drawn graphic with no colortones, making reproduction on low- and medium-resolution printers very accurate.

Line Chart Business-related graphic that displays values from one or more sets of data connected by lines.

Line Concentration Compressing multiple input lines into a lesser number of output lines.

Line Drawing Drawing made with solid lines and with no other features representing contour or mass.

Line Editor

Line Editor Cumbersome text editor that only allows for the editing of a single line of code at a time. The line editor has been replaced by the full-screen editor.

Line Feed Code sent by the computer to the printer to signal it to start a new line of print. The line feed character moves only the printed page down one line from the previously printed line; it does not move the print head or the cursor. To move the print head to the beginning of the next line along with advancing the line, you must also include a carriage return with the line feed.

Line Join Method in which two line segments are connected when they are printed.

Line Number Number assigned to a line in a line editor. By accessing the line number, you are able to edit, view, or print that line. The line numbers run in sequential order starting from one.

Line of Code Measurement of program length. Also refers to each individual line of type placed in a program file.

Line Printer High-speed printer, found mostly on mainframe computers, made of a chain of type elements for each column of print. This allows it to print an entire line of text at a time, in some cases up to 1,400 lines per minute.

Line Segment Part of a line defined by the beginning and ending points of the line.

Lines Per Minute Usually abbreviated LPM. Used in reference to printer speed. The term originated for line printers, since it took the same amount of time to print each given line. Dot-matrix printers are rated at characters per second and laser printers are rated at page per minute.

Line Style Shape and quality of a line in desktop publishing, printing, and high-end word processors. These lines are usually designated as a dotted line, a double line, or a hairline.

Line Surge Sudden change in amount of current or voltage being carried through a line. Storms are a known cause of surges in power lines. Surge protectors can be connected to a computer to protect the internal electronic components from damage due to these surges.

Line Voltage

Line Voltage Amount of voltage or electric energy present in a power line.

Line Width Length of a typed line, measured from the left to the right margin either on a computer monitor or on printed paper.

Link Connection path between two computers for communication. The ability of two programs to exchange and update data automatically is also called a link.

Linker Special program that links compiled program modules and related data files for the creation of executable programs.

Liquid Crystal Display (LCD) Type of display widely used in laptop computers, calculators, and digital watches. LCDs use liquid crystals made of chemicals whose properties change in the presence of electrical fields. With the use of a polarizing filter, the LCD can take on a dark or light appearance according to its electrical state. LCDs consume less energy than other types of displays, but they are sometimes hard to read because they lack contrast. A newer form of LCD, called "Supertwist," is an improved type that gives more contrast, making the screen more readable

List Group of data processed in a particular order, such as alphabetical or numerical. Also refers to displaying the contents of a file or program.

List Box Type of box that appears in a message box allowing for the selection of a grouping of choices.

Listing Printed list produced to show the lines of code from a program source code to allow the programmer to see the entire structure of the code on paper.

Literal Symbol in programming languages that stands for a value and is not programmer-defined. Literals are a stand-in for data that is entered at a later time.

Load Process of reading information into a computer from a storage device on the system so that it can be processed.

Loader Utility used to load the executable code of a program into memory to be executed, usually an invisible part of an operating program called up when a program is run.

Loader Routine

Loader Routine Program routine with the responsibility for loading executable code into memory and executing it. This loading routine can either be a part of the actual operating system or it can be a part of the program itself.

Load Module Executable portion of code loaded into memory by the loader module. A computer program can consist of one or more load modules that can be loaded and executed individually.

Load Point Start position of a valid data area on a magnetic tape.

Local Item or operation at or near the present location. In a communications session, this refers to having a device accessible directly without the means of a communication line. In reference to information processing, it means doing the processing on a computer readily available at the present location rather than doing the processing from a remote system.

Local Area Network (LAN) Connection of several computers located close to each other, such as in the same building, allowing all the computers to share files and computer devices such as printers. This is a very popular type of linking for offices that require several users to enter information into the system pertaining to the same data file.

Local Bypass Means of connecting computers in different locations through a phone connection that bypasses the telephone company.

Local Drive Drive that is part of the user's workstation in a network environment, as separate from the drive on the server of the network.

Local Echo Ability to display text on the screen of the local system being used, as well as to transmit it to another computer. This enables the user to see what is received by the other system.

Local Memory Memory located on the same card or on the same high-speed bus as a **processor.**

Local Printer Printer connected to the local workstation that a user is operating, instead of a printer that may be connected to the main server in a network.

Local Variable Variable that has a meaning in a given subroutine or function only. Using local variables in programming allows a

Local Variable

programmer to use the same variable name in more than one function or routine, each having a different meaning to the program.

Locking Ability to bar the use of a files in a database record, used widely in a database environment to prevent two people from accessing the same file at the same time. Locking the file enables one user at a time to edit a particular file; other users can see the file but cannot actually access it for manipulation until it has been unlocked by the other person.

Locked File File on a network server that has been locked out from being accessed by applications or users so they are unable to update or delete the file.

Lockout Act by which a user may be denied access to either a file or a system itself. Also refers to the access denial to a given resource, such as files, memory location, or an I/O port, to ensure that only one program can use the resource at a time.

Lock Up Condition causing processing to be halted or suspended; the program in process will accept no user input or recovery intervention.

Log Ability in some programs to keep track of procedures that take place while working on the computer. A tracking file is created to show what activity took place at a given time and which user produced the track file. A log can be viewed to track any misuse on a multi-user system. Also refers to changing from one disk drive to another, such as logging onto drive C: or logging onto drive D:.

Logic Board Main board in the system, also known as the motherboard, to which the memory and expansion cards are connected. This board contains all the main circuits that control system function.

Logical Operation or computing procedure based solely on true and false decisions, instead of entirely on arithmetic calculations of numbers.

Logical Drives Disk drives of a computer presented as identical devices that retrieve and save data using the same file-management commands.

Logic Gate Device that can accept binary digits as input and produce an output bit according to a special rule.

Logical Operator

Logical Operator Symbol for specifying a logical relationship of inclusion or exclusion between two quantities or concepts.

Logic Programming Program that uses the computer to make conclusions from data by logic reasoning. Sometimes referred to as artificial intelligence programming.

Log-In Security In network systems and BBSs, this is the procedure of gaining access to the system by typing in a previously defined password or code word pertaining to a particular account.

Log Off Procedure of completing a connection with another computer system in a designated, orderly fashion in which the connection is ended.

Log On Ability to connect to another computer and successfully gain access by entering the proper identification.

Log-On File Prewritten batch file, activated when the system is turned on, that automatically connects the computer to the network server.

Look-Up Function Procedure in which a program is able to consult and retrieve data stored in a data table or file.

Look-Up Table Special area set up with data that the program may access to determine the necessary information to use in a given task. This is a storage area for information to be selected by the program according to a set procedure.

Loop Programming procedure that causes a function to repeat itself until a given condition occurs or the number or repetitions required has been reached. A condition must be met to be able to exit from the loop, otherwise the loop function will continue indefinitely.

Loop Control Structure Well-written control structure of a loop that causes a set of instructions to be repeated until a defined condition occurs.

Lost Chain Section of a file that was once connected to other sections of the same file, but for some reason the (**FAT**) file allocation table no longer has information needed to reconnect the various file sections. In most cases lost chains are unrecoverable and the files must be deleted. If the lost chains are text files, some of the contents may be recoverable.

Lost Cluster

Lost Cluster Sectors on a disk that are not designated as free or open space but are not listed as belonging to any particular file or program. This results from interruption of file creation. These clusters take up valuable disk space and need to be cleared periodically by using the DOS command CHKDSK /F.

Lotus 1-2-3 Very popular business software package manufactured by the Lotus Development Corp., coupling the functions of a spreadsheet with the ability of data managing and graphics. Many large corporations are using this software package widely due to its range of functions.

Low-End Inexpensive products at or near the bottom of a company's merchandise, usually similar to their high-end equivalent but without some of the advanced features. Some low-end merchandise is actually outdated or obsolete, which accounts for the low cost.

Lowercase Letters in their noncapitalized form.

Low-Level Format Physical pattern of magnetic tracks and sectors located on a disk during the format procedure. This type of format is different from the high-level format, which establishes the housekeeping sections that keep track of free space on the disk as well as the used areas of the disk.

Low Memory Lowest memory locations on a computer system. Usually refers to the first 640K of memory that DOS recognizes. This low memory area is reserved for RAM that is used by DOS and application programs.

Low Resolution Computer monitors and printers unable to produce crisp, clear text or graphics, resulting in shapes being jagged around the edges.

LPT Device name in DOS that defines one of the parallel ports to which parallel printers can be connected.

Luminance Measurement of light radiated by a specified source, such as a computer monitor screen. When speaking of colors, luminance refers to the brightness of the color rather than its hue or saturation.

M Abbreviation for megabyte.

Machine Address Absolute address in the system.

Machine Code Code—produced when a written program in any language is compiled successfully—consisting of sequences of 1s and 0s that can be loaded and executed by the computer processor. Also called machine language because it is the only language that the machine can actually interpret and understand.

Machine Cycle Amount of time required or the fastest operation that a computer can perform.

Machine Dependent Program or device connected to a specific computer; due to unique characteristics, it most likely cannot be used on a different computer system.

Machine Errors Error in the system hardware device. Though seldom encountered, these errors are usually critical when they do occur. One such machine error could be a bad memory chip or the inability to read from a disk drive.

Machine Identification Code that can be accessed by executing applications so that it is able to determine the identity and machine characteristics of a computer and the other devices connected to it.

Machine Independent Applications or hardware that can be used on more than one type of computer, with little or no modification.

Machine Language Special coded instructions compiled into a form that the computer can understand and act upon.

Machine Readable Input in a format that the computer can read, such as bar codes that are scanned directly into the system to be used in an application. Also refers to the binary information stored onto magnetic media that the computer can access and read into the memory.

Macro Set of keystrokes or special instructions recorded and saved under a shorter key code combination. By pressing the designated key that contains the macro, the system will carry out the instructions contained in that macro. By creating keyed macros, the user is able to record frequently used functions and have one-key access to this function the next time it is needed. This saves time

Macro

since once the macro is set up, instructions do not have to be manually typed each time.

Macro Recorder Program able to record and store macros.

Magnetic Disk Computer disk enclosed in a protective metal case (hard drive) or plastic case or jacket (floppy disk). These disks are coated with a magnetic material that permits flux changes on small sections of the disk surface. These changes are changes in magnetic polarity and these are used to encode information in binary format. The changes in flux are created by the high-speed read-write head of the disk drive as it passes over the disk surface. Because of the nature of disk structure, it must be protected from exposure to any source of magnetism, which can destroy all the information contained on the disk.

Magnetic Storage Storage of information onto any magnetic media, such as disks or tapes.

Magnitude Size of a number without regard to its negative or positive sign. Positive 16 and negative 16 both have the same magnitude.

Mailbox Area designated on a network system into which electronic mail messages are stored on disk. Each user has his or her own private mailbox area.

Mail-Merge In a mass-mail environment, the ability to integrate names, addresses, and other pertinent information into form letters or other special types of document.

Main Body Base structure of a program to which other branches of the program are connected. Execution of programs start in the main body portion of the coding and usually end with the last statement contained in the main body.

Mainframe Computer High-level computer designed for very intensive computing tasks. Mainframe computers are usually shared by numerous users at connected terminals.

Male Connector Connector with pins that can be inserted into receptacles.

Management Information Service (MIS) Department within any organization that is responsible for handling all forms of information.

Management Information System

Management Information System Computer-based system for processing and organizing data for provide different levels of management, including accurate and timely reports for supervision of activities, tracking progress, making decisions, and solving problems.

Manager Program designed to perform a set of housekeeping tasks on a computer. File managers, for example, are used to maintain files.

Map Representation of the structure of an object, such as a map of the system memory, to show what, if anything, is taking up space in memory locations.

Margin Portions of a document along the top, bottom, and both sides, outside of the main body of the document.

Mark Symbol or other device used to distinguish one item from others like it, sometimes used to indicate the beginning or end of a data item. Most word processors allow the marking and unmarking of text so the user can block off a specific area to be deleted, moved, or otherwise manipulated without affecting any of the other information outside the marked area.

Mask Binary value used for screening out or letting through certain bits in a data value. Masking is used in some graphics program to allow the user to mark off a particular section of the graphic to be altered without affecting the rest of the graphic.

Mass Storage Either tape or disk storage of computer-related data. The name derives from the fact that huge amounts of data can be stored on this type of media.

Master File File that generally has all the most pertinent information of a database program, such as names and addresses, which normally remain permanent over a period of time.

Matching Process for testing whether two sets of data are identical. Also used to describe the process of finding a data item that matches an entered key word or code.

Math Coprocessor Processor chip that can be added to the motherboard that takes over all floating point calculations from the main processor, which speeds the system when doing mathematical procedures.

Mathematical Function

Mathematical Function Procedure in a program that performs a mathematical operation on one or several values or expressions and returns a numeric value.

Matrix Arrangement of rows and columns used in organizing related items such as numbers, dots, spreadsheet cells, or circuit elements. In computer applications, matrixes are used to arrange sets of data into a table format. In hardware use, matrixes of dots are used to create characters on the screen and to form characters for printing, such as on a dot-matrix printer.

MCGA Acronym for Multi-Color Graphics Array, a video adapter that emulates the **CGA** (Color Graphics Adapter) in addition to providing two additional graphics modes. One of these is the 640 by 480 mode, which means it can display a resolution of 640 horizontal pixels by 480 vertical pixels with the choice of two colors from a palette of 262,144 colors. The second is the 320 by 200 mode, which displays 320 horizontal pixels by 200 vertical pixels with a choice of 256 colors from a palette of 262,144 colors.

MDA Acronym for Monochrome Display Adapter, a video adapter capable of only one display mode, which is 25 lines of 80 characters per line, with underlining, blinking, and high-intensity character capabilities.

Mean Time Between Failures (MTBF) Average time frame—usually described in thousands or tens of thousands of hours—that elapses before a hardware component fails to the point of requiring service.

Mechanical Mouse Pointing device with a movable ball located under it; when moved on a surface the motion of the ball is translated to directional signals for the computer to use. When moved, the large ball mounted in the bottom of the mouse turns rollers mounted inside the mouse case. The movement of these rollers sends signals to the computer, which interprets these signals into movement. The mouse device has become very popular in graphical user interface software, which allows the user to move the cursor the mouse device to point at an object to activate or manipulate it. The use of a mouse eliminates numerous keystrokes since it can take over the keyboard input in most newer software packages.

Media

Media Physical material, such as paper, disks, and tapes, used to store computer-related information.

Media Eraser Device able to remove or make unusable the information on a storage media on a wholesale basis, sometimes by merely writing unintelligible information over the information.

Medium-Scale Integration Concentration of from 10 to 100 circuit elements on a single computer chip.

Meg Abbreviation for megabyte.

Megabyte Either 1 million bytes of information or 1,048,576 bytes.

Megahertz Measure of frequency equivalent to one million cycles per second.

Memo Field Database field that can contain nonstructured text.

Memory Electronic circuit that allows for the storage and retrieval of information. In a general sense, the term can also refer to external systems such as disk drives or tape drives. The most common usage of the term is to refer to the storage RAM that is directly connected to the processor.

Memory Cartridge Module that can be plugged into a system. This module contains RAM chips that can be used by the system for storing data and programs.

Memory Management Unit Unit of hardware that supports mapping of virtual memory addresses to physical memory addresses.

Menu Listing of options in a program from which the user can make a selection to perform a particular task. Many applications and almost all graphical interface programs use menus to supply the user with an easy means of using the software application, thus eliminating the necessity of memorizing program commands to work in a software package.

Menu Bar Bar usually displayed along the top of a screen by which the user can access the actual pull-down menus. The names of each available menu are shown in the menu bar; choosing one of these names will activate the pull-down menu for the next selection.

Menu-Driven

Menu-Driven Program that makes use of menus for presenting a choice of commands or available options, a program popular because it is user-friendly and is easier to learn than programs that demand command-line entries.

Menu Item Choice selectable from a menu by the user. These items can be selected either by keyboard entry or by clicking with a mouse. If a specific menu item is grayed out, it is unavailable at the present time.

Merge Combining two or more items in an orderly fashion without changing the basic structure of either item.

Message Unit of information in a communications environment that is transmitted electronically from one device to another. There are several connotations of the term.

1. In electronic mail, a message is a note from another user, organized similar to a memorandum (TO, FROM, SUBJECT, DATE) and received in an electronic mailbox.

2. To a computer or a communications network, a message is a transmission unit that transmits according to certain rules (protocols) that are followed by both the sending and receiving devices. A message can contain one or more blocks of text as well as beginning and ending characters, control characters, a software-generated header (destination address, type of message, and other such information), and error-checking or synchronizing information. A message can be routed directly from sender to receiver through a physical link, or it can be passed, either whole or in sections, through a switching system that sends it from one station to another. Most of the complexity of sending and receiving messages is not noticeable to the user because of the hardware and software involved.

3. In software, a message is a piece of information passed from the application or the operating system to the user to suggest an action that must be taken, to indicate a condition, or to inform that an event has occurred.

Message header Sequence of bits or bytes at the beginning of a message that usually provides a timing sequence and specifies such aspects pertaining to the message structure as its length, data format, and block identification number.

Message Queue

Message queue Ordered line of messages waiting for transmission, from which they are taken on a first in, first out (FIFO) basis.

Message switching Technique used on some communications networks in which a message, with appropriate address information, is routed through one or more switching stations before being sent to its destination. On a typical message-switching network, a central computer receives messages, stores them (usually briefly), determines their destination addresses, and then delivers them to the appropriate party. Message switching enables a network to regulate traffic and to use communications lines efficiently.

Metacharacter Character encoded in a program source or a data stream that sends information about other characters, rather than actually representing a character itself. The backslash (\) character, for example, which, when used in strings in the C programming language, indicates that the letter following the backslash is part of an escape sequence that enables C to display a nongraphic character.

Metacompiler Compiler that produces other compilers, or file that contains or defines other files. Many operating systems use metafiles to contain directory information about other files on a given storage device.

Metalanguage Language used to describe other languages. Backus-Naur Form (BNF) is a metalanguage commonly used to define programming languages.

Metal-Oxide Semiconductor (MOS) A semiconductor is a device based on the insulating properties of certain metal oxides, such as aluminum oxide or silicon dioxide. MOS designs are widely used both in discrete components and in integrated circuits. MOS integrated circuits have the advantages of high component density, high speed, and low power consumption. These devices are easily damaged by static electricity, so it is recommended that before they are inserted in a circuit they should be kept with their connectors placed in conducting foam to prevent the buildup of static charges.

MFLOPS Abbreviation for megaflops, a measure of computing speed.of a million floating-point operations per second.

MFM Acronym for Modified Frequency Modulation encoding, a form of hard drive setup code that tells the system the type of drive and the drive format.

MHz

MHz Abbreviation for **megahertz**.

Micro Short for microcomputer. Also used as a prefix meaning small or compact, as in microfloppy disk, microprocessor, and microcomputer. When used as a prefix referring to an exact measurement, micromeans one-millionth, as in microampere (one millionth of an ampere).

Micro Channel Architecture Design of the bus in IBM PS/2 computers (except Models 2S and 30). The Micro Channel is electrically and physically incompatible with the IBM PC/AT bus. Unlike the PC/AT bus, the Micro Channel functions as either a 1-bit or a 2-bit bus and can also be driven independently by multiple bus master processors.

Microcircuit Miniature electronic circuit similar to the germanium and silicon wafers characteristic of microprocessors and other products of the semiconductor industry. A microcircuit is made up of internally connected transistors, resistors, and other components; unlike earlier electronic equipment, it is fabricated as a unit, instead of as a set of tubes or other elements wired together. Also referred to as an **integrated circuit**.

Microcode Extremely low-level code (even lower than **machine code**) that defines the operation of a processor. Microcode specifies what the processor does when it executes a machine-code instruction.

Microcomputer Computer built around a single-chip microprocessor. Less powerful than minicomputers and mainframe computers, microcomputers have developed into very powerful machines capable of performing complex tasks. Technology is progressing so quickly that state-of-the-art microcomputers are every bit as powerful as the mainframes of only a few years ago, but are available at a fraction of the cost.

Microelectronics Technology of constructing electronic circuits and devices in small packages. The most significant advance in microelectronic technology has been the **integrated circuit**, which thirty years ago required a room full of energy-hungry vacuum tubes. They are now fabricated on a silicon chip smaller than a postage stamp, and require only a few milliwatts of power.

Microfiche

Microfiche Small sheet of film, about 4 by 6 inches, used to record photographically reduced images, such as document pages, in rows and columns that form a grid pattern. The results are images too small to read with the naked eye; a special microfiche reader is required to view the documents.

Microfilm Thin strip of film stored on a roll and used to record sequential data images. Just like microfiche, a special device is needed to magnify the images so that they can be read.

Microfloppy disk 3.5-inch floppy disk that most newer computer systems are capable of reading. A microfloppy disk is a round piece of Mylar coated with ferric oxide and enclosed in a plastic shell. On the Macintosh, a single-sided microfloppy disk can hold 400 kilobytes (KB); a double-sided (standard) disk can hold 800 KB; and a double-sided high-density disk can hold 1.44 megabytes (MB). On an IBM and compatible systems with 3.5-inch disk drive, a microfloppy can hold either 720 KB or 1.44 MB of information.

Microform Medium such as microfilm or microfiche on which a **microimage** is stored.

Micrographics Techniques and methods used for recording data on microfilm.

Microimage Photographically reduced image, usually stored on microfilm or microfiche, that is too small to be read without magnification. A microimage usually consists of text, such as archived documents.

Microinstruction Machine instruction that is part of the **microcode**.

Micrologic Set of electronic logic circuits or instructions, stored in binary format, that defines and oversees the operation within a microprocessor.

Microminiature Extremely small circuit or other type of electronic component, particularly one that is a refinement of an already miniaturized element.

Microprocessor Central processing unit (CPU) contained on a single chip. A modern microprocessor can have over 1 million transistors in an integrated circuit package that is roughly 1 inch. Microprocessors are the heart of all personal computers. When

Microprocessor

memory and power are added to a microprocessor, all the pieces other than the peripherals required for a computer are present. The most popular lines of microprocessors in existence today are the 680 x O group from Motorola, which powers the Apple Macintosh line, and the 80 x 86 group from Intel, which the core of all IBM PC-compatible and PS/2 computers.

Microprogramming Writing **microcode** for a processor. Some systems, primarily minicomputers and mainframes, allow modification of microcode for an installed processor.

Microsecond One millionth (10^{-6}) of a second.

Microsoft Disk Operating System Operating system developed and manufactured by the Microsoft Corporation, a software development company well known not only for the DOS operating system but also for various other high-end software packages. MS-DOS—similar to other operating systems—oversees such operations as disk input and output, video support, keyboard control, and many internal functions related to program execution and file maintenance. MS-DOS is a single-tasking, single-user operating system with a command-line interface. MSDOS.COM One of two hidden system files installed on an MS-DOS startup disk. MSDOS.COM, called IBMDOS.COM in IBM releases of MS-DOS, contains the software that makes up the heart (kernel) of the operating system.

Microsoft Windows Operating shell with a graphical-user interface, making the use of the computer a simple task. This shell is setup to use all system resources to maximum efficiency, and other program applications can be run through this shell just by clicking on an graphical icon that represents the application.

Microspace Justification Addition of thin spaces located between characters within words to fill out a line to make it justified instead of relying solely on adding space between words. Good microspace justification gives your justified text a more appealing and professional look. Also called microjustification.

Microspacing This term is used in relationship to printing which is the process of character placement by very small increments.

MIDI Acronym for **Musical Instrument Digital Interface**.

Milli

Milli Prefix meaning one-thousand, as in millisecond.

Millisecond Thousandth of a second in time.

Millivolt Amount of energy equaling one-thousandth of a volt.

Miniaturization Process of reducing the size of integrated circuits while also increasing the density of transistors and other elements on a semiconductor chip. By miniaturizing the semiconductors, power consumption is reduced, which in turn reduces the amount of heat generated within the system and thus greatly extends the life of the chips.

Minicomputer Mid-level type of computer built for performing complex computations while working with high-level input and output from other users connected by way of terminals. Minicomputers are also connected to other minicomputers in a network environment to process data among all systems in the network.

MIPS Acronym for Millions of Instructions Per Second, a common measurement of computer speed.

Mode Operational state of a computer system or application program.

Model Mathematical or a graphical representation of a real-world situation or object. Models can usually be altered so that the user can see the results immediately on the screen.

Modem Shortened form of modulator/demodulator, a communications device that enables a computer to convert data and send and receive it through regular phone lines. Modems can to transfer data at rates of 300 **baud** to 9600 baud or even 19,200 baud on leased phone lines. Modems contain such built-in features as automatic phone dialing, auto answering, and redialing capabilities. The modem is useless without an application that performs all function needed for a communications session.

Modem Eliminator Device that can connect two or more computers without the use of a modem.

Modified Frequency Modulation Encoding (MFM) Widely used form of storing data on a disk drive. MFM encoding stores more information on a disk than frequency modulation encoding.

Modify Structure

Modify Structure Operation available in some database management systems that allows fields (columns) to be added or deleted without needing to rebuild the entire database.

Modula-2 Modular high-level language designed in 1980 by Niklaus Wirth and derived from the Pascal language. Modula-2 is most recognized for its emphasis on modular programming, its early support for data abstraction, and its lack of standard functions and procedures.

Modular Design Approach in designing hardware or software in which a project is broken into smaller units, or modules, each of which can be developed, tested, and finished independently before being combined with the others to form the final product. Each unit is designed to perform a particular task or function and can then become part of a "library" of modules that can often be reused in other products having similar requirements. In programming, for example, one module might contain instructions for moving the cursor in a window on the screen. Because it is designed as a stand-alone unit that can work with other sections of a program, the same module might be able to perform the same task in another program as well, saving time in the developing and testing phase. The designer must build into each module the necessary means of working with other parts of the product. Modular design offers several tremendous benefits. Testing and debugging small units is much easier than working on one large unit; portions of the project can be written and developed by other individuals; modules provide for clear and accurate documentation; and modules are more easily upgraded or modified than component parts nested in or scattered through a single completed product.

Modular Programming Approach to programming in which the program is broken into several independently created and compiled modules. Each module creates and makes available specified elements (constants, data types, variables, functions, procedures); all the other elements remain private to the module. Other modules can use only the exported elements.

Modulate Ability to intentionally change an aspect of a signal, usually for the purpose of transmitting information. There are many forms of modulation, including amplitude modulation, frequency modulation, and pulse modulation.

Modulation

Modulation Operation of changing or regulation, the characteristics of a carrier wave vibrating at a certain amplitude (height) and frequency (timing) in such a way that the variations represent useful information. In computer communications, modulation is the means by which a modem can convert digital information from a computer to the audio form that it sends over a telephone line.

Module In programming, this term refers to a collection of routines and data structures that performs a particular task or uses a particular abstract data type. Modules usually consist of two parts: an interface, which lists the constants, data types, variables, and routines that can be used by other modules or routines; and an implementation, which is private (accessible only to the module) and which contains the source code that actually implements the routines in the module.

Modulo Arithmetic operation—used in programming—whose result is the remainder of a division operation.

Monitor Device on which images generated by the computer video adapter are displayed. Monitors are connected to the video adapter by a cable.

Monochrome Monitor that displays images only in black on white (standard on monochrome Apple Macintosh screens) or amber or green on black (standard on IBM and other monochrome monitors). Also refers to a monitor that displays only variable levels of gray. High-quality monochrome monitors are generally clearer and more readable than color monitors of the same resolution.

Monochrome Adapter Video adapter capable of generating a video signal for one foreground color or. sometimes a range of intensities in a single color, as for a gray-scale monitor.

Monochrome Display Video display capable of showing only one color. The color displayed depends on the phosphor of the display (often green or amber). Also refers to a display capable of rendering a range of intensities in only one color, such as in a gray-scale monitor.

Monochrome Display Adapter Video adapter able to generate video signals for one foreground color with some range of intensities.

Monographics Adapter

Monographics Adapter Generic term for any video adapter capable of displaying only monochrome text and graphics; any video adapter compatible with the Hercules Graphics Card.

Monospace Font Also referred to as a fixed-width font, a typewriter like font (a set of characters in a particular style and size) in which each character takes up the same amount of horizontal space regardless of its width. An "i," for example, would take up as much space as an "m."

Monospacing Type of print and display spacing in which each character occupies the same amount of horizontal space on a line, regardless of whether the character is wide (such as m) or narrow (such as i).

MOS Acronym for **Metal-Oxide Semiconductor**.

Most Significant Character Usually referred to as MSC, the high-order, or leftmost, character contained in a string.

Most Significant Digit Usually referred to as MSD, the highest-order digit in a sequence of one or more digits.

Motherboard Main circuit board containing the primary components of a computer system—the processor, main memory, support circuitry, and bus controller and connector. Other boards, including expansion memory and input/output boards, may be attached to the motherboard through the bus connector.

Mount Necessary parts that when assembled to a disk or tape drive enable it to be connected internally to a computer system. Any device mounted internally requires a mounting system to fasten it to the computer case.

Mouse Common pointing device, popularized by its inclusion as standard equipment with the Apple Macintosh. With the rise in popularity of graphical user interfaces in MS-DOS, UNIX, and OS/2, the use of the mouse is growing throughout the personal computer and workstation worlds. The basic features of a mouse are a casing with a flat bottom, designed to be held in one hand; one or more buttons on top; a multidirectional detection device (usually a ball) on the bottom; and a cable connecting the mouse to the computer. Moving the mouse on a surface (such as a desk), controls the on-screen cursor. A mouse is a relative pointing device because

Mouse

there are no defined limits to the mouse's movement and because its placement on a surface is not mapped directly to a specific screen location. To select items or choose commands on the screen, the user presses one of the mouse's buttons, which produces a "mouse click."

Mouse Sensitivity Relationship of mouse movement in reference to screen cursor movement. There are two ways in which mouse sensitivity can be adjusted or scaled. The first is by choosing a mouse that is more or less sensitive. A more sensitive mouse signals to the computer more "mouse moves" per inch of physical mouse movement than does a less sensitive mouse. The second way is by adjusting the sensitivity of the application program or of the mouse driver to make the cursor more sensitive to mouse movements. Increasing the sensitivity of the program or mouse driver can result in smaller cursor moves for a given mouse move, making it easier for the user to position the cursor more precisely. The program or the mouse driver's sensitivity decides the number of mouse moves in reference to screen coordinates. High sensitivity is good for exacting applications such as CAD/CAM and graphic art; low sensitivity is good for tasks in which the ability to move around the screen quickly is important and for applications such as HyperCard, word processors, and spreadsheets, in which the cursor is used mostly to select buttons or text.

Move To transfer information from one location to another. Depending on the operation involved, a move can affect data in a computer's memory or it can affect text or a graphical image in a data file. In programming, for example, a move instruction might transfer a single value from one memory location to another. In applications a move command may relocate a portion of text or a section of a graphic element from one place in a document to another. Unlike the copy procedure, the move function physically moves the object or text from one place to another, deleting the object from the old location.

ms Abbreviation for millisecond.

MSB Acronym for Most Significant Bit.

MSC Acronym for **Most Significant Character**.

MSD Acronym for **Most Significant Digit**.

MS-DOS Acronym for **Microsoft Disk Operating System**.

msec Abbreviation for millisecond.

MSI Acronym for **Medium-Scale Integration**.

MS-Windows Short form used when referencing the windows environment.

MTBF Acronym for **Mean Time Between Failures**.

Multibus Computer expansion bus designed by Intel Corporation and used extensively by designers of high-performance workstations. A high-bandwidth bus capable of extremely quick information exchange, it also allows multiple bus masters.

Multi-Color Graphics Array Enhanced video adapter similar to CGA.

Multifunction board Computer add-in board that provides more than one function. Multifunction boards for personal computers allow for the use of additional memory, serial/parallel ports, and a clock/calendar.

Multilayer In board designs, a printed circuit board consisting of two or more layers of board material. Each separate layer has its own metallic tracings to provide electrical connections among various electronic components and to provide connections to the other layers. These layers are laminated together to produce a single circuit board to which the components—such as integrated circuits, resistors, and capacitors—are attached. Multilayer design allows many more discrete paths between components than do single-layer boards.

In computer-aided design (CAD), the term refers to drawings, such as electronic circuits, that are built up using multiple layers, each with a different level of detail or a different object, so that specific parts of the drawing can easily be manipulated, overlaid, or peeled off.

Multimedia Combination of sound, graphics, animation, and video. In the world of computers, multimedia is a subset of hypermedia, which combines the elements of multimedia with hypertext to link the information.

Multipass Sort Sorting operation that requires two or more passes through the data before completion, similar to a **bubble sort**.

Multiple-Pass Printing

Multiple-Pass Printing Form of dot-matrix printing in which the print head makes more than one pass across the page for each printed line, thus printing each line a second time exactly on top of the first pass. Multiple-pass printing can be used with dot-matrix printers to darken the print and smooth out errors in alignment. On better printers, a second pass might occur after the paper is moved up slightly, so that the dots in the characters overlap to create a crisper, darker image.

Multiple-User System System set up to be accessed by numerous users for exchanging information.

Multiplexer Hardware circuit used for the selection of a single output from multiple inputs. Also refers to a device used for funneling several different streams of data over a common communications line. Multiplexers are used to attach many communications lines to a smaller number of communications ports or to attach a large number of communications ports to a smaller number of communications lines.

Multiplexer Channel One of the inputs in a multiplexer.

Multiplexing Technique used in communications and input/output operations for transmitting a number of separate signals at the same time over a single channel or line. To maintain the integrity of each signal on the channel, multiplexing is able to separate the signals by time, space, or frequency. The device used to combine the signals is a **multiplexer**.

Multiplicand In multiplication, a number that is multiplied by another number, the **multiplier**. In arithmetic, the multiplicand and the multiplier are interchangeable, depending on how the problem is stated, because the result is the same if the two are reversed; for example, 4 x 3 and 3 x 4. In arithmetic performed by computers the multiplicand is different from the multiplier because computer multiplication is usually performed as addition: 4 x 3 means "add 4 three times."

Multiplier In arithmetic, the number that indicates how many times another number (the **multiplicand**) is multiplied. In computing, multiplier also refers to an electronic device independent of the **central processing unit** (CPU) that performs

Multiplier

multiplication by adding the multiplicand according to the value of the digits in the multiplier.

Multiprocessing Mode of operation in which two or more connected and closely equal processing units each carry out one or more processes (programs or sets of instructions) in tandem. Each processing unit works on a different set of the same instructions (or on different parts of process) to achieve increased speed or computing power, the same as in parallel processing and in the use of special units called coprocessors. In **parallel processing**, however, multiple processes are carried out simultaneously, rather than concurrently, within a single system. In coprocessing, a separate unit such as a math **coprocessor** chip is designed to handle certain tasks with a high degree of efficiency. Definitions vary, however, and distinctions, particularly between multiprocessing and parallel processing, sometimes blur or overlap.

Multisync Monitor Monitor capable of responding to a wide range of horizontal and vertical synchronization rates. Such a monitor can be used with a variety of different video adapters because it can automatically adjust itself to the synchronization rates of the video signal.

Multisystem Network Communications network in which two or more host computers can be accessed by network users.

Multitasking Mode of operation offered by an operating system in which a computer works on more than one task at a time. There are several types of multitasking. Context switching is a very simple type of multitasking in which two or more applications are loaded at the same time but only the foreground application is given processing time; to activate a background task, the user must bring the window or screen containing that application to the front. In cooperative multitasking, exemplified by the Macintosh operating system, background tasks are given processing time during idle times in the foreground task (such as when the application is waiting for a keystroke), and only if this application allows it. In time-slice multitasking exemplified by OS/2, each task is given the micrcprocessor's attention for a fraction of a second. To maintain order, tasks are either assigned at priority levels or processed in sequential order. Because the user's sense of time is much slower than the processing speed of the computer, time-slice multitasking operations seem to be running at the same time.

Multithreading

Multithreading Ability to run several processes in rapid sequence (**multitasking**) within a single program. In data manipulation, multithreading is a technique in which nodes in a tree data structure contain pointers to higher nodes to make traversal of the structure more efficient.

Multiuser system Any computer system that can be used by more than one person. Although a microcomputer shared by several people can be considered a multiuser system, the term is usually reserved for machines that are accessed by several or many people through communications facilities or via network terminals.

Musical Instrument Digital Interface (MIDI) An serial interface standard that allows MIDI-capable musical instruments and synthesizers to be connected to a computer. The MIDI standard is based partly on hardware and partly on a description of the way in which music and sound are encoded and communicated between MIDI devices. The hardware portion of the standard defines these types of input/output channels, called MIDI ports, and designates a particular type of cable—a MIDI cable—that plugs into MIDI ports.

Mylar Polyester film product created by DuPont, often used as the base for magnetically coated storage media (disks and tape).

NAK Acronym for **Negative Acknowledgment**.

Nano Prefix representing the value called one billionth in the American numbering system and one thousand millionth the British numbering system. Abbreviated as n.

Nanosecond One billionth of a second, a measurement of time used to represent computing speed, particularly the speed that electrical signals travel through circuits within the computer. Abbreviated as ns.

National Television System Committee Standards-setting body for television and video in the United States. NTSC is the standard for an encoding system compatible with black-and-white signals and the first system used in color broadcasting in the United States.

Native Compiler Compiler that produces executable code for the system on which it is running, as opposed to a cross-compiler, which produces codes for another system or processor. Most compilers are native compilers.

Natural Language Any of the languages humans speak, as opposed to a program language or machine language. Understanding natural language and approximating it in a computer environment is one goal of research in artificial intelligence.

NCR Paper Special type of paper used for multicopy forms. NCR (no carbon required) paper is impregnated with a chemical that darkens the paper when pressure is applied to it; when a printer (or a pen or pencil) writes on the top sheet of a "set" of NCR paper, the writing appears on each of the sheets beneath.

Near-Letter-Quality More commonly known as NLQ, a printing mode on high-end dot-matrix printers that produces clearer, darker characters than normal (draft-mode) printing. Near-letter-quality printing, although sharper than plain dot-matrix printing, isn't as readable as output from a fully formed character printer, such as a daisy-wheel printer.

Negative Acknowledgment Control code transmitted to a sending station or computer by the receiving unit as a signal that transmitted information has arrived incorrectly. The ability to send and receive

Negative Acknowledgment

acknowledgment signals is built into software so that users of such software need not be concerned about sending or receiving them.

Nesting Process of embedding of one construct (such as a table in a database; a data structure, control structure, or routine in a program; or a document in a word-processing application) inside another; for example, a nested table (a table within a table), nested procedures (a procedure declared within a procedure), and nested records (a record containing a field that is itself a record).

NetBIOS Application program interface (API) that can be used by application programs on a local area network consisting of IBM and compatible microcomputers running MS-DOS, OS/2, or some version of UNIX. Primarily of interest to programmers, NetBIOS provides application programs with a uniform set of commands for requesting the lower-level network services required to conduct sessions between nodes on a network and to transmit information back and forth.

Network Group of computers and associated devices connected by means of communications facilities. A network can involve permanent connections, such as cables, or temporary connections made through telephone or other communications links. A network can be as small as a **local area network** consisting of a few computers, printers, and other devices, or it can consist of many small and large computers distributed over a vast geographic area. Small or large, a computer network exists to provide computer users with the means of transferring information electronically. Some types of communication are simple user-to-user messages; others, of the type known as distributed processes, can involve several computers and the sharing of workloads or cooperative efforts in performing a task.

Network Adapter Expansion card or other device designed to connect a computer to a **local area network**.

Network Administrator Person in charge of operations either on a wide area network system or a **local area network** system. Duties may be broad and might include such tasks as installing new workstations and other devices, adding and removing authorized users, archiving files, overseeing password protection and other security measures, monitoring usage of shared resources, and handling malfunctioning equipment. Also referred to as a system administrator.

Network Architecture

Network Architecture Underlying structure of a computer network, including hardware, functional layers, interfaces, and protocols (rules) used to establish communications and to ensure the reliable transfer of information. Since a computer network is a mixture of hardware and software, network architectures are designed to provide both philosophical and physical standards for enabling computers and other devices to handle the complexities of establishing communications links and transferring information without conflict. There are numerous network architectures in existence, among them the internationally accepted seven-layer **Open Systems Interconnection Model** (OSI) of the **International Organization for Standardization** (IOS) and IBM's Systems Network Architecture (SNA). Both the OSI and SNA architectures organize network functions in layers, with each layer dedicated to a particular aspect of communication or transmission and with the use of protocols that define how functions are carried out. The main objective of these and other network architectures is to create communication standards that will enable computers of various kinds to exchange information freely and (to the user) transparently.

Network Control Program In any communications network that makes use of a mainframe computer, this is a program that usually resides in a communications controller and is responsible for communications tasks such as routing, error control, line control, and polling (checking terminals for transmissions), leaving the main computer free for other functions.

Network Database Type of database in which data records can be linked (related to one another) in more than one way. A network database is similar to a hierarchical database in that it contains a progression from one record to another. It differs in being less rigidly structured, since any single record can point to more than one other record and, conversely, can be pointed to by one or more records. In effect, a network database allows more than one path between any two records, whereas a hierarchical database allows only one, from parent (higher-level record) to child (lower-level record).

Network Layer Third of the seven layers in the **Open Systems Interconnection** (OSI) model of the **International Organization for Standardization** (IOS) for standardizing computer-to-computer communications. The network layer is one level above the data-link

Network Layer

layer and ensures that information is sent to its intended destination. Information is not always transmitted in a direct path from the sender to the receiver; along the way, it might be routed from one circuit to another, or it might be broken into packets that are sent by different routes to the same destination. The function of the network layer is to establish, maintain, and keep open a path for information to travel and make the actual route of no use to any other layer. It is the middle of the three layers (data-link, network, and transport) concerned with actually moving information from one device to another.

Network Model Database structure or layout similar to a hierarchical model, except that records can have multiple parent records as well as multiple child records. A database management system that supports a network model can be used to simulate a hierarchical model.

Network Operating System Operating system installed on a server in a local area network that coordinates the activities of providing services to the computers and other devices attached to the network. Unlike single-user operating systems, which perform the basic tasks required to keep one computer running, a network operating system needs to acknowledge and respond to requests from many workstations, managing such details as network access and communications, resource allocation and sharing, data protection, and error control.

Network Server Main computer system in a network that stores the files needed by the workstations linked to it.

Network Structure Record organization used in a particular network model.

New Line Character Control character that causes the cursor on a display or the printing mechanism on a printer to move to the beginning of the next line. It is equivalent to an operation of a combination of the carriage return (CR) and linefeed (LF) characters. Abbreviated NL.

NLQ Acronym for **Near-Letter-Quality**.

NMI Acronym for **Nonmaskable Interrupt**.

NMOS Acronym for N-channel Metal-Oxide Semiconductor, a semiconductor manufacturing process in which the conduction

NMOS

channel is fabricated from N-type semiconductor material. NMOS relies on the movement of electrons rather than on holes (electron "vacancies" created as electrons move from atom to atom) and is faster than P-channel MOS. N-channel MOS is more difficult and more expensive to make than P-channel MOS but is used in microprocessors and memory hardware due to its speed.

Node A junction of some type. On local area networks, this is a device connected to the network and able to communicate with other network devices. In tree structures, a location (set of information) on the tree can have links to one or more nodes below it (child nodes). Some authors make a distinction between node and element, with an element being a given data type and a node comprising one or more elements as well as any supporting data structures (such as pointers).

Noise Broadly, any interference that affects the operation of a device. In communications, noise consists of random electrical signals—produced either naturally or by the circuitry—that reduce the quality or performance of a communications channel.

Nonbreaking Space In word processing or page layout applications, a character that replaces the standard space character in order to keep two words together on one line rather than allowing a line to break between them (such as Grand Canyon, for example). In some applications the size of a nonbreaking space is fixed and cannot be expanded in fully justified text to match the spaces between other words.

Nonconductor Another term for insulator.

Noncontiguous Data Structure In programming, a data structure whose elements are not stored in one whole piece in memory. Data structures such as graphs and trees, whose elements are connected by links, are noncontiguous data structures, as are data structures whose elements contain links (pointers) to parts of their data. Compare **contiguous** data structure.

Nondestructive Readout Abbreviated as either NDRO or as NDR, a reading operation that does not destroy the data read, either because the storage technology is capable of retaining the data or because the reading operation is accompanied by a data refresh (update) function.

Nonexecutable Statement

Nonexecutable Statement Program statement that cannot be executed because it is located outside of the flow of execution through the program. For example, a statement immediately following a return statement in the C programming language (and within the same block) is nonexecutable. The term is also applied to type definitions, variable declarations, preprocessor commands, comments, and other statements used in a program that are not translated into executable machine code.

Nonimpact Printer Any printer that makes marks on the paper without striking it mechanically. The most common types are **inkjet, thermal**, and **laser** printers; the only thing they have in common is the lack of direct impact.

Noninterlaced Display method on raster-scan monitors in which the electron beam scans each line of the screen once during each refresh cycle. Noninterlaced displays pay attention to every pixel on every line of the screen as the electron beam sweeps across and down the inner surface of the screen, to refresh the displayed image many times each second.

Nonmaskable Interrupt Abbreviated NMI. Hardware interrupt (request for service) called nonmaskable because it bypasses and takes priority over interrupt requests generated by software and by the keyboard and other such devices. A nonmaskable interrupt cannot be overruled (masked) by another service request. An NMI is issued to the microprocessor only in disastrous circumstances such as severe memory errors or impending power failures.

Nonreturn to Zero Abbreviated NKZ. In data transmission, a method of encoding data in which the signal representing binary digits alternates between positive and negative voltage when there is a change in digits from 1 to O or vice versa. In other words, the signal does not return to a zero, or neutral, level after transmission of each hit; tinting is used to distinguish one bit from the next, as when a succession of 1s is transmitted. In the recording of data on a magnetic surface, NRZ refers to a very similar method in which one magnetic state represents a 1 and, usually, the opposite state represents a 0; as in communications, there is no "neutral" state used as a reference condition.

Nontrivia Procedure that is either difficult or particularly meaningful, such as a complicated programmed procedure to handle a difficult problem, would represent a nontrivial solution.

Nonvolatile Memory Storage system that does not lose data when power is removed from it. Intended to refer to core, KOM, EPROM, bubble memory, or battery-backed CMOS RAM, the term is occasionally used in reference to disk subsystems as well.

No-Operation Instruction Abbreviated either NOP or NO-OP. Machine instruction that produces no results other than to cause the processor to use up a cycle or two of clock time. NOPs are useful in situations such as disabling a call to a subroutine (by replacing the call instruction with a NOP), padding out timing loops, or forcing subsequent instructions to align on certain memory boundaries.

Normal Distribution In statistics, a type of function that describes the probabilities of the possible values of a random variable. The function, whose graph is the familiar bell-shaped curve, can be used in determining the probability that the value of the variable will fall within a particular interval of values.

Normal Form In a relational database, an approach to structuring information. Normal forms avoid redundancy and inconsistency and promote efficient maintenance, storage, and updating of information. Several types of normalization are accepted, each refined than the preceding one. Of these, three forms are commonly used: first normal (1NF), second normal (2NF), and third normal (3NF).
 • First normal forms, the least structured, are groups of records (such as employee lists) in which each field (column) contains unique and nonrepeating information.
 • Second and third normal forms break down first normal forms, separating them into different tables by defining successively finer interrelationships between fields. Second normal forms do not include fields that are parts of other fields rather than of the primary (key) field; for example, a second normal form keyed to employee name could not include both job grade and hourly rate if pay were dependent on job grade.
 • Third normal forms do not include fields that provide information about fields other than the key field; a third normal form keyed to employee name would not include project name, crew number, and supervisor unless the crew number and supervisor were assigned only to the project on which the employee is working.

Normalize

Normalize In programming, to adjust the fixed-point and exponent portions of a floating-point number to bring the fixed-point portions into a specified range. In database management, this term refers to applying a body of techniques to a relational database in order to minimize the inclusion of duplicate information. Normalization simplifies query and update management, including security and integrity considerations. Due to the fact that normalization involves a technique called projection, which results in splitting a relation (table) into two or more relations, simplification is accomplished at the expense of producing a larger number of tables.

NOT Operator that performs **Boolean** (or logical) negation. In Boolean terms, NOT TRUE = FALSE and NOT FALSE = TRUE. In logical terms, if a value, for example, contains a binary value, then NOT value changes each O bit in value to 1 and each 1 bit in value to 0.

Notation Set of symbols and formats used to describe the elements of programming, mathematics, or a scientific field. In programming, notation describes elements such as constants, expressions, and statements within a language. A language's syntax is defined in part by notation.

Notebook Computer Small, laptop-type portable computer.

NTSC Acronym for **National Television System Committee**.

N-Type Semiconductor Semiconductor material in which electrical conduction is carried by electrons, in contrast to P-type semiconductors, in which conduction is carried by holes known as electron "vacancies." Whether a semiconductor is N-type or P-type depends on the kind of dopant added during manufacture. A dopant with an excess of electrons results in an N-type semiconductor, whereas a dopant with a shortage of electrons results in a P-type semiconductor.

NUL Character code with a null value; literally a character meaning "nothing." Although it is real in the sense of being recognizable, occupying space internally in the computer, and being sent or received as a character, a NUL character displays nothing, takes no space on the screen or on paper, and causes no action. NUL is used in many situations, such as to pad data fields, to terminate strings, or to separate blocks of information.

Null Cycle

Null Cycle Shortest amount of time required to execute a program; the time needed to cycle through the program without requiring it to process new data or loop through sets of instructions.

Null Modem Cable that enables two computers to communicate without the use of modems by crossing the sending and receiving wires so that the wire used by one device for transmitting is used by the other and vice versa for receiving.

Null Pointer Pointer to nothing, usually a standardized memory address, such as 0, which is clearly illegal and thus easily interpreted. A null pointer usually marks the last of a linear sequence of pointers or indicates that a data search operation has come up empty-handed.

Null String String containing no characters; a string whose length is zero.

Number Crunching Calculating large amounts of numeric data. Number crunching can be repetitious, mathematically complex, or both, and usually involves far more internal processing than input or output functions. Work that requires number crunching includes the calculation of large spreadsheets, scientific applications, and sophisticated graphics displays, as in CAD programs. Numeric coprocessors greatly enhance the ability of computers to perform these tasks.

Numerical Analysis Branch of mathematics devoted to finding ways to solve problems that can be expressed mathematically; the search for methods of finding concrete or approximate solutions to abstract mathematical problems. Computers with the speed and ability to perform calculations broaden and enhance such studies considerably.

Numeric Coprocessor Second processor that can be installed in most systems that performs the mathematical calculations for a system, saving the main processor from having to do these chores. This is better known as a math coprocessor.

Numeric Keypad Calculator-style block of keys on the right side of the keyboard that can be used to enter numbers, standard on many computer keyboards. Numeric keypads are also available as separate units. In addition to keys for the digits O through 9 and keys for indicating addition, subtraction, multiplication, and

Numeric Keypad

division, numeric keypads often include an Enter key, which is usually not the same as the Enter or Return key located on the main part of the keyboard. On most keyboards, many of the keys on the numeric keypad serve dual purposes.

Num. Lock Key Shortened form of Numeric Lock key, a toggle key that, when turned on, activates the numeric keypad so that its keys can be used for calculator-style data entry. When the Num. Lock key is toggled off, the keypad keys can be used for moving the cursor around the screen—allowing the user to scroll up and down in a document—and for inserting or deleting text. When the Num. Lock key is toggled on, the keypad keys can be used for entering numbers but not for cursor movement, scrolling, or editing functions.

Object Shorthand term for object code (machine-readable code). In object-oriented programming, a variable making use of both routines and data that is treated as a discrete entity. In graphics, the term refers to a distinct entity. For example, a bouncing ball might be an object in a graphics program.

Object code Code, generated by a compiler or assembler, that was translated from the source code of a program. Most commonly refers to machine code that can be directly executed by the system's central processing unit (CPU), but it can also be assembly language source code or a variation of machine code.

Object Computer Computer that is the target of a specific communications attempt.

Object file File containing an **object code**, usually the output of a compiler or an assembler and the input for a linker.

Objective-C An object-oriented version of the C language developed in 1984 by Brad Cox. Objective-C is most widely known as the standard development language for the Next system.

Object Module In the programming environment, the object-code (compiled) version of a source-code file, which is usually a collection of routines, ready to be linked with other object modules

Object-Oriented Any system or language that supports the use of objects.

Object-Oriented Graphics Also known as structured graphics. Computer graphics based on the use of "construction elements" (graphics primitives), such as lines, curves, circles, and squares. Object-oriented graphics that are used in applications such as CAD and drawing and illustration programs describe an image mathematically as a set of instructions for creating the objects in the image. This approach contrasts with bit-mapped graphics, the other widely used approach to creating images, which represents a graphic as a group of black and white or colored dots arranged in a certain pattern. Object-oriented graphics enable the user to manipulate objects as entire units—to change the length of a line or enlarge a circle, for example—whereas bit-mapped graphics require repainting individual dots in the line or circle. Since objects are

Object-Oriented Graphics

described mathematically, object-oriented graphics can also be layered, rotated, and magnified fairly easily.

Object-Oriented Interface Type of user interface in which elements of the system are represented by visible screen objects such as icons (pictorial representations), which are used to manipulate the system elements. For example, the Macintosh Finder presents an object-oriented interface to the file system by representing images of documents, file folders, and disk devices. Object-oriented display interfaces do not necessarily imply any relation to object-oriented programming.

Object-Oriented Programming Programming model in which a program is viewed as a collection of objects that are self-contained data structures and routines that interact with other objects. A class defines the data structures and routines of an object; an object is an instance of a class that can be used as a variable in a program. In some object-oriented languages, objects respond to messages, which are the principal means of communication. Other object-oriented languages retain the traditional procedure-call mechanism.

Oblique Style of text created by slanting a roman font to simulate italics when a true italic font doesn't exist on the computer or printer.

OCR Acronym for **Optical Character Recognition**.

Octal Base-8 number system (from the Latin "octo," meaning eight) consisting of the digits O through 7. The octal system is used in programming as a compact means of representing binary numbers. Because octal consists of eight digits and because 8 bits can form any of eight different combinations, binary numbers are commonly divided into groups of 8 bits for conversion to octal. The binary equivalents of the eight octal digits are as follows:

Thus the binary number 01010011 can be divided into groups of 3 bits, starting from the right and adding an extra O at the left, as 001 010 011. Converted to octal, the number becomes 123. Even though octal numbers may look like decimal numbers, their values differ because of the different meanings assigned to each number position. Since octal works with multiples of 3 bits but microcomputers commonly work in units of 4, 8, 16, 32, and so on, octal is more often encountered in minicomputers and mainframes than in personal computing, where hexadecimal, or base-16, arithmetic is far more widespread.

OEM Acronym for **Original Equipment Manufacturer**.

Office Automation Use of electronic and communications devices such as computers, modems, and FAX machines as well as any associated software to perform office functions mechanically rather than manually.

Offline State in which a device cannot communicate with or be controlled by a computer. Although a device is offline when it is disconnected or turned off, the term is not necessarily synonymous with being either physically disconnected or shut down. A printer, for example, can be offline (temporarily disengaged), yet still be turned on and connected to the computer by a printer cable.

Offline Storage Storage resource, such as a disk, that is not currently available to the system.

Offset Number that tells how far from a starting point a particular item is located. For example, in the search for a specific data item stored within a known area (segment) of memory, an offset is used to tell the microprocessor how many bytes past the beginning of the segment the item is located. Using an offset is similar to saying, "The loose stair is the fifth one from the bottom."

Off-the-Shelf Item that is ready to use right from the package. The term can refer to hardware or software.

Ohm Unit of measure for electrical resistance. A resistance of 1 ohm will pass 1 ampere of current when a voltage of 1 volt is applied. A 100-watt incandescent bulb has a resistance of approximately 130 ohms.

On-Board Computer Computer that resides within another device.

One-Pass Compiler Compiler that needs to read through a source file only once in order to produce the **object code**. The syntax of some languages makes it impossible to write a one-pass compiler for those languages.

Online Activated and ready for operation; capable of communicating with or being controlled by a computer. For

Online

example, a printer is online when it can be used for printing; a database is online when it can be used by a person who connects with the computer on which it is stored. Compare **offline**.

Online Help Special feature of most high-end applications that offers the user detailed help on program operation while working in the application. Most applications use a keystroke to bring up the online help. The F1 key is becoming a standard to represent help access.

Online State State of a modem when it is communicating with another modem.

OOP Acronym for **Object-Oriented Programming**.

Opcode Shortened form of operation code.

Open Reference to accessibility in many areas of computing. Open is used as an adjective or as a verb; for example, an open file is one that can be used because a program has issued an "open file" command to the operating system. Common uses of open in the sense of "accessible" or "not closed" include **open architecture**, **open system**, **open shop**, and **open subroutine**.

Open Architecture Any computer or peripheral design that has published specifications, which let third parties develop add-on hardware for an open architecture computer or device. Also refers to a design that provides for expansion slots on the motherboard, allowing the addition of boards to enhance or customize a system.

Open File File that can be read from or written to or both. A program must first open a file before the file's contents can be used, and it must close the file when done.

Open Shop Computer facility accessible to users and not restricted to programmers or other personnel, thus allowing users to work on or attempt to solve computer problems on their own rather than handing them over to a specialist.

Open Subroutine Program section that is copied, repeatedly if necessary, wherever it is needed in a program, as opposed to a closed subroutine, which is copied once and can then be called or jumped to from any other point in the program.

Open System In a communications environment, an open systems

Open System

interconnection model is a computer network designed to incorporate all devices regardless of manufacturer or model that can use the same communications facilities and protocols. In reference to individual pieces of computer hardware or software, an open system is one that can accept add-ons produced by third-party suppliers.

Operand Object of a mathematical operation or a computer instruction. An operand can be data or it can be the location (in memory or on disk) at which data is stored. For example, in the arithmetic operation 2 + 3, the numbers 2 and 3 are data that represent the operands of the add operation.

Operating System Abbreviated OS. The software responsible for controlling the allocation and usage of hardware resources such as memory, central processing unit time, disk space, and peripheral devices. The operating system is the foundation on which applications such as word processing and spreadsheet programs are built. Popular operating systems include MS-DOS, the Macintosh OS, OS/2, and UNIX.

Operation Code Abbreviated as opcode. The portion of a machine language or assembly language instruction that specifies the type of the instruction (that is, what sort of operation the instruction performs) and the structure of the data on which it operates.

Operations Research Use of mathematical and scientific approaches to analyze and improve efficiency in business, management, government, and other areas. Developed around the beginning of World War II, operations research was initially used to improve military operations during the war. The practice later spread to business and industry as a means of breaking down systems and procedures and studying their parts and interactions in order to improve overall performance. Operations research involves use of the critical path method, statistics, probability, and information theory.

Operator In programming and computer applications, this term defines a symbol or other character indicating an operation that acts on one or more elements. Mathematical operators, for example, include the familiar + and - of addition and subtraction; logical operators include the Boolean AND, OR, and NOT that enable programs to evaluate expressions, producing either true or false

Operator

results; concatenation operators combine strings of text, files, and other such elements.

Operator Associativity In programming, a characteristic of operators that determines the order of evaluation in an expression when adjacent operators have equal precedence. The two possibilities are left to right and right to left. The associativity for most operators is left to right. In a computer language with left-to-right associativity for addition and subtraction (and with equal precedence for addition and subtraction), the expression 7 - 4 + 1 means (7 - 4) + 1, or 4. In a language with right-to-left associativity for addition and subtraction (and with equal precedence for addition and subtraction), the expression 7 - 4 + 1 means 7 - (4 + 1), or 2.

Operator Overloading Assignment of more than one function to a particular operator, with the implication that the operation performed will vary depending on the data type (operands) involved. For example, the operator * might define multiplication for integers and floating-point values, but for vectors it might define cross-product, or for a number/vector combination, scaling. Some languages, such as Ada and C++, specifically allow for operator overloading.

Operator Precedence Priority of various operators when more than one is used in an expression. When there are no parentheses, operations with higher precedence are performed first. Operator precedence is usually set up so that expressions are evaluated intuitively. For example, most languages give the multiplication operator a higher precedence than the addition operator. This ensures that expressions such as 3 + 2 * 4 (three plus two times four) will evaluate to the accustomed result, 11. (If addition had a higher precedence than multiplication, 3 + 2 * 4 would evaluate to 20.) A few languages, such as Prolog:, allow arbitrary adjustment of operator precedence.

Optical Character Recognition Usually referred to as OCR. The process of examining printed characters on paper and determining their shapes by detecting patterns of dark and light. Once the scanner or reader has determined the shapes, character recognition methods—pattern matching with stored sets of characters—are used to translate the shapes into computer text. Sometimes OCR is done with special readers, but often it is done using a standard optical scanner and specialized software.

Optical Communications

Optical Communications Use of light and light-transmitting technology, such as optical filters and lasers, in sending and receiving voice, data, pictures, or sound.

Optical Disc Disc that can be read by a CD-ROM. This disk is capable of holding hundreds of megs of information.

Optical Fiber Thin strand of transparent material used to carry optical signals. Optical fibers are constructed from special kinds of glass and plastic and are designed so that a beam of light introduced at one end will remain within the fiber, reflecting off the inner surfaces as it travels down the length of the fiber. Optical fibers are inexpensive, compact, and lightweight and are often packaged many hundred to a single cable.

Optical Mouse Type of mouse that uses a pair of light-emitting diodes (LEDs) and a special reflective grid pad to detect motion. The two lights are of different colors, and the special mouse pad has a grid of lines in the same colors, one color for vertical lines and another for horizontal lines. Light detectors paired with the LEDs sense when a colored light passes over a line of the same color, indicating the direction of the movement.

Optical Reader Device that reads text from printed paper by detecting the pattern of light and dark on a page and then applying optical character recognition methods to identify the characters.

Optical Recognition Same as **Optical Character Recognition**.

Optical Scanner Input device that uses light-sensing equipment to scan paper or another medium, translating the pattern of light and dark (or color) into a digital signal that can be manipulated by either optical character recognition software or graphics software. A frequently encountered type of scanner is "flatbed," meaning that the scanning device moves across or reads across a stationary document. On a flatbed scanner such as the common office copier, such objects are placed face down on a flat piece of glass and scanned by mechanism that passes under them. Another type of flatbed scanner uses a scanning element place in a stationary housing above the document. Other scanners work by pulling in sheets of paper, which are scanned as they pass over a stationary scanning mechanism, as in the common office fax machine. Some specialized scanners work with a standard video camera, translating

Optical Scanner

the video signal into a digital signal to be processed by computer software. A very popular type of scanner is the hand-held scanner, so called because the user holds the scanner in the hand and moves it over the document to be scanned. These hand-held scanners have the advantage of relatively low cost; however, they are slightly limited by their inability to scan an area more than a few inches wide.

Optimization In programming, the process of producing more efficient programs through selection and design of data structures, algorithms, and instruction sequences. Also, the process of a compiler or assembler producing efficient executable code.

Optimizing Compiler Compiler able to analyze its output (assembly language or machine code) to produce more efficient (smaller and/or faster) instruction codes so that programs run as fast as possible.

Optomechanical Mouse Type of mouse by which motion is translated into directional signals through a combination of optical and mechanical means. The optical portion includes pairs of light-emitting diodes (LEDs) and matching sensors; the mechanical portion consists of rotating wheels with cut-out slits. When the mouse is moved, the wheels turn and the light from the LEDs either passes through the slits and strikes a light sensor or is blocked by the solid portions of the wheels. These changes in light contact are detected by the pairs of sensors and interpreted as indications of movement. Because the sensors are slightly out of phase with one another, the direction of movement is determined by which sensor is the first to regain light contact. Because it uses optical equipment instead of mechanical parts, an optomechanical mouse eliminates the need for many of the wear-related repairs and maintenance necessary with purely mechanical mice, but it does not require the special operating surfaces associated with optical mice.

Order When used as a verb, order refers to arranging of data in a sequence, such as alphabetic or numeric; when used as a noun, it refers to the type of sequence produced. In computing, order has two other related, but slightly different, meanings. When calculations are performed, order refers to the sequence in which arithmetic operations are performed—multiplication and division before addition and subtraction. This order of calculation is built into a program or programming language and is overridden by the

Order

use of parentheses that group items to be calculated together or in a certain sequence. In reference to numbers or to 2-byte groups of information, order is used to indicate the relative significance of a digit or byte: high order refers to the most significant (usually leftmost) digit or byte; low-order refers to the least significant (usually rightmost) digit(s) or byte. When used in reference to databases, order indicates the magnitude of a database in terms of the number of fields (attributes) it contains. For example, a database of order 5 contains five fields for holding data about each record.

Ordinal Number Number whose form indicates position in an ordered sequence of events.

Orientation Direction of the page layout—either **portrait** mode (vertical) or **landscape** mode (horizontal).

Original Equipment Manufacturer Usually referred to as OEM. The maker of a piece of equipment. In making computers and related equipment, OEMs typically purchase components from other OEMs, integrate them into their own products, and then sell the products to the public.

OS Acronym for **Operating System**.

OS/2 Protected-mode, virtual-memory, multitasking operating system for personal computers based on the Intel 80286, 80386, and 8046 processors. OS/2 can run most MS-DOS applications in a special session called the "compatibility box" and can read all MS-DOS disks. Several important OS/2 subsystems include Presentation Manager, which provides a graphical user interface, and LAN Manager, which provides networking facilities. OS/2 was developed from the start as a joint project of Microsoft and IBM.

Oscillation Broadly, any periodic change or alternation. The swinging of a pendulum is an oscillation, as is the vibration of a tuning fork. In electronics, oscillation refers to a periodic change in an electrical signal.

Oscillator Electronic circuit that produces a periodically varying output at a controlled frequency. Oscillators are an important type of electronic circuit, and can be designed to provide a constant or an adjustable output. Some oscillator circuits use a quartz crystal to generate a stable frequency. Personal computers use an oscillator

Oscillator

circuit to provide the "clock" frequency—typically 1 to 60 megahertz (MHz)—that drives the processor and other circuits.

Oscilloscope Also known as cathode-ray oscilloscope or scope. A test and measurement instrument that provides a visual display for an electrical signal. The most common use of oscilloscopes is to create a display of voltage vs. time. Circuits within the oscilloscope repeatedly sweep an electron beam across the display screen of a cathode-ray tube, from left to right, creating a spot of light on the screen. The speed of the sweep can be adjusted. The signal being measured controls the vertical position of the beam, with positive voltages causing an upward deflection and negative voltages a downward deflection. The resulting display shows the voltage and time characteristics of the signal.

Outline Font Font stored in a computer or printer as a set of outlines for drawing each of the alphabetic and other characters in a character set. Outline fonts are templates rather than actual patterns of dots and are scaled up or down to match a particular type size. Such fonts are most often used for printing—as with most PostScript fonts on a PostScript-compatible laser printer—rather than for displaying text on the screen.

Output Results of processing, whether sent to the screen or printer, stored on disk as a file, or sent to another computer in a network.

Output Buffer Portion of memory set aside for the temporary storage of information, which leaves the main memory for storage, display, printing, or transmission.

Output Stream Flow of information that leaves a computer system and is associated with a particular operation or destination. In programming, an output stream can be a series of characters sent from the computer's memory to a display or to a disk file.

Overflow Error Error that occurs when a number, usually the result of an arithmetic operation, is too large to be contained in the data structure provided for it by a program.

Overlay Section of a program designed to reside on a designated storage device such as a disk and to be loaded into memory when needed, usually overwriting one or more overlays already in memory. Use of overlays allows large programs to fit into a limited amount of memory, but at the cost of speed.

Overprint

Overprint Process of printing an element of one color over one of another color without removing, or knocking out, the material underneath.

Override To prevent something from happening or to initiate another response to a situation. For example, a user can often override and therefore abort a time-consuming sorting procedure in a database program by pressing the Escape key.

Overrun In the information-transfer process, an error that occurs when a device receiving data cannot handle or make use of the information as rapidly as it arrives.

Overscan Part of a video signal sent to a raster display that controls the area outside the rectangle containing visual information. The overscan area is sometimes colored to form a border around the screen.

Overstrike Typing or printing one character directly over another so that the two are superimposed.

Overtype To replace characters by other characters that are typed in the same location.

Overwrite Mode Text-entry mode in which newly typed characters replace existing characters under (or to the left of) the cursor or insertion point. This state is the opposite of insert mode, in which existing characters are pushed to the right and new characters are placed in front of them. The key or key combination used to toggle between these modes varies from one application to the next; the Insert key is often used.

Pack Storing information in a more compacted or compressed form, used by some programs to minimize storage requirements. Packing reduces the number of unnecessary spaces and other such characters and may use other special methods of compressing data as well. Although packed data is not necessarily readable in its compressed form, it can be unpacked and restored to its original appearance.

Package Computer application consisting of one or more programs sold together to perform a particular kind of work; for example, an accounting package or spreadsheet package. Software packages are designed to satisfy the needs of more than one organization; they are generally considered the same as "off-the-shelf" or "canned" programs.

Packaged Software Software program sold through a retail distributor, as opposed to custom software.

Packed Decimal Method of encoding decimal numbers in binary form that makes maximum use of storage space by using each byte to represent two decimal digits. For example, in binary form, the 1 in the decimal number 2 is represented as 0001, and the 2 is represented as 0010. If one byte is allotted to each decimal digit, decimal 12 is written 00000001 00000010 with extra 0's filling in the leftmost four bit positions in each byte. In the packed decimal method, however, where each byte represents two digits, the same number is written 00010010, thereby saving one full byte of storage. When signed decimal numbers are stored in packed decimal format, the sign appears in the rightmost four bits of the rightmost (least significant) byte.

Packet Broadly, a unit of information transmitted as a whole from one device to another on a network. In packet-switching networks, a packet is defined as a transmission unit of fixed maximum size that consists of binary digits representing both data and a header containing an identification number, source and destination addresses, and, sometimes, error-control data.

Packing Density Number of storage units per length or area of a storage device. Bits per inch is one measure of packing density.

Pad Character In data input and storage, an extra character

Pad Character

inserted as "filler" to use up surplus space in a predefined block of a specified length, such as a fixed-length field.

Padding In data storage, the addition of one or more bits (usually zeros) to a block of data in order to fill it, to force the actual data bits into a certain position, or to prevent the data from duplicating a bit pattern that has an established meaning, such as an embedded command.

Paddle Early type of input device most often used with computer games, especially for side-to-side or up-and-down movements of an on-screen object. A paddle is less sophisticated than a joystick because it permits the user to specify movement only along a single axis, by turning a dial. The paddle, first known as the paddle controller, got its name because its most popular use was to control the on-screen paddle bars in the simple early video games.

Page Fixed-size block of memory. In the context of a paging memory system, a page is a block of memory whose physical address can be changed with the use of mapping hardware. A page is usually associated with virtual memory hardware, although the 1G-kilobyte (KB) blocks mapped using the Expanded Memory Specification (EMS) are also called pages. In the memory management unit (MMU) of the 80386 and 80486, a page is 4 KB. In computer graphics, a portion of display memory that contains one complete full-screen image; the internal representation of a screen full of information.

Page Break Point at which the flow of text in a document moves to the top of a new page. Most word-processing programs create an automatic page break when the material on the page reaches a specified maximum depth. By contrast, a page break is a command or code that is inserted by the user to force a page break at a specific place in the text. In older word processors, a page break can be created by the insertion of a form-feed character.

Paged Address Term used in reference to the 80386 and 80486 paged memory architecture, an address in memory created by combining the processes of segment translation and page translation. In the paged memory scheme, which requires that the microprocessor's paging feature be enabled, logical addresses are transformed into physical addresses (actual locations in physical memory) by a two-step procedure: segment translation and page

Paged Address

translation. The first step, segment translation, converts a logical address (consisting of an segment selector and a segment offset) to a linear address (an address that refers indirectly to a physical address). After this linear address is obtained, the microprocessor's paging hardware converts the linear address to a physical address by specifying a page table (an array of 32-bit page specifiers), a page (a 4-KB unit of contiguous addresses within physical memory) within that table, and an offset within that page. This information, called a paged address, collectively refers to a physical address.

Page-Description Language Abbreviated PDL. A programming language, such as PostScript, used to describe output to a printer or a display device, which uses the instructions from the page-description language to layout text and graphics to create the required page image. PDLs are like other computer languages, with logical program flow allowing for alteration of the output. A page-description language, similar to a blueprint, sets out specifications (as for fonts and type sizes) but leaves the work of drawing characters and graphics to the output device itself. Because this approach dictates the detail work to the device that produces the output, a PDL is machine-independent, which means that any printer or other device that can understand the language can produce an image described by it. These abilities come at a price, however. Printers that use page-description languages require processing power and memory comparable to and often exceeding that of personal computers.

Paged Memory Management Utility Abbreviated PMMU. Hardware unit that performs tasks related to accessing and managing memory used by different applications or by virtual-memory operating systems. For example, the Motorola G885l, a PMMU available for Apple Macintosh II computers, translates memory addresses and supports demand-paged virtual memory, which makes an application behave as if it had as much memory available as the microprocess is capable of addressing. In this form of memory management, any attempt to access data that is not present in physical (system) memory causes the PMMU to send an interrupt signal to the CPU; the operating system then swaps the data in from other storage (such as a hard disk), without the application "knowing" about the transfer.

Page Down Key Key on the keyboard that performs various

Page Down Key

functions in different application programs but is most often used in word processing programs to scroll down in a document by one screen full of text at a time. On IBM PC and compatible keyboards, the Page Down key is overlaid on the 3 key in the numeric keypad (labeled PgDn) and can be used when Num Lock key is not on. On enhanced keyboards and Apple's Extended Keyboard, there is also a Page Down key in the editing keys between the numeric keypad and the main keyboard.

Page Fault Interrupt that occurs when software attempts to read from or write to a virtual memory location that is marked "not present." The mapping hardware of a virtual memory system is responsible for maintaining the status information about every page in the virtual address space. A page is either mapped onto a physical address or is not present in physical memory. When a read or write to an unmapped virtual address is detected, the memory management hardware generates the page fault interrupt. The operating system responds to the page fault by swapping in the data for the page and updating the status information in the memory management unit.

Page Frame Physical address to which a page of virtual memory may be mapped. In a system with 4096-byte pages, page frame O corresponds to physical addresses O through 40966.

Page-Image Buffer Memory in a page printer used for holding the bit map (image) of a page as the printer's raster image processor builds the page and as the printer produces the page.

Page-Image File File containing the code needed for a printer or another display device to create the page or screen image.

Page Layout Process of arranging text and graphics on the pages of a document. Page-layout programs excel in text placement and management of special effects applied to text. They are similar to word processing programs, and although generally slower than word processing programs, they can perform such advanced tasks as flowing text into complex multicolumn page designs, printing documents in signatures, managing color separations, and supporting sophisticated kerning (adjusting letter spacing) and hyphenation.

Page Makeup Assembling graphics and text on a page to prepare it for printing.

Page Mode RAM

Page Mode RAM Specially designed dynamic RAM that supports access to sequential memory locations with a reduced cycle time. This is especially attractive in video RAM, where each location is accessed in ascending order to create the screen image. Page mode RAM can also improve the execution speed of code because code tends to execute sequentially through memory.

Page Printer Any printer, such as a laser printer, that prints an entire page at once. Due to the fact that page printers must store the entire page in memory before printing, they require large amounts of memory. A common minimum amount of memory for laser printers, for example, is 512 kilobytes (KB). Even this is not enough to store a full page of graphics at the typical maximum laser-printer resolution of 300 dots per inch. Page printers that use page-description languages need even more memory, and require their own microprocessors.

Page Setup Set of choices that will affect how a file is printed on the page. Page setup might state the size of paper going into the printer, the page margins, the specific pages in the document needing to be printed, whether the image is to be reduced or enlarged when printed, and whether another file is to be printed immediately after the first file is printed. This stacking of files for printing is called a print queue, which is actually a batch print job.

Pages Per Minute Generally referred to as PPM. With printers—most commonly laser printers—this refers to the rating of output capacity, or simply the number of printed pages the printer can produce in one minute. A printer's PPM rating, which is provided by the manufacturer, is usually based on a "normal" page (a page having a single, usually built-in, typeface and containing no graphics or other special elements). Use of multiple or nonresident fonts, and particularly use of graphics or other nontext elements, can reduce a printer's PPM rate drastically.

Page Up Key Key on the keyboard that performs various functions in different application programs but is most often used in word processing programs to scroll up in a document by one screen full of lines at a time. On IBM PC and compatible keyboards, the Page Up key is overlaid on the 9 key in the numeric keypad (labeled PgUp) and can be used when Num Lock is not on. On enhanced keyboards and Apple's Extended Keyboard, there is also a Page Up

Page Up Key

key in the editing keys, which lie between the numeric keypad and the main keyboard.

Pagination Process of dividing a document into pages for printing; also, the process of adding page numbers. Most word processing programs can perform both types of pagination. Some also allow the user to scan or preview page breaks and alter those that are unacceptable (as when a heading would appear at the bottom of one page with the associated text at the top of the next).

Paging Technique for making use of a computer system's virtual memory. The virtual address space is divided into a number of fixed-size blocks called pages, each of which can be mapped onto any of the physical addresses available on the system. Special memory management hardware (MMU or PMMU) performs the address translation from virtual addresses to physical addresses.

Paint Color and pattern used with graphics programs to fill areas of a drawing, applied with either a paintbrush or a spray-can tool. Also refers to filling in a portion of a drawing with paint.

Paint Program Application program that creates graphics as bit maps—images stored as collections of pixels (dots) rather than as discrete lines, curves, and other such shapes. A paint program, since it treats a drawing as a group of dots, is particularly appropriate for freehand drawing. This type of program also provides tools for images requiring lines, curves, and geometric shapes but does not treat any shape as an entity that can be moved or modified as a discrete object without losing its identity. For fine details, paint programs often include a facility that enables pixel-by-pixel modification of a paint pattern or a small segment of a drawing.

Palette Collection of drawing tools, such as patterns, colors, brush shapes, and different line widths, from which the user of a paint program can choose. Also refers to a subset of the color look-up table that establishes the colors that can be displayed on the screen at a particular time. The number of colors in a palette is determined by the number of bits used to represent a pixel. For example, a pixel represented by 4 bits can have one of 16 colors. Likewise, the number of bits used to represent a pixel determines the size of the palette. Using the same example, a 4-bit pixel would allow a palette size with 16 entries.

PAM

PAM Acronym for **Pulse Amplitude Modulation**.

Panning In computer graphics, display method in which a viewing "window" on the screen scans horizontally or vertically, like a camera, to bring off-screen extensions of the current image smoothly into view, enabling the user to scroll on the screen to see an entire picture or graphic that will not completely fit on the screen.

Pantone Matching System Generally referred to as PMS. In graphic arts and printing, a standard system of ink-color specifications consisting of a swatch book in which each of about 500 colors is assigned a number.

Paper Feed Any mechanism that moves paper through a printer. In dot-matrix printers, the paper feed is usually a pin feed or tractor feed in which small pins drag or push paper with sprocket holes in it. Friction feed is another type of paper feed, in which the paper is gripped between the platen and pressure rollers and pulled by the rotation of the platen. In laser printers and other page printers, the paper feed is usually a series of rollers that firmly grip and align the paper.

Paperless Office Ideal office in which information is entirely stored, manipulated, and transferred electronically rather than on paper.

Paper-White Type of monochrome computer monitor whose default operating colors are black text on a white background (as opposed to white, green, or amber text on a black background, which is more common). Paper-white monitors are popular in desktop publishing and word processing environments because the monitor more closely resembles a white sheet of paper printed with black characters.

Paragraph In word processing, any part of a document preceded by one paragraph mark and ending with another. To the program, a paragraph represents a unit of information that can be selected as a whole or given formatting distinct from the surrounding paragraphs.
  On IBM and other computers built around the Intel 8086 microprocessor, paragraph refers to a 16-byte section of memory beginning at a location (address) that can be divided evenly by 16 (hexadecimal 10). In other words, a new paragraph begins at every hexadecimal address that ends in 0.

Parallel

Parallel In graphics, parallel refers to lines that run evenly, side by side. In other aspects of computing, parallel is used either in reference to data transfer, as in parallel interface, or in reference to data handling, as in parallel processing. In parallel data transfer, information is sent simultaneously in groups; for example, the 8 bits of a byte of data are transmitted at the same time over eight separate wires in a cable. In parallel processing and other such operations, more than one event is happening at a time; for example, multiple microprocessors in a single computer might be handling different aspects of a process (such as a complex calculation) at the same time.

Parallel Access Also called simultaneous access. Ability to store or retrieve all of the bits composing a single unit of information, such as a byte or a word (usually two bytes), at the same time.

Parallel Adder Logic device that processes the addition of several (typically 4, 8, or 16) binary inputs simultaneously rather than sequentially, as is the case with half adders and full adders. Parallel adders speed processing since they require fewer steps to produce the result.

Parallel Algorithm Algorithm in which more than one portion of the algorithm can be followed at one time. Parallel algorithms are usually used in multiprocessing environments.

Parallel Circuit Circuit in which the corresponding leads of two or more circuit components are connected. In the parallel circuit, there are two or more separate pathways between points. The individual components in a parallel circuit all receive the same voltage but they share the circuit load. This is different from a series circuit, in which all the circuit current passes through each component but the voltage is divided among the components.

Parallel Computer Computer that uses several processors connected in parallel (working concurrently). Software written for parallel computers can increase the amount of work done in a specific amount of time by dividing a computing task among several simultaneously functioning processors.

Parallel Interface Specification of a data-transmission scheme that sends multiple data and control bits simultaneously over wires connected in parallel. The most common parallel interface is the Centronics interface.

Parallel Port

Parallel Port Input/output connector for a parallel interface device. This port is most widely used for the connection of a printer to the system.

Parallel Printer Printer connected to the computer by use of a parallel interface. In general, a parallel connection can move data between devices faster than a serial connection can. However, in most microcomputer printers, the bottleneck is the printing itself. Provided the connection can move most data faster than the printer can handle it, there is no difference in print speed between serial and parallel printers. The parallel interface is preferred in the IBM PC world, however, because its cabling is more standardized than that of the serial interface and because the MS-DOS operating system assumes that the system printer is attached to the parallel port.

Parallel Processing Method of processing that can run only on a type of computer containing two or more processors running simultaneously. Parallel processing differs from multiprocessing in the way a task is distributed over the available processors; in multiprocessing, a process might be divided up into sequential blocks, with one processor managing access to a database, another analyzing the data, and a third handling graphical output to the screen.

Parallel Transmission Simultaneous transmission of a group of bits over separate wires. With microcomputers, parallel transmission refers to the transmission of 1 byte (8 bits). The standard connection for parallel transmission—for example, from a computer to a printer—is known as the Centronics interface.

Parameter In programming, parameter pertains to a value given to a variable, either at the beginning of an operation or before an expression is evaluated by a program. Until the operation is completed, a parameter is effectively treated as a constant value by the program. A parameter can be text, a number, or an argument name assigned to a value that is passed from one routine to another. Parameters are used as a means of customizing program operation. On MS-DOS machines, for example, the Directory command accepts filenames as parameters, as in dir.myfile.doc. This allows the user to limit the output of the command to a particular file, instead of listing all files on a disk or in a certain directory.

Parameter-Driven

Parameter-Driven Program or operation whose character or outcome is determined by the values of the parameters that are assigned to it.

Parameter Passing In programming, the substitution of an actual parameter value for a formal (dummy) parameter when a procedure or function call is processed.

Parameter RAM A few bytes of battery-backed CMOS RAM on the motherboards of Apple Macintosh computers that stores information about the configuration of the system.

Parent/Child Relationship between processes in a multitasking environment in which the parent process calls the child process and most often suspends its own operation until the child process aborts or is completed. Also, a relationship between nodes in a tree data structure in which the parent is one step closer to the root (that is, is one level higher) than the child.

Parity Quality of sameness or equivalence. In computer use, parity usually refers to an error-checking procedure in which the number of 1's must always be the same—either even or odd—for each group of bits transmitted without error. If parity is checked on a per-character basis, the method is called vertical redundancy checking, or VRC; if checked on a block-by-block basis, the method is called longitudinal redundancy checking, or LRC. Parity is used for checking data transferred within a computer or between computers. In typical modem-to-modem microcomputer communications, parity is one of the parameters that must be agreed upon by sending and receiving parties before transmission can take place. The following types of parity are used:
- **Even Parity** The number of 1's in each successfully transmitted set of bits must be an even number.
- **Odd Parity** The number of 1's in each successfully transmitted set of bits must be an odd number.
- **No Parity** No parity bit is used.
- **Space Parity** A parity bit is used and is always set to 0.
- **Mark Parity** A parity bit is used and is always set to 1.

Parity Bit Extra bit used in checking for errors in groups of data bits transferred within or between computer systems. With microcomputers, the term is frequently encountered in modem-to-modem microcomputer communications, in which a parity bit is

Parity Bit

often used to check the accuracy with which characters are transmitted. In this form of parity checking, the sending computer adds a parity bit to each group of data bits, each of which represents a single character. The setting of the parity bit depends on the type of parity used. With even parity, for example, the parity bit is set to 1 whenever it is needed to make the total number of 1's (data bits plus parity bit) an even number; with odd parity, the parity bit is set to 1 whenever it is needed to make the total number of 1's an odd number. The receiving device counts the number of 1's in each arriving group of data and parity bits; if the number is odd when it should be even, or vice versa, the device can assume that one of the bits was transmitted incorrectly and that an error occurred.

Parity Check Using parity to check the accuracy of transmitted data.

Parity Error Error in parity that indicates an error in transmitted data. When transferring files in a telecommunications linkup, a good protocol will transmit data over again if a parity error has been detected. This is referred to as an error-correcting protocol.

Park Ability to position the read/write head over a portion of a disk that stores no data (and therefore can never be damaged) or beyond the surface of the disk, prior to shutting down the drive, mainly used in preparation for moving it. Parking can be performed manually, automatically, or (as is typical) by a disk utility program.

Parse Breaking input into smaller chunks so that a program can act upon the information. Compilers have parsers for translating the commands and structures entered by a programmer into machine language. A natural-language parser accepts text in a human language such as English, attempts to determine its sequence structure, and translates its terms into a form the program can use. Database management programs and expert systems often support natural-language parsing.

Partition Logically distinct portion of memory or a storage device that functions as though it were a physically separate unit. The MS-DOS operating system, for example, can divide a hard disk into a primary partition and an extended DOS partition, each of which behaves as if it were physically distinct from the other.

In database programming, partition refers to a subset of a database, table, or file. In a horizontal partition, data is separated by rows or records; in a relational database management system, horizontal partitions can usually be created based on primary key values. In a vertical partition, data is separated by columns or fields. Vertical partitioning (or projection of columns) often occurs during normalization of database design. Database files may be horizontally or vertically partitioned across multiple nodes in a distributed database.

Pascal Concise procedural programming language, designed by Niklaus Wirth. Pascal, a compiled, structured language, simplifies syntax while adding data types and structures such as subranges, enumerated data types, files, records, and sets. Acceptance and use of Pascal exploded with Borland International's introduction in 1984 of Turbo Pascal, a high-speed, low-cost Pascal compiler for MS-DOS systems that has sold over a million copies in its various versions. Even so, Pascal appears to be losing ground to C as a standard development language on microcomputers.

Pass In programming, carrying out one complete sequence of events; for example, one pass through a program loop ("WHILE x is less than 10, DO this") or one scan of a program by a compiler or an assembler (in preparation for converting program instructions into a form the computer can carry out). In another sense, pass means to forward a piece of data from one part of a program to another.

Password Security measure used to restrict access to computer systems and sensitive files. A password is a unique string of characters that a user types in as an identification code. The system compares the code against a stored list of authorized passwords and users; if the code is legitimate, the system allows the user access, at whatever security level has been approved for the owner of that password.

Password Protection Use of passwords as a means of allowing only authorized users access to a computer system or its files.

Paste To insert text or graphics cut or copied from one document into a different location in the same or a different document.

Patch In programming, to repair a deficiency in the functionality of an existing routine or program, generally in response to an unforeseen need or set of operating circumstances. Patching does

Patch

not necessarily imply sloppiness in implementing a solution to a problem; it is a common means of adding a feature or a function to an existing version of a program until the release of the next version of the software, which presumably will have that feature or function included in its design.

Path Route from one point to another. In communications, a path is a link between two nodes (stations) in a network. In other contexts, a path is a route through a structured collection of information, as in a database, a program, or files stored on disk. In a database, for example, a path is the selection of branches and nodes to be traversed in a tree structure in order to progress from the root node of the tree to any other node.

In programming, a path is the sequence of instructions a computer carries out in executing a routine. In information processing, such as the theory underlying expert (deductive) systems, a path is a logical course through the "branches" of a tree of inferences (this AND that, this OR that) leading to a conclusion.

In file storage, a path is the route followed by the operating system in finding, storing, and retrieving files on a disk. In hierarchical file systems, such as that used by the MS-DOS operating system, a path is the course leading from the root directory of a drive, such as C, to a particular file; the path can include any number of named subdirectories up to the maximum length of the pathname allowed by the system (64 characters in MS-DOS).

In graphics, a path is an accumulation of line segments or curves, to be filled or overwritten with text.

Pathname In a hierarchical filing system, a listing of the directories or folders that lead from the current directory to a file.

Pattern Recognition Broad technology describing the ability of a computer to identify patterns. The term usually refers to computer recognition of visual images or sound patterns that have been converted to arrays of numbers. This type of pattern recognition involves two main activities: translation of the image or sound into a digital signal that can be processed by the computer (possibly followed by fine-tuning for better recognition) and matching of the input against a set of stored patterns. Uses of this type of pattern recognition range from optical character recognition systems, such as those used by the U.S. Postal Service, to more exotic

Pattern Recognition

applications such as robotic vision, artificial-intelligence research, speech recognition, fingerprint analysis, medical analysis, satellite surveillance, and handwriting analysis.

Pattern recognition can also refer to recognition of purely mathematical or textual patterns. Early spell-checking programs, for example, performed a simple form of pattern recognition by recognizing which text patterns in a document matched the text pattern in the program's dictionary. Patterns not in the dictionary were considered misspelled words.

Pause Key Key on the keyboard that temporarily stops the operation of a program or a command. The Pause key is used, for example, to halt scrolling so that a multiscreen listing or document can be read. The term can also refer to any key that pauses the current operation. Many game programs have a Pause key—often simply the P key—that temporarily suspends the game.

PC Common abbreviation for personal computer. Depending on the context, PC often refers to IBM's Personal Computer line; thus PC-compatible refers to a computer that can run the same programs as an IBM PC.

PCB Acronym for **Printed Circuit Board**.

PC Board Same as PCB.

PC-DOS Version of MS-DOS sold by IBM. MS-DOS and PC-DOS are virtually identical, although filenames or utility programs sometimes differ in the two versions. See also **MS-DOS**.

PCL Acronym for **Printer Control Language**.

PCM Acronym for **Pulse Code Modulation**.

PC/XT Keyboard Original keyboard for the IBM PC. Strong, reliable, and equipped with 83 keys, the PC/XT keyboard offers a typist both an audible click and clear kinesthetic feedback. Most touch typists did not like the keyboard because of its departures from the standard layout of the office typewriter, as typified by the IBM Selectric. The Enter and Shift keys, for example, are notably smaller than on the Selectric; there is an extra key (with a backslash and vertical bar) between the Z key and the left shift key; and another extra key (with the grave accent and the tilde) between the quote key and the Enter key. Other annoyances on the keyboard included the lack of lights to indicate the status of the Caps Lock, Scroll Lock, and Num Lock keys.

PDL Acronym for **Page-Description Language**.

PDM Acronym for **Pulse Duration Modulation**.

Peek Ability to read a byte from an absolute memory location. PEEK and POKE (store a byte in memory) commands are often found in programming languages, such as BASIC, that do not normally allow access to specific memory locations. PEEK can also refer to the act of looking at the next character in a buffer associated with a keyboard or other sequential input device without actually removing the character from the buffer.

Peer Any of the devices on a layered communications network that operate on the same protocol level.

Pel Rare term used in reference to a picture element (pixel).

Pen Light pen, or stylus, a form of pointing device.

Pen Plotter Traditional graphics plotter that uses pens to draw on paper, as opposed to an electrostatic plotter, which works with toner to create images made up of dot patterns. Pen plotters use one or more colored pens, either fiber-tipped pens, or for highest-quality output, drafting pens. Many systems use a carousel that can hold pens of various colors. A gripping arm holds the pen for drawing; to change colored pens, the arm returns the pen in use to the carousel, which then rotates to offer the new color.

Performance Monitor Process or program that appraises and records status information about various system devices and other processes.

Period Length of time required for an oscillation to complete one full cycle. The period of a clock pendulum, for example, is the time required for it to swing from the leftmost position to the right and then back again. For an oscillating electrical signal, the period is the time between waveform repetitions, as shown in the illustration. If "f" is the frequency of oscillation in hertz, and "t" is the period in seconds, then $t = 1/f$.

Peripheral Device such as a disk drive, printer, modem, and joystick connected to a computer and controlled by its

Peripheral

microprocessor. Although peripheral often implies "additional but not essential," many peripheral devices are critical elements of a fully functioning and useful computer system. Few people, for example, would argue that disk drives are nonessential, although computers can function without them. Keyboards, monitors, and mice are also strictly considered peripheral devices, but because they represent primary sources of input and output in most computer systems, they can be considered more extensions of the system unit than peripherals.

Permanent Storage Recording medium that retains the data recorded on it for long periods of time without power. Paper is by far the most widely used permanent storage, but data can be transferred from paper to a computer only with difficulty. Typically, some form of magnetic medium, such as floppy disk or tape, is preferable. Magnetic media are generally accepted as permanent, even though the magnetic fields that encode data in the media tend to fade eventually (in five years or more).

Perpendicular Recording Also called vertical recording. A method of increasing storage capacity on magnetic media by aligning the magnetic dipoles, whose orientation determines bit values, in a direction that is perpendicular to the recording surface.

Persistence Characteristic of some light-emitting materials (such as the phosphors used in CRTs) that causes an image to remain for a short while after being irradiated (for example, by an electron beam in a CRT). The decay in persistence is sometimes called luminance decay. If the persistence of a phosphor is too short, the tendency of an image to flicker is increased; if the persistence is too long, images tend to smear on the screen.

Personal Computer Computer designed for use by one person at a time. Personal computers do not need to share the processing, disk, and printer resources of another computer, although they can at the user's option. When capitalized (Personal Computer), the term refers to a computer manufactured by IBM Corporation.

Personal Identification Number Unique code number assigned to the authorized user, as with automatic teller machine cards.

Perspective View In computer graphics, a display method that shows objects in three dimensions (height, width, and depth), with

Perspective View

the depth aspect rendered according to the desired perspective. A drawing program that produces a perspective view of a cube, for example, shows the sides in relation to one another but shows the height as growing smaller with distance. An advantage of perspective view is that it presents a more accurate representation of what the human eye perceives.

PgDn Key Abbreviation for **Page Down key**.

PgUp Key Abbreviation for **Page Up key**.

Phase Relative measurement that describes the temporal relationship between two signals that have the same frequency. Phase is measured in degrees, with one full oscillation cycle having 360 degrees. The phase of one signal can either lead or follow the other by 0 through 180 degrees. If two clock pendulums are swinging at the same frequency, they are in phase if they are at corresponding positions at the same instant. However, if one is at its leftmost position when the other is pointing straight down, they are said to be 90 degrees out of phase.

Phase-Change Recording In optical media, a recording technique that uses a laser beam focused on a microscopic portion of metallic crystal to alter the reflectiveness of its structure in such a way that the change can be read as a 0 bit or a 1 bit, depending on whether the resulting structure reflects or absorbs the laser light.

Phase Encoding Process of placing digital information on an analog carrier wave while periodically changing the phase of the carrier, in order to increase the bit density of the transmission. The term can also refer to a recording technique (sometimes called phase-modulation recording) used with magnetic storage devices in which each data-holding unit (cell) is divided into two parts, each of which is magnetized so that it is opposite to the other. Depending on the sequence of magnetization (positive/negative or negative/positive), the cell represents a binary 1 or 0.

Phase-Locked Relationship between two signals whose phases relative to each other are kept constant by a controlling mechanism such as an electronic device.

Phase Modulation Method of imposing information onto a waveform signal by shifting the phase of the wave (the position of

Phase Modulation

the wave relative to time and a baseline value) to represent information, such as the binary digits O and 1.

Phase-Shift Keying Abbreviated PSK. In communications, a method used by modems to encode data that relies on phase shifts in a carrier wave to represent digital information. In its most simple form, phase-shift keying allows for the phase of the carrier wave to be in either of two states: shifted 0 degrees or shifted 180 degrees, effectively reversing the phase of the wave. One of these states can be used to represent a binary 0; the other can represent a binary 1.

This straightforward phase-shift keying, however, is useful only when each phase can be measured against an unchanging reference value, so a more sophisticated technique, called differential phase-shift keying, or DPSK, is used in many modems, such as those conforming to the CCITT V.22 standard. In differential phase-shift keying, the phase of the carrier wave is shifted to represent more than two possible states, and each state is interpreted as a relative change from the state preceding it. No reference values or timing considerations are required, and because more than two states are possible, more than one binary digit can represent each state. For example, a modem using differential phase-shift keying might recognize four possible states: no change, a 90-degree change, a 180-degree change, or a 270-degree change. Because there are four states rather than two, each can represent a unique combination of 2 bits, known as a dibit, as follows:

PhaseShift	Dibit
0-degree change	00
10-degree change	01
180-degree change	11
270-degree change	10

A V.22 modem engineered to transmit at the rate of 6OO baud (6OO signal changes per second) can use four-state differential phase-shift keying to encode data as dibits and to transmit the information at the rate of 1200 hits per second 6OO signal changes per second times 2 bits per change. See also **phase modulation**.

Phone Connector Attachment, usually an RJ-II connector, used to join a telephone line to a device such as a modem.

Phoneme

Phoneme In linguistics, the smallest unit of speech that distinguishes one word sound from another. For example, c and r, as in the words cat and rat, represent different phonemes in English. Phonemes are the elements on which computer speech is based.

Phono Connector Attachment used to connect a device such as a microphone or a pair of headphones to a piece of audio equipment or to a computer peripheral or adapter with audio capability.

Phosphor Any substance capable of emitting light when struck by radiation. The inside surface of a CRT screen is coated with a phosphor that, when excited by an electron beam, displays an image on the screen.

Photocomposition In traditional typesetting, the use of photographic and electronic equipment in laying out (and producing) a printed page. In desktop publishing, the use of phototypesetters to accomplish the same ends.

Photoelectric Device Device that uses light to create or modulate an electrical signal. Photoelectric devices use semiconductor material, and they fall into two categories. In one type, light falling on the semiconductor generates an electrical current. This type is used in the photovoltaic, or solar, cells found in solar-powered watches and calculators. In the second type of device, light changes the resistance of the semiconductor material, modulating an applied voltage. This type is used in camera exposure meters.

Photolithography Technique used in the fabrication of integrated circuits. The circuit pattern drawn is photographed and reduced to a negative (referred to as the photomask) of the desired final size. Light is passed through the photomask onto a wafer of semiconductor material that has been coated with a photosensitive material. Wherever light strikes this photosensitive material, the composition of the material is changed. After this step, the photosensitive material not effected by the light is washed off. The semiconductor material is then exposed to an etching solution that eats away the surface not protected by the photosensitive material, which creates the desired circuit pattern on the surface of the wafer.

Photomask Photographic negative image of a circuit pattern used in fabrication of integrated circuits.

Photorealism

Photorealism Process of creating images as close to photographic or "real-life" quality as possible. In computer graphics, photo realism requires powerful computers and highly sophisticated software and is heavily mathematical. Large numbers of calculations are required to determine, for example, the correct positioning and intensity of light, color, reflections, and shadows for each element in the image, accounting for their position both in relation to other objects in the image and to a light source at a specified location (which might or might not be in the image itself). Movement of objects further complicates the process. Photorealism, particularly in color images, is not yet in the mainstream of microcomputer applications. Computer-generated images of this type, when done well, are almost indistinguishable from photographs. See also **ray tracing**.

Photoresist Compound used in photolithographic fabrication of integrated circuits and printed circuit boards. When exposed to ultraviolet light through a photomask, the photoresistive material exposed to the light polymerizes (hardens); the areas not exposed can be washed away, leaving the pattern of traces on the substrate (a silicon chip or a copper-clad circuit board). Subsequent etching removes areas not protected by the polymerized photoresist.

Phototypesetter Printer similar to a laser printer, but capable of resolutions over 2000 dots per inch (vs. 300 dpi for most laser printers). Phototypesetters also differ in their medium. Rather than playing a laser or other light-generating device against a photosensitive drum that converts the energy to an electromagnetic charge, phototypesetters apply light directly to photographic film or photosensitive paper.

Physical In computing, having to do with a "real" as opposed to a conceptual piece of equipment or frame of reference. Physical is linked to hardware in some way. For example, a physical disk drive is the actual hardware in the computer; a physical record in a database is a record as stored at a particular location; a physical address is the location of a portion of memory or a device attached to a computer; a physical network layer encompasses the hardware that connects two or more computers. The complement of physical in the computing sense is logical, which refers to elements that exist conceptually but not necessarily in reality. For example, a single physical hard-disk drive can be divided into several logical

Physical

drives, each of which appears to the user to be a separate disk drive although all reside on the same (physical) piece of equipment. Software within a computer is responsible for translating logical references to physical ones and, when necessary, physical references to logical ones.

Physical Address Address that corresponds to a hardware memory location. In simple processors such as the 8088 and the 68000, every address is a physical address. In processors such as the 80386/486, 68030, or 68040, which support virtual memory, programs reference virtual addresses, which are then mapped by memory management hardware onto physical addresses.

Physical Layer First, or lowest, of the seven layers in the International Organization for Standardization's Open Systems Interconnection (OSI) model for standardizing computer-to-computer communications. The physical layer is totally hardware-oriented and deals with all aspects of establishing and maintaining a physical link between communicating computers. Among specifications covered on the physical layer are cabling, electrical signals, and mechanical connections.

Physical Memory Memory actually present in the system, as opposed to virtual memory. A computer might have only 4 megabytes (MB) of RAM but support a virtual memory of 20 MB. Compare **virtual memory**.

Pica Either of two units of measure used with printed type. In one sense, as on typewriters, pica refers to fixed-width type that fits 10 characters to the linear inch; in this respect, a pica is a measure of pitch, or number of characters per horizontal inch. In the sense used by typographers, a pica is a unit of measure equal to 12 points, or approximately 1/6 inch.

Pico Abbreviated as p, prefix meaning one trillionth. In the British numbering system, one million millionth.

Picosecond Usually seen as psec, one trillionth of a second.

Pie Chart Type of graph that presents values as percentages (slices) of a whole (a pie).

Piezoelectric Certain crystals that can convert between mechanical and electrical energy. An electrical potential applied to a

Piezoelectric

piezoelectric crystal causes a small change in the shape of the crystal. Likewise, physical pressure applied to the crystal creates an electrical potential difference between the surfaces of the crystal. Piezoelectric crystals are used in some microphones to convert the mechanical energy of the sound waves to an electrical signal, and in crystal oscillators, where the mechanical properties of the crystal serve to control the frequency of oscillation.

Piggyback Board Circuit board that plugs into an expansion card rather than into an expansion slot to enhance its capability or to provide additional capability. A piggyback board is sometimes used to replace a single chip (such as a microprocessor); in this case, the chip is removed and the piggyback board is inserted into the empty socket. Sometimes referred to as a daughterboard.

Pin Slender prong. Pins are commonly encountered as the contacts protruding from a male connector. Connectors are often identified by the number of pins they have; for example, a 5-pin or a 9-pin connector. Other types of pins are the spidery, leglike metal appendages that connect computer chips to sockets on a circuit board or directly to the circuit board; for example, memory chips on a computer's system board (motherboard).

PIN Acronym for **Personal Identification Number**.

Pinch Roller Small cylindrical pulley that presses magnetic tape against the drive's capstan to move the tape over the tape machine's heads.

Pin-Compatible Chip or electronic device having pins equivalent to the pins on another chip or device. A chip, for example, might have different internal circuitry from that used in another chip, but if the two use the same pins for input and output of identical signals, they are pin-compatible. Some chips are pin-compatible with their predecessors but are more powerful; to upgrade the system, one simply replaces the older chip. Compare **plug-compatible**.

Pin Feed Method of feeding paper through a printer using small pins, mounted on rollers on the ends of the platen, that engage holes near the edges of continuous-form paper. Pin feed is often used mistakenly as a synonym for **tractor feed**, which also uses small pins or sprockets. See also **continuous-form paper**.

Ping Pong

Ping Pong In communications, a technique that changes the direction of transmission so that the sender becomes the receiver and vice versa. In information processing and transfer, the technique of using two temporary storage areas (buffers) rather than one to hold both input and output (also called double buffering).

Ping-Pong Buffer Double buffer in which each part is alternately filled and flushed, resulting in a more or less continuous stream of input and output data.

Pin Grid Array Abbreviated PGA. Method for mounting chips on boards; preferred for chips with a very large number of pins. PGA packages have pins protruding from the bottom of the chip, as opposed to dual in-line packages and leaderless chip carrier packages, which have pins protruding from the sides of the chip. Both IBM and Compaq used the pin grid array version of the 80286 microprocessor in their personal computers, whereas many clone makers opted for the less expensive LCC (leaderless chip carrier) mounting method.

Pinout Description or diagram of the pins of a chip or connector.

Pipe Portion of memory that can be used by one process to pass information along to another. Essentially, a pipe connects two processes so that the output of one can be used as the input to the other. Pipes are symbolized in the MS-DOS and OS/2 operating systems by the colon (:), as in the command dir : sort : more, which calls for a directory listing, pipes the output to the sort command, and pipes the results of the sort command to the more command, which displays its output one screen full at a time.

Pipelining Method of fetching and decoding instructions (preprocessing) in which, at any given time, several program instructions are in various stages of being fetched or decoded. Ideally, pipelining speeds execution time by ensuring that the microprocessor does not have to wait for instructions; when it completes execution of one instruction, the next is ready and waiting.

In parallel processing, pipelining can also refer to a method in which instructions are passed from one processing unit to another, as on an assembly line, and each unit is specialized for performing a particular type of operation.

On a level more easily visible to a computer user, pipelining

Pipelining

can refer to the use of pipes in passing the output of one task as input to another until a desired sequence of tasks has been carried out.

Piracy Either theft, as in the appropriation of a computer design or a program, or unauthorized distribution and use of a computer program. The latter form of piracy, in which programs are purchased, copied without permission, and then given away without charge, was widely practiced by individuals in the early days of microcomputing. The practice resulted in the copy protection applied to many software products of the time. Piracy still exists, but instead of copy protection many developers use the legal system to stop pirates or add incentives to persuade them to become registered users.

Pitch Measure, generally used with monospace (fixed-width) fonts, that describes the number of characters that fit in a horizontal inch. For example, 30-pitch means that 10 characters can be printed per inch. Pitch is a measurement not only of the character but also of the space between characters. A single character and its accompanying blank space in a 10-pitch font would be 1/10 inch wide. In monospace fonts, sizes are usually described by pitch. In proportional fonts, size is usually described in points, which measure height rather than width. In pitch measurements, a higher number means smaller characters; in points, a higher number means larger characters.

Pixel Picture element; sometimes called a pel. It refers to one spot in a rectilinear grid of thousands of such spots that are individually "painted" to form an image produced on the screen by a computer or on paper by a printer. Just as a bit is the smallest unit of information a computer can process, a pixel is the smallest element that display or print hardware and software can manipulate in creating letters, numbers, or graphics. If a pixel has only two color values (typically black and white), it can be encoded by 1 bit of information. If more than 2 bits are used to represent a pixel, a larger range of colors or shades of gray can be represented: 2 bits for four colors or shades of gray, 4 bits for sixteen colors, and so on. Typically, an image of two colors is called a bit map, and an image of more than two colors is called a pixel map.

Pixel Image Representation of a color graphic in a computer's memory. A pixel image is similar to a bit image, which also describes a screen graphic, but differs in having an added

Pixel Image

dimension, sometimes called depth, that describes the number of bits in memory assigned to each on-screen pixel. For example, a pixel image with a depth of 8 bits uses 8 bits to describe the attributes, such as color, of each individual pixel on the screen

Pixel Map Generally, same as **pixel image**.

Plastic Leaderless Chip Carrier Abbreviated PLCC. Inexpensive variation of the leaderless chip carrier (LCC) method of mounting chips on boards. Although the two carriers are similar in appearance, PLCCs are physically incompatible with LCCs, which are made from a ceramic material.

Platen Cylinder in most impact printers and typewriters around which the paper wraps and against which the print mechanism strikes the paper. The paper bail, a spring-loaded bar with small rollers, holds the paper smoothly against the platen just above the print mechanism.

Platform Foundation technology of a computer system. Because computers are layered devices composed of a chip-level hardware layer, a firmware and operating-system layer, and an applications program layer, the bottommost layer of a machine is often called a platform, as in "an IBM PC platform." However, designers of applications often view both the hardware and systems software as the platform because both provide support for the application.

Platter One of the individual metal data storage disks within a hard-disk drive. Most hard disks have from two to eight platters.

PLCC Acronyn for **Plastic Leaderless Chip Carrier**.

Plotter Any device used to draw charts, diagrams, and other line-based graphics. Plotters use either pens or electrostatic charges and toner. Pen plotters draw on paper or transparencies with one or more colored pens. Electrostatic plotters "draw" a pattern of electrostatically charged dots on the paper and then apply toner and fuse it in place, much as laser printers do. Plotters use three basic types of paper handling: flatbed, drum, and pinch-roller. Flatbed plotters hold the paper still and move the pen along both x and y axes. Drum plotters roll the paper over a cylinder. The pen moves along one axis while the drum, with the paper attached, moves along the other. Pinch-roller plotters are a hybrid of the two, in which the pen moves only along one axis while the paper is moved

Plotter

back and forth by small rollers. Most plotters use a graphics language, such as Hewlett-Packard's HPGL, to define graphics primitives such as lines, circles, and squares. This simplifies the job of the graphics software.

Plugboard Board that permits users to control the operation of a device by plugging cables into sockets.

Plug-Compatible Hardware equipped with connectors that are equivalent both in structure and in usage. For example, most modems having DB-25 connectors on their rear panels are plug-compatible; that is, one can be replaced by another without the cable having to be rewired.

PMMU Acronym for **Paged Memory Management Utility**.

PMS Acronym for **Pantone Matching System**.

PNP Transistor Type of transistor in which a base of N-type material is sandwiched between an emitter and a collector of P-type material. The base, emitter, and collector are the three terminals of the transistor through which current flows. In a PNP transistor, holes (electron "vacancies") are the majority of the charge carriers, and these holes flow from the emitter to the collector.

Point In reference to printed output, a typographical unit of measure equal to approximately 1/72 inch, often used to indicate character height and the amount of space (leading) between lines of text. In programming and video graphics, a point can be either a single pixel on the screen (as in the all-points-addressable mode on IBM computers) or a location in a geometric form (as in a point on a line or a point in a circle). This term is also used in reference to moving an arrow or other such indicator to a particular item or position on the screen by using direction keys or by maneuvering a pointing device such as a mouse.

Pointer In a graphics-based environment, an on-screen symbol, such as an arrowhead, controlled by a mouse or other input device and used as a means of indicating (and selecting) locations or choices on the screen. When used in reference to programming and information processing, it refers to a variable that contains the memory location (address) of some data rather than the data itself. This allows the memory for that data to be dynamically allocated (and deallocated).

Pointing Device

Pointing Device Input device used to control an on-screen cursor for such actions as "pressing" on-screen buttons in dialog boxes, choosing menu items, and selecting ranges of cells in spreadsheets or groups of words in a document. A pointing device is also often used to create drawings or graphical shapes. The most common pointing device is the mouse, which was popularized by its central role in the design of the Apple Macintosh. Other pointing devices include the graphics tablet, the stylus, the light pen, the joystick, the puck, and the trackball.

Point-to-Point Configuration Communications link in which two stations are directly joined.

Poke Ability to store a byte into an absolute memory location. PEEK (read a byte from memory) and POKE commands are often found in programming languages, such as BASIC, that do not normally allow access to specific memory locations.

Polarity Sign of the potential (voltage) difference between two points in a circuit. When a potential difference exists between two points, one point has a positive polarity and the other a negative polarity. Electrons flow from negative to positive, but by convention current is considered to flow from positive to negative. Polarity also refers to the orientation of the north and south magnetic poles.

Polarized Component Circuit component that must be installed with its leads in a particular orientation with respect to the polarity of the circuit. Diodes, rectifiers, and some capacitors are examples of polarized components. Examples of nonpolarized components are resistors, inductors, and most capacitors.

Polarizing Filter Transparent piece of glass or plastic, usually dark gray or brown, that polarizes the light passing through it—that is, it allows only waves vibrating in a certain direction to pass through. Polarizing filters are often used to reduce glare on monitor screens.

Polygon Any two-dimensional closed shape with multiple sides, such as a hexagon, an octagon, or a triangle. Computer users encounter polygons—or tools for creating polygons—in graphics programs such as MacPaint and Windows Paint. Graphical interfaces can include polygons as geometric primitives (objects that programs can create and manipulate as discrete entities).

Polyline

Polyline In computer graphics, a line consisting of multiple connected segments, such as the lines connecting the stars in a representation of the handle of the Big Dipper. Polylines are used in CAD and other graphics programs. Graphical interfaces can include polylines as geometric primitives (objects that programs can create and manipulate as discrete entities).

Polymorphism In object-oriented programming language, the ability to redefine a routine in a derived class (a class that inherited its data structures and routines from another class). Polymorphism allows the programmer to define a base class that includes routines that perform standard operations on groups of related objects, without regard to the exact type of each object. The programmer can redefine the routines, taking into account the type of the object, in the derived classes for each of the types.

Pop Ability to fetch the top (most recently added) element of a stack and remove that element from the stack in the process. A stack is a data structure generally used to temporarily hold pieces of data being transferred or the partial result of an arithmetic operation.

Populate To fill the sockets of a circuit board.

Port In computer hardware, location for passing data in and out of a computing device. Microprocessors have ports for sending and receiving data bits; these ports are usually dedicated locations in memory. Full computer systems have ports for connecting peripheral devices such as printers and modems. In programming, this term refers to the ability to change a program in order to run it on a different computer, such as the ability to move documents, graphics, and other files from one computer to another.

Portability In computer programs, ability of a program to run on or be changed to run on more than one computer system or under more than one operating system. Highly portable software can be moved to other systems with little effort; moderately portable software can be moved only with substantial effort; and nonportable software can be moved only with effort similar to or greater than the effort of writing the original program.

Portable Program capable of being moved to various systems. With reference to computers, portable commonly refers to a computer that can be moved or carried with ease.

Portable Computer

Portable Computer Any computer designed to be moved easily, characterized by size and weight.

Port Expander Hardware mechanism used for connecting several devices to a single port. Although several devices might be connected, only one can use the port at any given moment.

Portrait Mode Vertical print orientation in which a document is printed across the narrower dimension of a rectangular sheet of paper—the print mode typical of most letters, reports, and other such documents.

Portrait Monitor Monitor with a screen shape higher than it is wide. The proportion (but not necessarily the size) of the screen is usually the same as that of a sheet of 8 1/2-by-11-inch paper. Portrait monitors are often preferred by people working with desktop-publishing applications.

PostProcessor Device or software routine, such as a linker, that operates on data manipulated first by another processor.

PostScript Page-description language from Adobe Systems that offers flexible font capability and high-quality graphics. The best-known page-description language, PostScript uses English-like commands to control page layout and to load and scale outline fonts. Because PostScript uses scalable outline fonts, it can create a font of any size, giving the user flexibility in creating documents. PostScript is used in many printers, either as the only print mode or as one alternative among several.

Adobe also makes Display PostScript, a graphics language for computer displays that gives users of both PostScript and Display PostScript absolute WYSIWYG (what-you-see-is-what-you-get), which is difficult when different methods are used for displaying and printing.

PostScript Font Font defined in terms of the PostScript page-description language rules and intended to be printed on a PostScript-compatible printer. PostScript fonts are distinguished from bit-mapped fonts by their smoothness, detail, and faithfulness to standards of quality established in the typographic industry. Fonts that appear on the screen—for example, as bit-mapped characters in a graphical user interface—are called screen fonts. When a document displayed in a screen font is sent to a PostScript

PostScript Font

printer, the printer uses the PostScript version if the font exists. If the font doesn't exist but a version is installed on the computer, that font is downloaded. If there is no PostScript font installed in either the printer or the computer, the bit-mapped font is translated into PostScript and the printer prints text using the bit-mapped font.

Potentiometer Commonly called a pot. Circuit element that can be adjusted to provide varying amounts of resistance. The twist-knob and slider-type volume controls found on many radios and television sets are potentiometers.

Power In mathematics, the number of times a value is multiplied by itself; for example, 10 to the third power means 10 times 10 times 10. When used in computing, this term refers to the electricity used to run a computer; or it can be used to reference the action of turning a computer on (power up) or off (power down). In terms of computing ability, the speed at which a computer performs and the availability of various features.

Power Down To shut down; to turn off the power.

Power Failure Loss of electricity, which causes a loss of unsaved data in a computer's random-access memory (RAM) if no backup power supply is connected to the machine.

Power-On Key Special key on the Apple ADB and Extended Keyboards used for turning on a Macintosh II. The Power-on key is marked with a left-pointing triangle and is used in lieu of the on/off switch. There is no Power-off key; the system is shut down by choosing the Shut Down command from the Special menu. When the Apple Extended Keyboard or the ADR keyboard is connected to a Macintosh SE or Apple IIGS, the Power-on key is useless unless a third-party accessory takes advantage of it.

Power-On Self Test Abbreviated as POST. A set of routines stored in a computer's read-only memory (ROM) that tests various system components such as RAM, the disk drives, and the keyboard to see if they are properly connected and operating. If problems are found, the POST routines alert the user by displaying a message, often accompanied by a diagnostic numeric value, to the standard output or standard error device (usually the screen). If the POST is successful, it passes control to the system's bootstrap loader.

Power Supply

Power Supply Electrical device that transforms standard wall outlet electricity (115-120 volts AC in the United States) into the lower voltages (typically 5 to 12 volts DC) required by computer systems. Personal computer power supplies are rated by wattage; they usually range from about 90 watts at the low end through 250 watts at the high end.

Power Up Starting up, or beginning of a cold boot procedure; to turn on the power.

Power User Person adept with computers, particularly on an applications-oriented level rather than on a programming level. A power user is someone who knows a considerable amount about computers and is comfortable enough with applications to be able to work with their most sophisticated features. In many cases, power users are especially familiar with a specific type of application, such as spreadsheets or word processors, and can push these products to the limits of their capabilities.

PPM Acronym for **Pages Per Minute**, or **Pulse Position Modulation**, depending on the topic being discussed.

Precedence In applications, the order in which values in a mathematical expression are calculated. In general, application programs perform multiplication and division first, followed by addition and subtraction. Sets of parentheses can be placed around expressions to control the order in which they are calculated. Programming languages, like the programs created with them, also follow orders of precedence. The operations, however, are more complex than those encountered with applications because of the languages' need to evaluate program code in terms of relationships, logic, and various internal rules of order.

Precision Refers to the extent of detail used in expressing a number. Precision is related to accuracy, and indicates the degree of detail.

When used in reference to programming, numeric values are often referred to as single-precision values, for example, might be contained in 4 bytes, double-precision values in 8 bytes. More storage space means that a number can be expressed with more precision. Hence, double-precision allows more exact values.

Preprocessor Device or routine that performs preliminary operations on input before passing it on to further processing. A

Preprocessor

program written in C, for example, is first examined by a preprocessor that performs operations such as replacing alphanumeric constants with values, expanding macros, and inserting specified files. The preprocessed version is then passed to the main part of the compiler for translation into machine code.

Presentation Graphics Representation of business information, such as sales figures and stock prices, in chart form rather than as lists of numbers. Capitalizing on the idea that a picture is worth a thousand words (or numbers), presentation graphics are used to give viewers an immediate grasp of business statistics and their significance. Common examples are area charts, bar charts, line charts, and pie charts. Although they may incorporate drawings and decorative type, presentation graphics have a different purpose than graphics created for engineering, architectural, or ornamental purposes.

Presentation Layer Sixth of the seven layers in the International Organization for Standardization's Open Systems Interconnection (OSI) model for standardizing computer-to-computer communications. The presentation layer is responsible for formatting information so it can be displayed or printed. This task generally includes interpreting codes (such as tabs) related to presentation, but it can also include converting encryption and other codes and translating different character sets.

Presentation Manager Graphical user interface provided with OS/2 versions 1.1 and later. The Presentation Manager derives from the MS-DOS-based Windows environment and provides similar capabilities. The user sees a graphical, window-oriented interface, and the programmer uses a standard set of routines for handling screen, keyboard, mouse, and printer input and output, no matter what hardware is attached to the system.

Pressure-Sensitive Device in which pressing on a thin surface produces an electrical connection and causes an event to be registered by the computer. Pressure-sensitive devices include touch-sensitive drawing pens, membrane keyboards, and some touch screens.

Preventive Maintenance Routine servicing of hardware intended to keep equipment in good operating condition and to find and correct problems before they develop into severe malfunctions.

Primary Channel

Primary Channel Data-transmission channel in a communications device, such as a modem.

Primary Key Also referred to as the major key. In databases, the key field that serves as the unique identifier of a specific tuple (row) in a relation (database table).

Primary Storage Refers to random-access memory (RAM), the main general-purpose storage region to which the microprocessor has direct access. A computer's other storage options, such as disks and tape, are called secondary storage or (sometimes) backing storage.

Primitive In computer graphics, a shape, such as a line, circle, curve, or polygon, that can be drawn, stored, and manipulated as a discrete entity by a graphics program. Primitives, also called geometric primitives, are the elements from which large graphic designs are created. In programming, primitive refers to a fundamental element in a language that can be used to create larger procedures that do the work a programmer wants to do. At the machine language level, a primitive is also a fundamental machine instruction.

Print In computing, to send information to a printer. Also sometimes used in the sense of "show me" or "copy this." For example, the PRINT statement in BASIC causes output to be displayed (printed) on the screen. Similarly, an application program that can be told to "print" a file to disk interprets the command as an instruction to route output to a disk file instead of to a printer.

Print Buffer Section of memory to which print output can be sent for temporary storage until the printer is ready to handle it. A print buffer can exist in a computer's random-access memory (RAM), in the printer, in a separate unit between the computer and the printer, or on disk. Regardless of its location, the function of a print buffer is to free the computer for other tasks by taking print output at high speed from the computer and passing it along at the much slower rate required by the printer. Print buffers vary in sophistication: Some simply hold the next few characters to be printed, and others can queue, reprint, or delete documents sent for printing. Print buffers often become noticeable when a print command is canceled; the printer may continue printing for quite a while, working its way through the contents of the buffer until the Cancel command becomes effective.

Printed Circuit Board

Printed Circuit Board More commonly referred to as PCB. Flat board made of nonconducting material, such as plastic or fiberglass, on which chips and other electronic components are mounted, usually in predrilled holes designed to hold them. The components on a printed circuit board—or, to be more specific, the holes that hold them—are connected electrically by predefined conductive metal pathways printed on the surface of the board. The metal leads protruding from the electronic components are soldered to the conductive metal pathways to form a connection. A printed circuit board should be held by the edges and protected from dirt and static electricity to avoid damage.

Printer Computer peripheral that puts text or a computer-generated image on paper or on another medium, such as a transparency. Printers can be categorized in several ways. The most common distinction is impact vs. nonimpact. Impact printers physically strike the paper, exemplified by pin dot-matrix printers and daisy-wheel printers; nonimpact printers refer to every other type of print mechanism, including laser, inkjet, and thermal printers. Other possible methods of categorizing printers include (but are not limited to) the following:

- **Print technology**: Chief among these, with microcomputers, are pin dot-matrix, inkjet, laser, thermal, and (although somewhat outdated) daisy-wheel or thimble printers. Pin dot-matrix printers can be further classified by the number of pins in the print head: 9, 18, 24, and so on.
- **Character formation**: Fully formed characters made of continuous lines (for example, those produced by a daisy-wheel printer) vs. dot-matrix characters composed of patterns of dots (such as those produced by standard dot-matrix, inkjet, and thermal printers). Laser printers, while technically dot-matrix, are generally considered to produce fully formed characters because their output is very clear and the dots are extremely small and closely spaced.
- **Method of transmission**: Parallel (byte-by-byte transmission) vs. serial (bit-by-bit transmission). These categories refer to the means by which output is sent to the printer rather than to any mechanical distinctions. Many printers are available in either serial or parallel versions, and still other printers offer both choices, yielding greater flexibility in installation options.
- **Method of printing**: Character by character, line by line, or page by page. Character printers include standard dot-matrix, inkjet,

Printer

thermal, and daisy-wheel printers. Lineprinters include the band, chain, and drum printers that are commonly associated with large computer installations or networks. Page printers include the electrophotographic printers, such as laser printers.

• **Print capability**: Text-only vs. text-and-graphics. Text-only printers, including most daisy-wheel and thimble printers and some dot-matrix and laser printers, can reproduce only characters for which they have matching patterns, such as embossed type, or internal character maps. Text-and-graphics printers—dot-matrix, inkjet, laser, and others—can reproduce all manner of images by "drawing" each as a pattern of dots.

Printer Control Language Commonly abbreviated as PCL. Printer control language from Hewlett-Packard, used in its LaserJet, DeskJet, and RuggedWriter printer lines. Because of the LaserJet dominance in the laser printer market, PCL has become a defacto standard.

Printer Controller The printer, typically a processing hardware in a page printer. It includes the raster image processor, the memory, and any general-purpose microprocessors. A printer controller can also reside in a personal computer, attached with the use of a high-speed cable to a printer that simply carries out its instructions.

Printer Driver Software program designed to enable other programs to work with a particular printer without concerning themselves with the specifics of the printer's hardware and internal "language." Different printers require different codes and commands to operate properly and to provide access to their special features and abilities. Application programs can communicate properly with a variety of printers by using printer drivers, which handle all the subtleties of each printer so that the application program doesn't have to. Today, graphical user interfaces offer their own printer drivers, eliminating the need for an application that runs under the interface to have its own printer driver.

Printer Engine Part of a page printer, such as a laser printer, that actually performs the printing. Most printer engine's are self-contained cartridges that can be easily replaced. The engine is distinct from the printer controller, which includes all the processing hardware in the printer. The most widely used printer engines are manufactured by Canon.

Printer File

Printer File Output that would normally be destined for the printer but has been diverted to a computer file instead. A printer file is created for one of several reasons. It allows output to be transferred to another program or to another computer. It also allows additional copies to be made at any time by simply copying the print image to the printer. Occasionally, the term printer file is used, incorrectly, to refer to the printer driver.

Printer Font Font residing in or intended for a printer. A printer font can be internal, downloaded, or on a font cartridge. Printer fonts are distinct from screen fonts, which are designed for displaying text on a computer screen. Compare **screen font**.

Print Head Part of a printer that mechanically controls the imprinting of characters on paper. In pin printers, including 9-pin, 24-pin, line, and other printers, the print head contains pins that mark the paper by firing against the ribbon and pressing it against the paper. In inkjet printers, the print head contains a group of jets that shoot ink at the page. In electrostatic plotters, the print head contains pins that transfer a charge to the paper.

Print Job Single batch of characters printed as a unit. A print job usually consists of a single document, which can be one page or hundreds of pages long. To avoid having to print individual documents separately, some software can group multiple documents into a single print job.

Print Quality Quality and clarity of characters produced by a printer. Print quality varies with the type of printer. Generally, dot-matrix printers produce lower-quality output than laser printers. The printer mode can also affect quality. Dot-matrix printers, for example, may operate in different modes with names such as draft quality, near-letter-quality, correspondence quality, or best quality. Draft quality, at the low end, is rapid but uses fewer dots to produce each character; near-letter-quality or best quality, at the high end, is relatively slow but uses more dots to form smoother characters.

Print Screen Key Key on the keyboard that, on IBM PC and compatible keyboards, normally causes the computer to send a character-based "picture" of the screen contents to the printer. The print screen feature works only when the display is in text mode or in CGA graphics mode (the lowest-resolution color and graphics mode available on IBM compatibles). It will not work properly in

Print Screen Key

other graphics modes; for example, with a Microsoft Windows-based word processor in EGA mode. Some programs use the Print Screen key to capture a screen image and record it as a file on disk. These programs typically can work in any graphics mode and record the file as a graphics image.

On some keyboards, such as the enhanced keyboard used with IBM PC and compatible computers, the Print Screen key alone is pressed. On other keyboards, including the original AT key board and the original PC/XT 89-key keyboard, the Print Screen key works only in combination with the Shift key. When the user is working directly with the MS-DOS operating system, and with some programs, the combination Control-Print Screen toggles the printer on or off. With printing turned on, the system sends every character to the printer as well as to the screen. The Print Screen key on the Apple Extended Keyboard is included for compatibility with operating systems such as MS-DOS.

Print Server Workstation dedicated to managing the printers on a network. The print server can be any station on the network.

Print Spooler Computer software that intercepts a print job on its way to the printer and sends it to disk or memory instead, where the print job is held until the printer is ready for it. Spool is actually an acronym for Simultaneous Print Operations On Line. In operations where a printer has more than one simultaneous user or where a single user sends multiple print jobs to the printer, the spooler might use a simple first-come, first-served method, or it might assign different priorities to different print jobs, juggling them in order to give preferential treatment to some. In operations with one user and one print job, the print spooler still serves a purpose: by diverting the entire print job to disk or memory and then coordinating with the printer at the printer's speed, the spooler frees the user from waiting for the printer to finish before moving on to another task.

Priority Precedence in receiving the attention of the microprocessor and the use of system resources. Within a computer, unseen and unnoticed levels of priority are the means by which many different types of potential clashes and disruptions are avoided. Devices such as the timer, keyboard, modem, disk drives, and mouse have different interrupt priorities, both so that their individual requests for service do not conflict and so that none can interrupt the microprocessor at critical moments. Similarly, tasks

Priority

running on a computer can be assigned priorities that determine when and for how long they receive time from the microprocessor. On networks, stations can be assigned priorities that determine when and how often they can control the communications line, and messages can be assigned priorities that indicate how soon they must be transmitted.

Privileged Instruction Instruction (usually a machine instruction) that can be executed only by the operating system. Privileged instructions exist because the operating system needs to perform certain operations that applications should not be allowed to perform; therefore, only the operating system routines have the necessary privilege to execute these instructions.

Privileged Mode Mode of execution supported by the protected mode of the Intel 80286 and higher microprocessors in which software can carry out restricted operations that manipulate critical components of the system, such as memory and input/output ports (channels). Application programs cannot be executed in privileged mode; the heart (kernel) of the OS/2 operating system can be, as can the programs (device drivers) that control devices attached to the system.

PRN Logical device name for printer, reserved by the MS-DOS operating system for the standard print device. PRN usually refers to a system's first parallel port, also known as LPT1.

Probability Likelihood that an event will happen, which can often be estimated mathematically. In mathematics, statistics and probability theory are related fields. In computing, probability is used to determine the likelihood of failure or error in a system or device.

Problem Solving Process of devising and implementing a strategy for finding a solution or for transforming a less desirable condition into a more desirable one. The term is also used to refer to an aspect of artificial intelligence when the task of problem solving is performed solely by a program.

Procedural Language Programming language in which the basic programming element is the procedure (a named sequence of statements, such as a routine, subroutine, or function). The most widely used high-level languages (C, Pascal, BASIC, FORTRAN, COBOL, Ada) are all procedural languages.

Procedure

Procedure In a program, a named sequence of statements, often with associated constants, data types, and variables, that usually performs a single task. A procedure can usually be called (executed) by other procedures, as well as by the main body of the program. Some languages distinguish between a procedure and a function, with the latter returning a value. See also **function, parameter, routine, subroutine**.

Process Program or part of a program; a coherent sequence of steps undertaken by a program; for example, an internal or external data-transfer operation, handling of an interrupt, or evaluation of a function. As a verb, process refers to the manipulation of data with a program.

Process Color Method of handling color in a document in which each block of color is separated into its subtractive primary color components for printing: cyan, magenta, and yellow (as well as black). All other colors are created by blending layers of various sizes of halftone spots printed in cyan, magenta, and yellow to create the image.

Processing Manipulating data within a computer system. Processing is the vital step between receiving data (input) and producing results (output)—the task for which computers are designed.

Processor Short for central processing unit (CPU) of a computer system that carries out the functions and operations on a system.

Product Operator in relational algebra used in database management that, when applied to two existing relations (tables), results in the creation of a new cable containing all possible ordered concatenations (combinations) of tuples (rows) from the first relation with tuples from the second. The number of rows in the resulting relation is the product of the number of rows in the two source relations. In mathematics, product is the result of multiplying two or more numbers.

In general computer usage, product is an entity conceived and developed for the purpose of competing in a commercial market. Although computers are products, the term is more commonly applied to software, peripherals, and accessories in the computing arena.

Production System

Production System In an expert system, an approach to problem solving based on an "IF this, THEN that" approach that uses a set of rules, a database of information, and a "rule interpreter" to match premises with facts and form a conclusion.

Professional Graphics Adapter Video adapter introduced by IBM, primarily for CAD applications. The PGA is capable of displaying 256 colors, with a horizontal resolution of 640 pixels and a vertical resolution of 480 pixels.

Professional Graphics Display Analog display introduced by IBM, intended for use with their Professional Graphics Adapter.

Program Mostly refers to software that pertains to a sequence of instructions that can be executed by a computer. The term can refer to the original source code or the executable (machine language) version. Program implies a degree of completeness in that a source code program comprises all statements and files necessary for complete interpretation or compilation, and an executable program can be loaded into a given environment and executed independently of other programs.

Program Creation Process of creating a program—that is, an executable file. Normally program creation comprises three steps: (1) compiling the high-level source code into assembly language source code; (2) assembling the assembly language source code into machine-code object files; (3) linking the machine-code object files with various data files, run-time files, and library files into an executable file. Some compilers go directly from high-level source to machine-code object, and some integrated development environments compress all three steps into a single command.

Program File Disk file that contains the executable portion(s) of a computer program, such as a word processor, spreadsheet, or communications package. Depending on its size and complexity, an application or other program, such as an operating system, can be stored in several different files, each containing the instructions necessary for some part of the program's overall functioning. A word processor, for example, might have its text-entry and editing functions in a main program file, its spell checking abilities in a separate file, and its built-in dictionary or thesaurus in yet another file. All of these, however, are program files, as opposed to letters, reports, and other user-generated materials, which are document (or data) files.

Program Generator

Program Generator Program that creates other programs (usually in source code) based on a set of specifications and relationships given by the user. Program generators are often used to simplify the task of creating an application. See also **application generator**.

Program Listing Copy, usually on paper, of the source code of a program. Some compilers can generate program listings with line numbers, cross references, and so on.

Program Logic Logic behind the design and construction of a program—the reasons it works the way it does.

Programmable Capable of accepting instructions for performing a task or an operation. Programmability is a characteristic of computers.

Programmable Function Key Any of several, sometimes unlabeled, keys on some third-party keyboards that allow the user to "play back" previously stored key combinations or sequences of keystrokes called macros. The same effect can be achieved with a standard keyboard and a keyboard enhancer, the latter of which intercepts the keyboard codes and substitutes modified values; but programmable function keys accomplish this without requiring RAM-resident software that might not work with some application software.

Program Maintenance Process of supporting, debugging, and upgrading a program in response to information from individual or corporate users or the marketplace in general.

Programmer Individual who writes and debugs computer programs—the sometimes lengthy sequences of instructions that determine the work performed by a computer. Depending on the size of the project and the work environment, a programmer might work alone or as part of a team, be involved in part or all of the process from design through completion, or write all or a portion of the program.

In hardware, a device used to program read-only memory chips. See also **PROM, ROM**.

Programming Art and science of creating computer programs. Programming begins with knowledge of one or more programming languages, such as BASIC, C, Pascal, or assembler. Knowledge of a language alone does not make a good program. Much more can be involved: expertise in the theory of algorithms, user interface

Programming

design, and characteristics of hardware devices. General knowledge in the field in which the program is to be applied—word processing or molecular biology, for example—is also desirable.

Computers are rigorously logical machines, and programming requires a similarly logical approach to designing, writing (coding), testing, and debugging a program. Low-level languages, such as assembly language, also require familiarity with the capabilities of a microprocessor and the basic instructions built into it. In the modular approach advocated by many programmers, a project is broken into smaller, more manageable modules: stand-alone functional units that can be designed, written, tested, and debugged separately before being incorporated in the larger program. Finished programs are in many ways reflections of their creators. A finely crafted program is often called "elegant" for the clarity of its design and execution; a poorly structured program is often called a "kludge" for its haphazard and ill-conceived design.

Programming Language Any artificial language that can be used to define a sequence of instructions that can ultimately be processed and executed by the computer. Defining what is or is not a programming language can be tricky, but general usage implies that the translation process—from the source code expressed using the programming language to the machine code that the computer needs to work with—be automated by means of another program, such as a compiler. Thus English and other natural languages are ruled out, although some subsets of English are used and understood by some fourth-generation languages.

Program Statement Statement defining the name, briefly describing the operation, and possibly giving other information about a program. Some languages, such as Pascal, have an explicit program statement; others do not, or they use other forms (such as the main function in C).

PROM Short form for programmable read-only memory, a type of read-only memory (ROM) that allows data to be written into the device with hardware called a PROM programmer. After a PROM has been programmed, it is dedicated to that data, and it cannot be reprogrammed. Because ROMs are cost-effective only when produced in large volumes, PROMs are used during the prototyping stage of the design. New PROMs can be created and discarded as needed until the design is perfected.

Prompt

Prompt Displayed text that indicates that a computer program is waiting for input from the user.

Proportional Font Set of characters in a particular style and size in which a variable amount of horizontal space is allotted to each letter or number. In a proportional font, the letter i, for example, is allowed less space than the letter m.

Proportional Spacing Form of character spacing in which the horizontal space each character occupies is proportional to the width of the character. The letter w, for example, takes up more space than the letter t.

Proprietary Software Program owned or copyrighted by an individual or a business and made available for use only through purchase or by permission of the owner. Compare **public-domain software**.

Protected Mode Operating mode of the Intel 80286 and higher microprocessors that supports larger address spaces and more advanced features than real mode. When started in protected mode, these CPUs provide hardware support for multi-tasking, data security, and virtual memory. The OS/2 operating system runs in protected mode, as do most versions of UNIX for these microprocessors.

Prototyping Creation of a working model of a new computer system or program for testing and refinement, used in the development of both new hardware and software systems and new systems of information management. Tools used in the former include both hardware and support software; tools used in the latter can include databases, screen mockups, and simulations that, in some instances, can be developed into a final product.

PrtSc Key Short for **Print Screen Key**.

Pseudolanguage Nonexistent programming language, one for which no implementation exists. The term can refer either to the machine language for a nonexistent processor or to a high-level language for which no compiler exists.

Public-Domain Software Program donated for public use by its owner or developer and freely available for copying and distribution.

Puck Pointing device used with a graphics tablet. Often used in engineering applications, a puck is a mouselike device with buttons for selecting items or choosing commands and a clear plastic section extending from one end with crosshairs printed on it. The intersection of the cross hairs on the puck points to a location on the graphics tablet, which in turn is mapped to a specific location on the screen. Because the puck's cross hairs are on a transparent surface, a user can easily trace a drawing by placing it between the graphics tablet and the puck and moving the cross hairs over the lines of the drawing.

Pull-Down Menu Type of menu that is pulled down from the menu bar and remains available as long as the user holds it open.

Pulse Amplitude Modulation Usually referred to as PAM. Method of encoding information in a signal by varying the amplitude of pulses. The unmodulated signal consists of a continuous train of pulses of constant frequency, duration, and amplitude. During modulation, the pulse amplitudes are changed to reflect the information being encoded.

Pulse Code Modulation Abbreviated PCM. The term refers to a method of encoding information in a signal by varying the amplitude of pulses. Unlike pulse amplitude modulation (PAM), in which pulse amplitude can vary continuously, pulse code modulation limits pulse amplitudes to several predefined values. Because the signal is discrete, or digital, rather than analog, PCM is more immune to noise than PAM.

Pulse Duration Modulation Abbreviated PDM. Also known as pulse width modulation or pulse length modulation, a method of encoding information in a signal by varying the duration of pulses. The unmodulated signal consists of a continuous train of pulses of constant frequency, duration, and amplitude. During modulation, the pulse durations are changed to reflect the information being encoded.

Punched Card Outdated computer-input medium made of stiff paper that stores data bits in columns containing patterns of punched holes. The method for creating the patterns used for different byte values is called Hollerith coding. Punched cards are often called Hollerith cards.

Pure Procedure

Pure Procedure Any procedure that modifies only data that is dynamically allocated (usually on the stack). A pure procedure cannot modify either global data or its own code. This restriction allows a pure procedure to be called simultaneously by separate tasks.

Purge Ability to eliminate old or unneeded information systematically; to clean up.

QAM Acronym for either Quadrature Amplitude Modulation or Queued Access Method.

Quadbit Set of 4 bits representing one of 16 possible combinations. In communications, quadbits are used by modems that use quadrature amplitude modulation and operate at speeds of 2400 bits per second or more. Quadbits are a means of increasing transmission rates by encoding 4 bits at a time, rather than 1 or 2. The 16 quadbits are 0000, 0001, 0010, 0011, 0100, 0101, 0110, 0111, 1000, 1001, 1010, 1011, 1100, 1101, 1110, and 1111.

Quadrature Amplitude Modulation Abbreviated as QAM. In communications, an encoding method used by modems that operate at rates of 2400 bits per second or more. QAM combines amplitude modulation and phase modulation to create a constellation of signal points, each representing one unique combination of bits that can be identified with one possible state that the carrier wave can be in. For example, modems conforming to the CCITT V.22bis standard use a combination of 4 phase changes and 2 amplitudes to provide a total of 16 distinct states (signal changes) that can be represented on the carrier wave. Because there are 16 states, each state can also represent a unique combination of 4 bits (a quadbit). Transmitting at 600 baud (600 signal changes per second), the modem can thus transmit 2400 bits per second (600 signal changes times 4 bits per change). QAM is also used by faster modems to transmit at rates up to 9600 bits per second.

Quadrature Encoding Most common method used to determine the direction in which a mouse is moving. In mechanical mice, movement of the mouse ball is translated into horizontal or vertical movement by a pair of turning disks (one disk for horizontal movement and another disk for vertical movement), each of which makes and breaks contact with two sensors located on it. The two sensors are placed out of phase with each other, and the mouse notes which sensor receives contact first. The term derives from the fact that each sensor sends a square-wave signal 90 degrees out of phase with the other; if the first signal occurs before the second, the mouse is assumed to have been moved in one direction: if the second signal occurs before the first, the mouse is assumed to have been moved in the opposite direction.

Quantity

Quantity Number, either positive or negative, whole or fractional, that is used to indicate a value.

Quantize To divide an element into separate, distinct units (quanta) and assign a value to each resulting unit, particularly in the domain of time. Quantization is used in communications and CD-ROM technology to divide analog signals (such as voice and music) into discrete units of time that can be assigned binary values.

Quantum In communications, the unit resulting from division of a signal by quantization. In other areas, a quantum is, variously, a portion of time allotted on a timesharing system (an equivalent term in microcomputer areas is time slice); an amount of something; or, in physics, a unit of radiant energy. The plural of quantum is quanta

Quartz Crystal Precisely shaped and sized piece of the mineral quartz, used for its piezoelectric properties. When a voltage is applied to a quartz crystal, it vibrates at a frequency determined by its size and shape. Quartz crystals are commonly used to control the frequency of oscillator circuits, such as the clocks in microcomputers.

Quasi-Language Derogatory term for any programming language that, because of deficiencies, is not suitable for any serious work.

Query Process of extracting data from a database and presenting it for use. Also, a specific set of instructions for extracting particular data repetitively. In this latter context, for example, a query might be created to present sales figures for a particular region of the country. This query could be run periodically to obtain current reports.

Query By Example Abbreviated as QBE. Simple-to-use query language implemented on several relational database management systems. Using QBE, the user specifies fields to be displayed, intertable linkages, and retrieval criteria directly onto forms displayed on the screen. These forms are a direct pictorial representation of the table and row structures that make up the database. Thus, the construction of a query becomes a simple "checkoff" procedure from the viewpoint of the user.

Query Language Subset of the data-manipulation language, specifically that portion relating to the retrieval and display of data from a database.

Query Language

In loose form it is sometimes used to refer to the entire data-manipulation language.

Question Mark In some operating systems and applications, a wildcard character often used to represent any other single character. For example, in MS-DOS, the filename specification B?G.DOC could apply to BAG.DOC, BEG.DOC, BIG.DOC, BOG.DOC, and BUG.DOC. The question mark is one of two wildcard characters supported by the MS-DOS and OS/2 operating systems, the other being the asterisk (*), which represents one or more other characters.

Queue Multielement data structure from which elements can be removed only in the same order in which they were inserted; that is, following a first-in-first-out (FIFO) constraint. The two basic queue operations are add (a new element to the queue) and remove (fetch and remove the oldest element from the queue). There are also several types of queues in which removal is based on factors other than order of insertion. In a priority queue, for example, the elements are removed according to some priority value assigned to each.

Queued Access method Programming technique that minimizes input/output delays by synchronizing the transfer of information between the program and the computer's input and output devices.

Quicksort Efficient sort algorithm, described by C.A.R. Hoare in 1962, in which the essential objective is to "divide and conquer." A quicksort begins by scanning the list to be sorted for a median value. This value, called the pivot, is then moved to the final position in the list. Next, all items in the list whose values are less than the pivot value are moved to one side of the list, and the items with values greater than the pivot value are moved to the other side. Finally, both sides are sorted and the result is a sorted list.

Quit To stop in an orderly manner; to execute the normal shutdown of a program and return control to the operating system.

QWERTY Keyboard Standard layout of most typewriters and computer keyboards, named for the six leftmost characters in the top row of alphabetic characters. An alternative layout, the Dvorak keyboard, is considered more efficient, but the QWERTY keyboard has the advantage of familiarity and is by far the more widespread of the two.

Race Condition Condition in which a feedback circuit coincides with the internal circuit processes in a way that produces chaotic output behavior.

Rack-Mounted Piece of equipment built for installation in a metal frame or cabinet, typically in one of two standard widths, 19 inches or 23 inches.

Radian In trigonometry, the length of arc intercepted by an angle in a circle; specifically, a unit of angular measurement equal to the angle between two radii such that the length of the arc between them is equal to the radius, approximately 7.2958 degrees. Radians can be related both to pi and to the number of degrees in a circle. Multiplying radians by l80/pi gives degrees, and multiplying degrees by pi/l80 gives radians.

Radio Button In graphical user interfaces, a means of selecting one of several options, usually within an option-selection area such as a dialog box. The presence of radio buttons in a list of options means that only one of the options can be selected at any given time. Check boxes, another means of selecting options, are used when more than one option can be selected at the same time. Visually, a radio button is a small circle that, when selected, has a smaller, filled circle inside it. Radio buttons are so named because their behavior mimics that of the buttons on a radio: selecting one button deselects the previously selected button.

Radio Frequency Commonly referred to as RF. The portion of the electromagnetic spectrum with frequencies between 10 kilohertz and 3000 gigahertz, corresponding to wavelengths between 30 kilometers and 1 millimeter.

Radix Base of a number system, such as 2 in the binary system, 10 in the decimal system, 8 in the octal system, and 16 in the hexadecimal system.

Radix Point Period or other character that separates the integer portion of a number from the fractional portion. In the decimal system, the radix point is the decimal point, as in the number 1.33.

Radix Sorting Algorithm Sorting algorithm that performs a sort by grouping elements according to successive parts of their keys. A simple example is sorting a list of numbers in the range 0-993. First the list is sorted by the 100's digit into a set of (up to) 10 lists; then each list, one at a time, is sorted into a set of (up to) 10 lists based on the 10's digit; and finally, each of those lists is sorted by the 1's digit. This algorithm is usually most efficient when the sorting is done using binary values, which simplifies comparisons (whether a given bit is on or off) and reduces the number of lists (each pass produces at most two lists).

Rag Irregularity along the left or right margins on a printed page. Rag is an alternative to justification, in which text is aligned along the margin. Word-processed letters and other documents are commonly left-justified, with ragged-right margins. Ragged-left text is used infrequently/typically, in advertisements for visual effect.

RAM Acronym for **Random-Access Memory**.

RAM Card Add-in circuit board that contains RAM memory and the interface logic necessary to decode memory addresses.

RAM Chip Semiconductor storage device. RAM chips are the memory of a computer system and can be either dynamic or static memory.

RAM Disk Simulated disk drive whose data is actually stored in RAM memory. A special program fools the operating system into believing that an additional disk drive is present. The operating system reads and writes to the simulated device, and the program stores and retrieves data from memory. RAM disks are extremely fast, but they require that system memory be given up to their use. RAM disks usually use volatile memory, and because of this the data stored on them disappears when power is turned off. Many portables offer RAM disks that use battery-backed CMOS RAM to avoid this problem.

RAM-Resident Program More commonly called terminate-and-stay-resident program, which means that the program is loaded into a portion of memory and remains there in a more or less permanent state until the system is rebooted or reset. These programs are usually helpful, needed utilities such as drivers or the like, but they do take up much of the system memory if several are loaded.

Random Access

Random Access Ability of a computer to find and go directly to a particular storage location without having to search sequentially from the beginning location. With microcomputers, the term is often used in reference to a computer's memory, in which certain general locations are reserved for different types of information (applications, operating system, and so on) but specific items can be located directly through the use of numbers (addresses) that identify individual locations in memory. The term is also used to describe access to files stored on disk. This type of access is best used for files in which each set of information has no intrinsic relationship to what comes before or after it, such as in databases of client records, inventories, and so on. The human equivalent of random access would be equivalent to finding a desired address in an address book without having to proceed sequentially through all the addresses.

Random Access Memory Abbreviated as RAM. Semiconductor-based memory that can be read and written by the microprocessor or other hardware devices. The storage locations can be accessed in any order. Note that the various types of ROM memory are capable of random access. The term RAM, however, is generally understood to refer to volatile memory, which can be written as well as read.

Random Noise Signal in which there is no relationship between amplitude and time and in which many frequencies occur randomly, without pattern or predictability.

Random Number Generation Creation of a number or sequence of numbers characterized by unpredictability so that no number is any more likely to occur at a given time or place in the sequence than any other. Because truly random number generation is generally viewed as impossible, the process would be more properly called "pseudorandom number generation."

Range In general usage, the spread between specified low and high values. Range checking is an important method of validating data entered into an application. In spreadsheets, range refers to a block of cells selected for similar treatment. A range of cells can extend across a row, down a column, or over a combination of the two, but all cells in the range must be contiguous, sharing at least one common border. Ranges allow the user to affect many cells with a single command; for example, to format them similarly, enter the same data into all of them, give them a name in common and treat them as a unit, or select and incorporate them into a formula.

Raster Rectangular pattern of lines; on a video display, the horizontal scan lines from which the term raster scan is derived.

Raster Display Video monitor (usually a CRT) that displays an image on the screen from top to bottom as a series of horizontal scan lines. The scan lines are as wide as the smallest visible image on the screen. Within each scan line, individual pixels can be illuminated. Television screens and most computer monitors are raster displays.

Raster Graphics Method of generating graphics in which images are stored as multitudes of small, independently controlled dots (pixels) arranged in rows and columns. Raster graphics treats an image as a collection of such dots. Compare **vector graphics**.

Raster Image Display image formed by patterns of light and dark pixels in a rectangular array.

Raster Image Processor Device consisting of computer chips (including a microprocessor) and software, that converts vector graphics and/or text into a raster (bit-mapped) image. RIPs are used in page printers, phototypesetters, and electrostatic plotters: they identify each dot on the page, either leaving the dot blank or filling it in. The resulting pattern of dots re-creates the vector graphics and text originally described.

Rasterization Conversion of vector graphics (images described mathematically as points connected by straight lines) to equivalent images composed of pixel patterns that can be stored and manipulated as sets of bits. See also **pixel**.

Raw Data Unprocessed and usually unformatted data; a stream of bits that has not been filtered for commands or special characters. More generally, information that has been collected but not evaluated.

Raw Mode One of two ways in which the MS-DOS operating system "sees" the handle, or identifier, for a character-based device. If the handle is in raw mode, the operating system does not filter input characters or give special treatment to carriage returns, end-of-file markers, and linefeed and tab characters.

Ray Tracing

Ray Tracing Sophisticated and complex approach to producing high-quality computer graphics. Ray tracing is used to calculate the brightness, transparency level, and reflectivity of each object in an image that will be shown on the computer screen. These attributes are calculated by tracing single rays of light backward to see the way the rays were affected as they traveled from the defined source of light illuminating the object to the object and to the viewer's eye. The attributes of the object are then used to calculate the color and intensity of the pixels that create the image on the screen. Ray tracing therefore calculates the attributes of each pixel in relation to the viewer, to other objects in the image, and to the light source for the image. It is demanding in terms of processing capability because the computer must account not only for the reflection or absorption of individual rays but also for the intensity of each ray with respect to the brightness of the object, the position of each pixel, and the positions of the viewer and the light source.

RCA Connector Connector used for attaching audio and video devices such as stereo equipment or a composite video monitor to a computer's video adapter.

Read Gathering of information from an input source to be used by the computer. Reading is the means by which a computer receives information, typically from a disk drive; the opposite is writing—transferring information to storage such as a disk or to a device such as a printer or the screen. A disk read means that information is transferred from disk into memory. A computer can also be said to read the keyboard when it accepts keystrokes from the user.

Read Error Error encountered while a computer is in the process of retrieving information from storage or from another source of input. The opposite is a write error, a problem in sending information to storage or to an output device.

README Name traditionally used on MS-DOS machines for a file containing information that the user either needs or will find informative and that might not have been included in the documentation. README files are placed on disk in plain-text form (without extraneous or program-specific characters) so that they can be read easily by word processing programs.

Read-Only Information stored in such a way that it can be played back (read) but cannot be changed (written). Read-only can apply to

Read-Only

a file or document that can be displayed or printed but not altered in any way; it can apply to a type of memory-holding program (read-only memory, or ROM) that cannot be changed; or it can apply to a storage medium, such as CD-ROM, that can be played back but cannot be used for recording information. See also **authorization**.

Read-Only Memory Abbreviated ROM. Semiconductor-based memory that contains instructions or data that can be read but not modified. To create a ROM chip, the designer supplies a semiconductor manufacturer with the instructions or data to be stored; the manufacturer then produces one or more chips containing those instructions or data. Because creating ROM chips involves a manufacturing process, it is economically viable only if the ROM chips are produced in large quantities; experimental designs or small volumes are best handled using PROM or EPROM. In general usage, ROM often means any read-only device, including PROM and EPROM.

Read/Write Designation applied to memory or to any device that can be both read from and written to. R/W can also refer to the types of operations that can be performed on a file—in this case, both reading and writing, as opposed to read-only, which does not allow changes to be recorded.

Read/Write Memory Type of memory that can be both read from and written to (modified). RAM and core memory are typical read/write memory systems.

Real Address Absolute (machine) address, a real (specific) location in memory.

Real Mode Native or default operating mode in IBM and other computers based on the Intel 8086 family of microprocessors; the only operating mode supported by MS-DOS. Real mode refers to the microprocessor and the way it handles memory, but it can be characterized as providing the user with a single-tasking (one-program-at-a-time) working environment in which programs can freely access system memory and input/output devices. Real mode is one of two incompatible modes designed into Intel 80286, 80386, and i486 microprocessors. Unlike the more versatile protected mode, real mode does not offer features for memory management and memory protection, two important ingredients in the multitasking environment supported by the OS/2 operating system.

Real Number

Real Number Number that can be represented by digits in a number system with a fixed base (radix), such as the decimal system. A real number can be made up of either a finite or an infinite set of digits; for example, 1.1 is a real number, as is 0.33333. Real numbers are a data type used for storing measurements and other values to some limit of precision in programming languages such as C and Pascal.

Real Storage Amount of RAM memory in the system, as opposed to virtual memory.

Real-Time Either those operations in which the machine's activities match the human perception of time or those in which computer operations proceed at the same rate as a physical or external process. Real-time operations are characteristic of transaction-processing systems, aircraft guidance systems, scientific applications, and other areas in which a computer must respond to situations as they occur; for example, animate a graphic in a flight simulator or make corrections based on measurements.

Real-Time Animation Computer animation in which images are updated on the screen at the same rate at which the objects simulated might move in the real world. This is different from animation done in virtual time, in which image frames are first calculated and stored and later replayed at a higher rate to achieve smoother movement. Real-time animation allows dynamic involvement by the user because the computer can accept and incorporate keystrokes or controller movements as it is drawing the next image in the animation sequence. Arcade-style animation (such as in a flight-simulator program) makes use of real-time animation in translating game plays into on-screen actions.

Real-Time Operating System Operating system designed or optimized for the needs of a process control environment.

Real Time System Computer and/or software system that reacts to events before the events become obsolete; for example, airline-collision-avoidance systems must process radar input, detect a possible collision, and warn air traffic controllers or pilots while they still have time to react.

Reboot To restart a computer by reloading the operating system.

Recompile

Recompile To compile a program again, usually because of changes that needed to be made in the source code in response to error messages generated by the compiler.

Record One definition for this term is the ability to retain information, usually in a file. Another refers to a data structure that is a collection of fields (elements), each with its own name and type. Unlike an array, whose elements are accessed using an index, the elements of a record are accessed by name. A record can be accessed as a collective unit of elements, or the elements can be accessed individually.

Record Head Device in a tape machine that places data on the tape. In some tape machines, the record head is combined with the read head.

Record Layout Organization of data fields within a record.

Record Length Amount of space required to store a record, typically given in bytes.

Record Locking Strategy employed in distributed processing and other multiuser situations to prevent more than one user at a time from writing data to a record.

Record Number Unique number assigned to a record in a database. A record number can identify an existing record in relation to an entire group of records (for example, the tenth record from the beginning of a database), or it can be a number assigned dynamically to a record when it is generated and added to a database.

Record structure Ordered list of the fields that compose a record, together with a definition of the domain of each field.

Recover To return to a stable condition after some error has occurred. When a program recovers from an error, it stabilizes itself and continues carrying out instructions without user intervention. When a computer user recovers lost or damaged data, a recovery program searches for and salvages whatever information remains in storage. When a database is recovered, it is returned to a previous stable condition after some problem, such as abnormal termination of the database management program, has caused the data to lose its integrity.

Recoverable Error

Recoverable Error Nonfatal error or meaning one that can be successfully managed by software, as when the user enters a number when a letter is required.

Rectifier Circuit component that passes current flowing in one direction but stops current flowing in the other direction. Rectifiers are used to convert alternating current to direct current.

Recursion Ability of a routine to call itself. Recursion allows the implementation of certain algorithms with small, simple routines, but it does not guarantee speed or efficiency; in fact, excessive use of recursion can cause a program to run out of stack space during execution, usually resulting in a halt in the program and sometimes causing the entire system to crash.

Redirection Process of writing to or reading from a file or device different from the one that would normally be the target or the source; for example, redirecting a directory listing from the screen to the printer, as in the MS-DOS or OS/2 command dir >prn.

Reduced Instruction Set Computing Type of microprocessor design that focuses on rapid and efficient processing of a relatively small set of instructions. RISC design is based on the premise that most of the instructions a computer decodes and executes are simple. As a result, RISC architecture limits the number of instructions that are built into the microprocessor but optimizes each so it can be carried out very rapidly, usually within a single clock cycle. RISC chips therefore execute simple instructions faster than microprocessors designed to handle a much wider array of instructions. They are, however, slower than general-purpose CISC (complex instruction set computing) chips when executing complex instructions, which must be broken down into many machine instructions before they can be carried out by RISC microprocessors. Families of RISC chips that are gaining popularity include Sun Microsystems' SPARC, Motorola's 88000, and Intel's i860.

Redundant Code Code that duplicates a function performed elsewhere, such code to sort a list that has already been sorted.

Reference One meaning of this term refers to accessing a variable, often said of elements in an array or in a record. Another meaning is a reference to a form of pointer in the C++ programming

Reference

language that can be used to access a variable. When such a reference is declared, it must be associated with a variable. The reference then becomes an alias for that variable.

Reference Parameter Parameter that has been passed by reference; in other words one whose address has been passed to the called routine.

Reformat In reference to applications, this term means to change the look of a document by altering stylistic details, such as font, layout, indention, and alignment. In reference to data storage, reformat means to prepare for reuse a disk that already contains programs or data, effectively destroying the existing contents.

Refresh To reenergize. In reference to computer monitors, it means to retrace the screen at frequent intervals to irradiate the phosphors and maintain a constant image. With computer memory, refresh means to recharge dynamic random-access memory chips (DRAMs) so that they continue to retain the information they contain; logic on the memory board automatically performs this function. In programming, refreshable refers to a type of program module that can be replaced in memory without affecting processing or information.

Refresh Cycle With dynamic semiconductor random-access memory, this term refers to the process in which the RAM controller circuitry provides repeated electric pulses to the chips in order to renew the electric charges contained in storage locations that represent a binary 1. Each pulse is one refresh cycle. Without constant refreshing, dynamic semiconductor RAM loses any information stored in it, as it does, for example, when the computer is turned off (or when the power fails).

Refresh Rate In video hardware, the frequency with which the entire screen is redrawn to maintain a constant, flicker-free image. On TV screens and raster-scan monitors, the electron beam that lights the phosphor coating on the inner surface of the screen typically refreshes the entire image area at a rate of about 60 hertz, or 60 times per second. (Interlaced monitors, which redraw alternate lines during each sweep of the electron beam, actually refresh any particular line only 30 times per second. Since odd and even lines are refreshed on successive sweeps, however, the effective refresh rate is 60 times per second.)

Region

Region Area dedicated to, or reserved for, a particular purpose. In video programming, a region is a contiguous group of pixels that are treated as a unit. On the Apple Macintosh, for example, a region is an area in a grafPort that can be defined and manipulated as an entity. The visible working area within a window is an example of a region

Region Fill In reference to computer graphics, the technique of filling a defined region on the screen with a selected color, pattern, or other attribute.

Register Small, named region of high-speed memory located within a microprocessor or any electronic device capable of storing binary data. A register is usually large enough to hold only a few bytes of information and is referenced in programs by a name such as AX or SP. It is used as a holding area for specific, sometimes critical, pieces of data or information related to activities going on within the system. For example, a register might be used to hold the results of an addition operation or to hold the address of a particular location in the computer's memory.

Registration Process of precisely aligning elements or superimposing layers in a document or a graphic so that everything will print in the correct relative position.

Registration marks Marks placed on a page so that in printing, the elements or layers in a document can be arranged correctly with respect to each other. Each element to be assembled contains its own registration marks; when the marks are precisely superimposed, the elements are in the correct position.

Relational Database Type of database or database management system that stores information in tables—rows and columns of data—and conducts searches by using data in specified columns of one table to find additional data in another table. In a relational database, the rows of a table represent records (collections of information about separate items) and the columns represent fields (particular attributes of a record). In conducting searches, a relational database matches information from a field in one table with information in a corresponding field of another table to produce a third table that combines requested data from both tables.

Relational Expression Expression that uses a relational operator such as "less than" or "greater than" to compare two or more

Relational Expression

expressions. A relational expression resolves to a Boolean (true/false) value.

Relational Model Data model, implemented in most modern database management systems, in which the data are organized in relations (tables).

Relational Operator Operator that allows the programmer to compare two (or more) values or expressions. Typical relational operators are greater than (>), equal to (=), less than (<), not equal to (<>), greater than or equal to (>=), and less than or equal to (<=).

Relational Structure Record (tuple) organization used in the implementation of a relational model relative address, sometimes referred to as an indirect address. A location, as in a computer's memory, that is calculated in terms of its distance (displacement) from a starting point (base address). A relative address is typically computed by adding an offset to the base in everyday terms; this is similar to creating the address 2001 Main Street, in which the base is the 2000 block of Main Street and the offset is 1, which specifies the first house from the beginning of the block.

Relative Coordinates Coordinates defined in terms of their distance from a given starting point, rather than from the origin (intersection of two axes), as are absolute coordinates. For example, from a starting point on the screen, a square defined by relative coordinates can be drawn as a series of lines, each representing a displacement in distance and direction from the end of the preceding point. The entire square can be redrawn at another location simply by changing the coordinates of the starting point rather than by recalculating the coordinates of each corner with reference to the origin.

Relative Movement Motion whose distance and direction are relative to the starting point; for example, when a mouse pointer is moved on the screen, the coordinates of its new position are relative to the previous location of the pointer. In computer graphics and cinematography, relative movement can also refer to the movement of one object in relation to another, such as the movement of horse A from the perspective of horse B on a racetrack.

Relative Pointing Device Cursor-control device, such as a mouse or a trackball, in which the movement of an on-screen cursor is

Relative Pointing Device

associated to the movement of the device but not to the position of the device. For example, if a user picks up a mouse and puts it down in a different location on a desk, the position of the on-screen cursor does not change because no movement (rolling) is detected. When the user rolls the mouse again, the cursor moves to reflect the mouse movement against the surface of the desk. Relative pointing devices differ from absolute pointing devices, such as graphics tablets, in which the device's location within a defined area is always associated with a predefined on-screen position.

Relay Switch activated by an electrical signal. A relay allows another signal to be controlled without the need to route the other signal to the control point, and it also allows a relatively low-power signal—the signal used to activate the relay—to control a high-power signal.

Release Particular version of a piece of software, most commonly associated with the most recent version (as in "the latest release"). Some companies—for example, Lotus Development Corporation—use the term as an integral part of the product name (as in Lotus 1-2-3 Release 2.2). Release also refers to the process of an application relinquishing control of a block of memory, a device, or other system resource, thereby "releasing" it to the operating system.

Reliability Possibility of a computer system or device continuing to function over a given period of time and under specified conditions. Reliability is measured by different performance indexes; for example, the reliability of a hard disk is often given as mean time between failures (MTBF), the average length of time the disk can be expected to function without failing.

Relocatable Address In programming, an address (reference to a memory location) that can be adjusted to reflect the actual portion of memory into which a program is loaded for execution. This convention is comparable to describing the "address" of a parked car as "level 2, row C" on one day and "level 5, row B" on another.

Relocatable Code Program written in a way that enables it to be loaded into any part of available memory. In relocatable code, address references can be adjusted when the program is readied for execution so that they reflect the program's physical location in memory and so that program instructions can be carried out correctly.

Relocate

Relocate In reference to programs and blocks of memory, the ability to move about within available space to use memory resources flexibly and efficiently. A relocatable program is one that can be loaded by the operating system into any part of available memory rather than one that must be loaded into one specific area. A relocatable block of memory is a portion of memory that can be moved around by the operating system as required; for example, the system might collect several available, relocatable blocks of memory to form one larger block of the size requested for use by a program.

Remark Commonly abbreviated REM. Used to add a comment to a line of code. When the system senses this statement, it skips that particular line of code and continues to the next line.

Remote Used to describe a computer or other device located in another place (room, building, or city) that is accessible through some type of cable or communications link.

Remote Access Use of a remote computer.

Remote Communications Interacting with a remote computer through a telephone connection or another communications line.

Remote Terminal Terminal located at a site removed from the computer to which it is attached. Remote terminals rely on modems and telephone lines to communicate with the host computer.

Removable Disk Disk that can be taken from a disk drive. Floppy disks are removable, whereas hard disks are not.

REM Statement Statement in the BASIC programming language and the MS-DOS and OS/2 batch file languages that is used to add comments to a program or batch file. Any statement beginning with REM is ignored by the interpreter or compiler or the command processor.

Rendering Creation of an image containing geometric models, using color and shading to give the image a realistic look. Usually part of a geometric modeling package such as a CAD program, rendering uses mathematics to describe the location of a light source in relation to the object and to calculate the way in which the light would create highlights, shading, and variations in color. Realism can range from opaque, shaded polygons to images approximating photographs in their complexity.

Repaginate

Repaginate Ability to recalculate the page breaks in a document.

Repeat Counter Loop counter; typically, a register that holds a number representing how many times a repetitive process has been or is to be executed.

Repeater Device used on communications circuits that decreases distortion by amplifying or regenerating a signal so that it can be transmitted onward in its original strength and form. On a network, a repeater connects two networks or two network segments at the physical layer of the ISO/OSI model and regenerates the signal.

Repeat Key Key that must be held down at the same time as a character key to cause the character key's key code to be sent repeatedly. On most computer keyboards, however, a repeat key is not needed because a key automatically repeats if held down, after a brief delay timed to avoid accidental repeats.

Replace Process of putting new data in the place of other data, usually after conducting a search for the data to be replaced. Text-based applications such as word processors typically include search-and-replace commands. In such operations, both old and new data must be specified, and search-and-replace procedures may or may not be sensitive to uppercase and lowercase, depending on the application program.

Report Presentation of information about a given topic, typically in printed form. Reports prepared with computers and appropriate software can include text, graphics, and charts. Database programs can include special software for creating report forms and generating reports. Desktop publishing software and laser printers or typesetting equipment can be used to produce publication-quality output.

Report Generator Type of application, commonly part of a database management program, that uses a report "form" created by the user to lay out and print the contents of a database. A report generator is used to select specific record fields or ranges of record, to make the output attractive, and to specify such features as headings, running heads, page numbers, and fonts.

Request To Send. Usually referred to as RTS. A signal used in serial communications; sent, as from a computer to its modem, to request permission to transmit. RTS is a hardware signal sent over line 4 in **RS-232-C** connections.

Reserve Character

Reserve Character Keyboard character that has a special meaning to a program and normally cannot be used in assigning names to files, documents, and other user-generated tools such as macros. Characters commonly reserved for special uses include the asterisk (*), forward slash (/), backslash (\), question mark (?), and broken vertical bar (|).

Reserved Word Word that has special meaning to a program or in a programming language. Reserved words usually include those used for control statements (IF, FOR, END), data declarations, and the like. A reserved word can be used only in certain predefined circumstances; it cannot be used in naming documents, files, labels, variable names, or user-generated tools such as macros.

Reset Button Mechanism that restarts a computer without turning off its power. Many PC compatibles have a button on the front panel of the system unit for this purpose. Most Apple Macintosh computers have two buttons, one for resetting the computer and one (called the programmer's switch) to allow programmers to use the system monitor.

Resident Font Internal font built into a printer.

Resistor Circuit component designed to provide a specific amount of resistance to current flow.

Resolution Clarity or fineness of detail attained by a monitor or a printer in producing an image. In relation to printers, resolution generally refers to the output of printers like dot-matrix, inkjet, and laser models that form characters from small, closely spaced dots. Print resolution is measured in dots per inch, or dpi, and ranges from about 125 dpi for low-quality dot-matrix printers to about 300 dpi for a laser printer. In comparison, typesetting equipment can print at resolutions of 1000 dpi or more.

In relation to computer monitors, resolution is defined as the number of pixels per unit of measurement (such as inch or centimeter) on a video display. Resolution commonly denotes the total number of pixels displayed horizontally or vertically on the video display. By this definition, common screen resolutions for IBM PCs and compatible computers and Apple Macintosh computers are as follows:

IBM and compatibles:
• Monochrome Display Adapter (MDA): 720 pixels across by 350

Resolution

pixels down
- Color/Graphics Adapter (CGA): 640 pixels across by 200 pixels down
- Enhanced Graphics Adapter (EGA): 640 pixels across by 350 pixels down.
- Professional Graphics Adapter (PGA): 640 pixels across by 480 pixels down
- Multi-Color Graphics Array (MCGA): 640 pixels across by 480 pixels down
- Video Graphics Array (VGA): 720 pixels across by 400 pixels down in text mode; 640 pixels across by 480 pixels down in graphics mode.

Apple Macintosh:
- Macintosh Plus, Macintosh SE: 512 pixels across by 342 pixels down.
- Macintosh II: 640 pixels across by 480 pixels down on Apple's 12-inch black-and-white and 13-inch color monitors

Resource Any part of a computer system or a network, such as a disk drive, printer, or memory, that can be allotted to a program or a process while it is running. In some types of programming, a resource can be used by more than one program or in more than one place in a program. The use of resources allows alteration of many features in a program without the necessity of recompiling the program from source code. On the Apple Macintosh, in a program such as HyperCard, a programmer could add the sound of a car horn as a resource and play the sound from inside HyperCard by using a statement such as play carBee. If this were not possible, the HyperCard program itself would have to be recompiled from scratch, incorporating the sound data to be added. The sound resource can also be copied and pasted into any other program or document that can handle it.

Resource Data Data structures, templates, definition procedures, management routines, icon maps, and so forth associated with a particular resource such as a Menu, window, or dialog box.

Resource File File that consists of resource data and the resource map that indexes it.

Resource ID Number that identifies a particular resource within a given resource type in the Macintosh Operating System, such as a particular menu among many resources of type MENU that a program might use.

Response Time

Response Time Time, usually an average, that elapses between the issuance of a request and the provision of the data requested. Also refers to the time required for a memory circuit or a storage device to furnish data requested by the central processing unit (CPU).

Restricted Function Function or operation that can be executed only under certain circumstances, particularly when the processor is in privileged mode.

Retrace Path followed by the electron beam in a raster-scan computer monitor as it returns either from the right to the left edge of the screen or from the bottom to the top of the screen. The retrace positions the electron beam for its next sweep across or down the screen; during this interval, the beam is briefly turned off to avoid drawing an unwanted line on the screen. Retracing occurs many times each second and uses tightly synchronized signals to ensure that the electron beam is turned off and on during the retrace.

Retrieve Ability to obtain requested data. Computers can retrieve information from any source of storage, such as disks, tapes, or memory. In general, retrieve refers to locating a specific item or set of data, as from a database, and returning it to a program or to the user.

Return Act of transferring control of the system from a called routine or program to the calling routine or program. Some languages support an explicit return or exit statement; others allow return only at the end (last statement) of the called routine or program. See also **call**.

Return Code In programming, a code used to report the outcome of a procedure or to influence subsequent events when a routine or process terminates (returns) and passes control of the system to another routine. Return codes can, for example, indicate whether an operation was suc-cessful or not and can thus be used to determine what is to be done next.

Return Key Main Enter key on IBM and most compatible keyboards. The name is a holdover from the typewriter, where this key causes the carriage holding the print mechanism to return to the beginning of the line and then advance to the next line.

Reverse Video Reversal of light and dark in the display of selected characters on a video screen. For example, if text is normally

Reverse Video

displayed as white characters on a black background, reverse video presents text as black letters on a white background. Programmers commonly use reverse video as a means of highlighting text or special items (such as menu choices or the cursor) on the screen.

Revert Ability to return to the last saved version of a document. Choosing this command tells the application to abandon all changes made in a document since the last time it was saved.

Revisable-Form-Text DCA Standard within Document Content Architecture (DCA) for storing documents in such a way that the formatting can be changed by the receiver. A related standard is Final-Form-Text DCA.

Rewind To return a magnetic tape spool or cassette to its beginning.

Rewrite Ability to write again, particularly in situations where information is not permanently recorded.

RF Shielding Material, usually metal or metallic foil, designed to prevent the passage of radio frequency (RF) electromagnetic radiation. RF shielding is intended to keep RF radiation either in a device or out of a device. Without proper RF shielding, devices that use and/or emit RF radiation can interfere with each other; for example, running an electric mixer might cause interference on the television. Personal computers generate RF radiation and, to meet Federal Communications Commission standards, must be properly shielded to prevent this RF radiation from leaking out. The metal case of a PC provides most of the needed RF shielding. Devices meeting FCC type A standards are suitable for business use. Devices meeting the more stringent FCC type B standards are suitable for home use.

RGB Acronym for Red-Green-Blue, a mixing model or method of describing colors, used with many color monitors (or other light-based media as opposed to print media). RGB uses the additive primaries method, mixing percentages of red, green, and blue to get the desired color. Adding no color produces black, and adding 100 percent of all three colors results in white.

RGB Monitor Color monitor that receives its signals for red, green, and blue levels over separate lines. An RGB monitor generally produces sharper and cleaner images than those produced

RGB Monitor

by a composite monitor, which receives levels for all three colors over a single line.

Ribbon Cable Flat cable, usually carrying from 8 to 100 parallel data and control lines. The broad, flat bands connected inside the system to a computer's disk drives are ribbon cables.

Ribbon Cartridge Disposable module that contains an inked fabric ribbon or a carbon-coated Mylar ribbon. Many impact printers use ribbon cartridges to make ribbon changing easier and cleaner.

Right-Justified Having text aligned along the right margin.

RJ-ll Connector Connector such as the type found on all modular phone jacks.

RLL Encoding Shortened form of **Run-Length Limited Encoding**, one of several types of encoding used on hard drives.

Robot Machine that can sense and react to input and cause changes in its surroundings with some degree of intelligence, ideally without human supervision. Robots are seldom humanlike in appearance, although they are often designed to mimic human movements in carrying out their work. Robots are commonly used in manufacturing, as in the construction of automobiles and most computers.

Robotics Branch of engineering devoted to the creation and training of robots. Roboticists work within a wide range of fields, such as mechanical and electronic engineering, cybernetics, bionics, and artificial intelligence, all toward the end of endowing their creations with as much sensitivity, independence, and flexibility as possible.

Rollback Return to a previous stable condition, as when the contents of a hard disk are restored from a backup after a destructive hard-disk error.

ROM Acronym for **Read-Only Memory**.

Roman Typeface or type style in which the characters are upright.

ROM BIOS Acronym for Read-Only Memory Basic Input/Output System, a set of software routines shipped with IBM and compatible computers, providing low-level routines for performing

ROM BIOS

simple input/output operations. In the IBM PC, the BIOS takes up 64 kilobytes (KB) of address space, beginning at location OFOOOOH. In the PS/2 series, the BIOS is expanded to 128 KB, beginning at location OEOOOOH. For both the IBM PC and PS/2, the ROM BIOS also includes that portion of the BASIC interpreter—commonly called cassette BASIC—that does not provide disk support or support for advanced graphics.

ROM Card Plug-in module that contains one or more printer fonts, programs, or games or other information stored in ROM (read-only memory). A typical ROM card is about the size of a credit card and about three times as thick. It stores information directly on integrated circuit boards.

ROM Cartridge Plug-in module that contains one or more printer fonts, programs, games, or other information stored in ROM (read-only memory). The ROM is in the form of one or more computer chips mounted on a printed circuit board. The board is enclosed in a plastic case with a connector exposed at one end so that it can easily plug into a printer, computer, game system, or other device. For example, a cartridge that plugs into a Nintendo or similar game system is a ROM cartridge.

ROM Emulator Special circuit containing RAM memory that is connected to a target computer where the target computer's ROM chips would normally be installed. The contents of the RAM memory are supplied by a separate computer; after the RAM chips are programmed, they are used as ROM in the target computer. Before the advent of EPROMs, using a ROM emulator was the only economical way to debug ROM-resident software, owing to the high cost of creating ROM chips. Today, an EPROM can be used in the prototype circuit and replaced with a ROM when the software is completed. Since a ROM emulator's memory contents can be changed much more quickly than those of an EPROM, developers often prefer using a ROM emulator even though doing this is more expensive than programming an EPROM.

Root Main or uppermost level in a hierarchically organized set of information. The root is the point from which subsets branch in a logical sequence that moves from a broad focus to narrower perspectives.

Root Directory In a disk-based hierarchical directory structure, the

Root Directory

point of entry into the directory "tree." Branching from this root are various directories and subdirectories, each of which can contain one or more files and subdirectories of its own. The root directory is identified by the backslash character (\), and is the main directory on a drive.

Routine Generic term for any section of code that can be invoked (executed) within a program. A routine usually has a name (identifier) associated with it and is executed by referencing that name. Related terms, which might or might not be exact synonyms, depending on the context, are function, procedure, and subroutine.

Row Series of items arranged horizontally within some type of framework; for example, a continuous series of cells running from left to right in a spreadsheet; a horizontal line of pixels on a video screen; or a set of data (text or numeric values) aligned horizontally in a table, a mathematical array, or some other row-and-column type of matrix.

RS-232-C Accepted industry standard for serial communications connections. Adopted by the Electrical Industries Association, this Recommended Standard (RS) defines the specific lines and signal characteristics used by serial communications controllers to standardize the transmission of serial data between devices. The "C" denotes that the current version of the standard is the third in a series.

RTS Acronym for **Request To Send**.

Rubber Banding In computer graphics, changing the shape of an object made up of connected lines by "grabbing" a point on an anchored line and "pulling" it to the new location.

Rule Line printed above, below, or to the side of some element, either to set that item off from the remainder of the page or to improve the look of the page. Footnotes, for example, often appear below a short rule that sets them off from the main text on the page. The thickness of a rule is typically measured in points (1/72 inch). In expert systems, a rule is a statement that can be used to verify premises and to enable a conclusion to be drawn.

Ruler In some application programs, such as word processors, this refers to an on-screen ruler, marked off in inches or other units of measure, used to show line widths, tab settings, paragraph indents,

Ruler

and so on. In programs in which the ruler is "live," the on-screen ruler can be used with the mouse or with the keyboard to set, adjust, or remove tab stops and other settings.

Run To execute a program.

Run Around Page composition pertaining to the ability to position text so that it flows around an illustration or other display.

Run-Length Limited Encoding Generally referred to as RLL encoding, a fast and highly efficient method of storing data on a disk (usually a hard disk) in which patterns in the bits representing information are translated into codes rather than being stored literally bit by bit and character by character. RLL encoding uses a coding scheme built upon a "run length," in which changes in magnetic flux are based on a certain number of zeros occurring in sequence. Essentially, RLL encoding allows data to be stored with fewer changes in magnetic flux than would otherwise be needed for the number of data bits involved and results in considerably higher storage capacity than is possible with older technologies, such as frequency modulation (FM) and modified frequency modulation (MFM) encoding.

Run Time Either the time period during which a program is running or the amount of time needed to execute the program. Also, a reference to events that occur after a program is executed, such as evaluation of variable expressions and dynamic allocation of memory.

Run-Time Library File that contains one or more prewritten routines to perform specific, commonly used functions. A run-time library, used primarily in high-level languages such as C, saves the programmer from having to write the routine himself or herself.

Run-Time Version Program code ready to be executed. Usually, this code has been compiled and can operate without error under most user command sequences and over most ranges of data sets. In software, a special release that provides the computer user with some, but not all, of the capabilities available in the full-fledged software package.

Sampling Process of gathering data from some source. The term has two senses. In statistics, sampling is gathering data from a representative subset of a larger group (called a population), such as determining a country's presumed voting pattern by polling a demographic cross section of voters. Other uses of this type of sampling might include checking the accuracy and efficiency of computerized transactions by reviewing every hundredth transaction or predicting traffic volumes by measuring traffic flow in a few strategic streets. There are many procedures used for estimating how accurately a given sample reflects the behavior of a routine as a whole.

The second sense of the term pertains to the conversion of analog signals to a digital format; samples are taken at periodic intervals to measure and record some parameter, such as a signal from a temperature sensor or microphone. Analog-to-digital converters are used in computers to sample analog signals as voltages and convert them to the binary form a computer can process. The two primary characteristics of this type of sampling are the sampling rate (usually expressed in samples per second) and the sampling precision (expressed in bits; 8-bit samples, for instance, can measure an input voltage accurate to 1/256 of the measured range).

Sampling Rate Frequency with which samples of a physical variable, such as sound, are taken. The higher the sampling rate (the more samples taken per unit of time), the more closely the digitized result resembles the original. See also **sampling**.

Sans Serif Any typeface in which the characters have no **serif**s. A sans serif typeface usually possesses a more straightforward, geometric appearance than a typeface with serifs and typically lacks the contrast between thick and thin strokes found in serif faces. Sans serif typefaces are used more frequently in display type, such as headlines, than in large bodies of text.

Satellite Computer Computer connected to another computer; the two communicate over a communications link. As its name indicates, a satellite computer is of lesser "stature" than the main, or host, computer; the host controls either the satellite itself or the tasks the satellite performs.

Saturated Mode

Saturated Mode State in which a switching device or amplifier is passing the maximum possible current. A device is in saturated mode when increasing the control signal does not result in output of additional current.

Saturation During saturation, a device is passing the maximum possible current. The term is most commonly used with reference to circuits containing bipolar or field-effect transistors. When used in color graphics and printing, this term refers to the amount of color in a specified hue, often specified as a percentage from 0% to 100%.

Save Ability to write data (typically a file) to a storage medium, such as a disk or tape.

Scalable Font Any font that can be scaled to produce characters in varying sizes. Examples of scalable fonts are screen fonts in a graphical user interface, stroke fonts (such as Courier) and outline fonts common to most PostScript printers, and the new method for screen font definition used in Macintosh System 7. In contrast, most text-based interfaces and printing devices (such as daisy-wheel printers) offer text in only one size.

Scale Horizontal or vertical line on a graph that shows minimum, maximum, and interval values for the data plotted. Also, the ability to enlarge or reduce a graphic display, such as a drawing or a proportional character font, by adjusting its size proportionally; also, to alter the way in which values are represented so as to bring them into a different range; for example, to change linear feet to quarter inches on a blueprint drawing of a house. In programming, to scale is to determine the number of digits occupied by fixed-point or floating-point numbers.

Scaling In computer graphics, the process of enlarging or reducing a graphical image-scaling a font to a desired size or scaling a model created with a CAD program, for example. See also **scale**.

Scan In television and computer display technologies, the ability to move an electron beam across the inner surface of the screen, one line at a time, to light the phosphor that creates a displayed image. In facsimile and other optical technologies, scan means to move a light-sensitive device across an image-bearing surface such as a page of text, converting the light and dark areas on the surface into binary digits that can be interpreted by a computer.

Scan Code

Scan Code Code number transmitted to an IBM or compatible computer whenever a key is pressed or released. Each key on the keyboard has a unique scan code. This code is not the same as the ASCII code for the letter, number, or symbol shown on the key; it is a special identifier for the key itself and is always the same for a particular key. When a key is pressed, the scan code is transmitted to the computer, where a portion of the ROM BIOS (**read-only memory basic input/output system**) dedicated to the keyboard translates the scan code into its ASCII equivalent. Because a single key can generate more than one character (such as a lowercase "a" and uppercase "A"), the ROM BIOS also keeps track of the status of keys that change the keyboard state, such as the Shift key, and takes them into account when translating a scan code.

Scan Head Device in many scanners, including fax machines, that sweeps across the item being scanned and sends a bit-mapped (dot-by-dot) image of the material to the scanning system for processing. A scan head can be designed to distinguish levels of light and dark, shades of gray, or different colors.

Scan Line On a television or raster-scan computer monitor, one of the horizontal lines on the inner surface of the screen that is traced by the electron beam to form an image. Also, a row of pixels read by any scanning device, such as a full-page scanner or a fax machine.

Scheduler Operating-system process that manages other concurrently running processes and tasks, responding to their requests for system services, tracking each one's progress, and allocating system resources, including CPU time, for their use. This term can also refer to a project-management program that allocates human resources to a series of tasks.

Schematic Diagram that shows a circuit's components and the connections between them. Schematic diagrams use lines to represent connections (wires) and standard, unique symbols to represent circuit components such as resistors, transistors, and integrated circuits.

Scientific Notation Method of representing a number, especially a very large or very small one, as a mantissa, which shows the number of significant digits in the number, and an exponent (a power of 10). Widely used in science and engineering, scientific

Scientific Notation

notation is similar to, and is often considered synonymous with, the floating-point notation commonly used in computing.

Scrambler Device or a program for reordering a sequence of signals in order to render them indecipherable. This is a form of encryption.

Scratch Also called scratch file. Memory region or file used by a program as a place to keep work in progress. The scratch is created and maintained by the program, usually without the user's knowledge, and is needed only until the current session is terminated, at which time the work saved in the scratch is either recorded on disk or discarded. The scratch is similar to the temporary storage facility called the scrap. The scrap, however, usually stores data that has been copied or deleted by the user rather than data used by the program.

Scratchpad Temporary storage area used for calculations, data, and other work in progress. In a microprocessor, scratchpad refers to a special high-speed memory circuit used to hold small items of data for rapid retrieval.

Screen Buffer Buffer area that holds the screen image in memory; also known as a video buffer.

Screen Dump Duplicate of a screen image; in other words, a "snapshot" of the screen, either sent to a printer or saved as a file on disk. Because it literally dumps the screen contents to another output location, a screen dump preserves a screen image for later use or reference.

Screen Flicker Flickering effect seen on some computer monitor screens. Flicker seems to be more noticeable on a noninterlaced monitor.

Screen Font Type size designed for display on a computer screen. On the Macintosh, for example, screen fonts are bit maps (pixel-by-pixel designs) that are used for the display and for printing on an ImageWriter or a LaserWriter printer. Often a screen font has a corresponding PostScript font for printing to a PostScript-compatible printer.

Script Type of program that consists of a set of instructions to an application or utility program, usually expressed with the

Script

application's or utility's rules and syntax, combined with simple control structures such as loops and if/then expressions.

Scroll Bar In many types of graphical user interfaces, a vertical or horizontal bar at the side or bottom of a window that can be used with a mouse for moving around in a document. A scroll bar has three active areas; a vertical scroll bar in a word processing application, for example, has two scroll arrows for moving up and down by one line and a scroll box for moving to an specific location in the document. Clicking in one or the other of the gray areas in the scroll bar moves up or down through the document in increments of one window.

Scrolling Process of moving a document in a window to permit viewing of any desired portion. Scrolling is so named because it is the electronic equivalent of reading through a rolled (scrolled) document rather than flipping through the pages of a book. The keyboard provides a number of "scroll-control" keys, such as the up, down, left, and right arrow keys. Application programs often offer additional methods of scrolling such as combining the Control and Page Up keys to move to the beginning of a document.

Scroll Lock Key Key on the top row of the numeric keypad on the IBM PC/XT and original AT and compatible keyboards that governs the effect of the cursor-control keys. On the enhanced keyboard, this key is to the right of the function keys in the top row. When toggled on, the Scroll Lock key affects the cursor-control keys on the numeric keypad or, with an enhanced keyboard, the cursor-control keys between the numeric keypad and the main keyboard. The operation of the cursor keys with the Scroll Lock key toggled on depends on the application program; a word processing program, for example, might scroll a document around the cursor when the cursor keys are used and Scroll Lock is on, whereas the cursor keys would move the cursor around the document if Scroll Lock is off. Although the name of this key suggests that pressing it stops the screen from scrolling, it does not do this in all situations. Instead, Pause (on the enhanced keyboard only), Ctrl-Num Lock, and Ctrl- S are the keys that stop scrolling on a DOS screen.

SCSI Acronym for **Small Computer System Interface**.

Seamless Integration Desired result that occurs when new hardware, a new program, or a program addition blends smoothly

Seamless Integration

into the overall working of a system. Seamless integration is the result of careful design or programming and attention to detail. It occurs, for example, when a modem and its controlling software settle into a system without interfering with other software or hardware, or when a spelling module added to a word processor works flawlessly without requiring considerable effort in installation or program adjustments.

Search Ability to seek the location of a file, or to search a file or data structure for specific data. A search is carried out by comparison or calculation to determine whether a match to some specified pattern exists or whether some other criteria have been met; for example, a search might or might not be sensitive to uppercase and lowercase letters, depending on the program. See also **replace**, **search and replace**, **wildcard character**.

Search and Replace Process typical of application programs such as word processors in which the user can specify two strings of characters, one string for the program to find and replace with the second string. For example, a program might be instructed to find the word "company" and replace it with the word "corporation." Search-and-replace procedures might or might not be sensitive to uppercase and lowercase, depending on the program.

Search Key Particular field (or column) of the records to be searched in a database, or the value that is to be found in a document or any collection of data. See also **primary key**, **secondary key**.

Search String String of characters to be matched in a search, typically (but not necessarily) a text string.

Secondary Channel Transmission channel in a communications device, such as a modem, that carries testing and diagnostic information rather than actual data.

Secondary Key Field that is to be sorted or searched within a subset of the records having identical primary key values.

Secondary Storage Any data storage medium other than a computer's random-access memory, such as a tape or disk.

Sector Portion of the data storage area on a disk. A disk is divided into sides (top and bottom), tracks (rings on each surface), and

Sector

sectors (sections of each ring). Sectors are the smallest physical storage units on a disk and are of fixed size, typically, capable of holding 512 bytes of information apiece.

Sector Map Map indicating the unusable sectors on a disk; also, a table used to translate sector numbers requested by the operating system into physical sector numbers. Sector mapping is a different method of performing sector interleaving. When a sector map is used, the sectors are formatted on the disk in sequential order. Sector mapping enables the system to read sectors in a nonsequential order. For example, using a 3-to-1 sector interleaving map, a system request for sectors 1 through 4 will result in the disk drive driver reading physical sectors 1, 4, 7, and 10.

Security Protection of a computer system and its data from harm or loss. A major focus of computer security, especially on systems accessed by many people or through communications lines, is the prevention of system use by unauthorized individuals.

Seed Starting value used in generating random or pseudorandom numbers.

Seek Process of moving the read/write head in a disk drive to the proper site, typically for a read or write operation.

Seek Time Amount of time required to move a disk drive's read/write head to a specific location on a disk. See also **access time**.

Segment Section of a program that, when compiled, occupies a contiguous address space and is usually position-independent; that is, it can be loaded anywhere into memory. With Intel-based microcomputers, a native-mode segment is a logical reference to a G4-KB contiguous portion of RAM in which the individual bytes are accessed by means of an offset value. Collectively, the segment offset values reference a single physical location in RAM.

Segmentation Breaking a program into several sections.

Segmented Address Space Address space that is logically divided into chunks called segments. To address a given location, a program must specify both a segment and an **offset** within that segment. Because segments may overlap, addresses are not unique; there are many logical ways to access a given physical location. The Intel

Segmented Address Space

8086 real-mode architecture is segmented; most other microprocessor architectures are flat.

Segmented Addressing Architecture Memory-access methodology typified by the Intel 80 x 86 family of microprocessors, which implement a segmented memory model in which system memory is divided into 64-KB segments. In the native mode of these processors (real mode), the address of any byte consists of two l6-bit values: a segment address and an offset. The segment component of an address is multiplied by 16 and added to the offset component, producing a 20-bit physical address. In the protected mode of the 80286, 8086, and i486 microprocessors, the segment register selects an entry from a descriptor table; that entry contains the beginning address, a segment length, and permission bits. In both modes, memory objects larger than 64 KB occupy all or part of several segments.

On the 80286 and earlier Intel microprocessors, an application cannot access large memory objects simply by incrementing a pointer to the memory as if the objects composed a single contiguous block. Instead, the application can increment only the offset portion of the address, taking care not to exceed the 64-KB boundary of the segment. The 80386 microprocessor introduced 32-bit registers that parallel the 16-bit registers of older members of the 80 x 86 family. These registers make it possible to access memory in segments larger than 64 KB. In fact, the maximum segment size is potentially so large (2^{32} bytes, or 4 gigabytes) that a flat memory model utilizing a single segment is feasible, which enables an application to manipulate the 32-bit offset portion of the address as though it were a simple pointer. Compare **linear addressing architecture**.

Select In general computer use, to specify an item displayed on screen by highlighting or otherwise marking it, with the intent of manipulating information in some way. Selecting generally indicates only that a choice has been made; a program does not act on a selection until instructed to do so.

In database management, select refers to the ability to choose records according to one or more specified criteria; for example, all customers in Arizona or all job applicants with 12 or more years of schooling.

In information processing, select refers to choosing an

Select

alternative based on a particular condition, to activate the channel to an input/output device for reading or writing, or to choose from a collection of subroutines.

Selection In applications, the highlighted portion of an on-screen document. In communications, the initial contact made between a computer and a remote station that is to receive a message.

Self-Adapting Distinguishing characteristic of a system's devices, or processes that can adjust their operational behavior according to environmental conditions.

Self-Checking Digit Digit appended to a number during its encoding that serves to confirm the encoding's accuracy.

Semiconductor Substance that ranks between a conductor and a nonconductor (insulator) in its ability to conduct electricity. The resistance of a semiconductor material is moderate to high, depending on impurities (dopants) added during manufacture. The most common semiconductor materials used in electronics are silicon and germanium. The term semiconductor is also loosely used to refer to electronic components such as transistors and integrated circuits fabricated from semiconductor materials.

Sensor Device that detects or measures something by converting nonelectrical energy into electrical energy. For example, a photocell detects or measures light by converting light energy into electrical energy. A sensor is one kind of transducer.

Sequence Ordered arrangement, as in a set of numbers.

Sequence Check Process that determines that data or records conform to a particular sort order.

Sequential Access Method of storing or retrieving information that requires the program to start reading at the beginning and continue until it finds the desired data. The data could be a linked sequence in which each access to a file or record points to the next file or record in the sequence. The term can be used to describe access to sequential-access files stored on disk. This type of access is best used for files in which each piece of information is related to what comes before it, such as mailing-list files and word processing documents. Sequential access is analogous to the process of finding a particular song on an audio tape. The search must start at the beginning of the tape and continue sequentially until the song is found.

Sequential Execution Executing routines or programs in linear sequence, as opposed to concurrent execution, which simultaneously executes two or more routines or programs.

Sequential Logic Element Logic circuit element that has at least one input and one output and in which the output signal depends on the present and past state(s) of the input signal(s).

Sequential Processing Processing in the order in which items of information are stored or input, such as in the order of storage location or in order of values contained in fields of records. In terms of computer operations, sequential processing is the execution of one instruction, routine, or job followed by the execution of the next in line. Such processing follows a first-in, first-out order and is the simplest form in which information is processed.

Serial In data transfer, the sending of information one bit at a time over a single wire, as through a serial port. In other aspects of computing, serial (or sequential) access refers to finding information based on the location of the last item found; a serial computer is one with a single arithmetic logic unit; serial addition is digit-by-digit addition of the sort people usually perform, as opposed to parallel addition, in which all digits are added at the same time.

Serial Communications Transmission of information between computers or between computers and peripheral devices one bit at a time over a single line. Serial communications can be synchronous (controlled by some time standard such as a clock) or asynchronous (managed by the exchange of control signals that govern the flow of information. One important aspect of serial communications—and a potential source of difficulty—is that both sender and receiver must use the same **baud rate**, **parity**, and control information. See also **stop bit**.

Serial Interface Data-transmission scheme that sends data and control bits sequentially over a single transmission line. In reference to a computer's serial input/output connection, the term usually implies the use of an RS-232 or RS-422 interface.

Serial Mouse Mouse that attaches to the computer through a standard serial port of the type that can also be used for other

Serial Mouse

purposes, such as attaching a modem. If a serial port is unavailable or another serial port cannot be added to the system, however, a bus mouse, which uses its own computer card, might be used instead.

Serial Port Input/output location (channel) for serial data transmission.

Serial Printer Printer connected to the computer via a serial interface. In the microcomputer world, a serial printer or printer port is almost always an RS-232-C or compatible interface. The most common connector for a serial port on a printer is a female D-shaped connector with 25 pin holes. Connectors on the computer side are more varied. Before IBM introduced the PC, the most common connector on the computer side was also a female D-shaped connector with 25 pin holes.

The IBM PC, XT, PS/2, and virtually all compatible systems use a male D-shaped connector with 25 pins; the IBM AT and compatibles use a 9-pin male D-shaped connector. This variety in connectors, along with the need for printer-specific cabling, is one reason why serial printers are less popular than parallel printers in the IBM world. In addition, the MS-DOS operating system assumes that the system printer is attached to the parallel port.

Serif Any of the short lines or ornaments at the upper and lower ends of the strokes that form a character in a typeface; also an adjective describing any face with serifs.

Server In a **local area network**, a computer running administrative software that controls access to all or part of the network and its resources (such as disk drives or printers). A computer acting as a server makes resources available to computers known as clients acting as workstations on the network.

Service Customer-based or user-oriented function; for example, technical support service for purchasers of a computer or a software package, or network service for users of a communications network. Within a computer, service is sometimes used to refer to a program or routine that provides support to other programs, particularly at a low (close to the hardware) level.

Session Time during which a program is running. With the interactive programs typical of microcomputers, a session represents the time during which the program accepts input,

Session

processes information, and responds to user commands. In communications, session refers to the time during which two computers (or a computer and a terminal) maintain a connection and, usually, are engaged in transferring information. In this context, session also refers to a specific protocol layer in the ISO/OSI networking model that manages communication between remote users or processes.

Setup In hardware terminology, the computer and the devices that are attached to it, such as a computer with a color monitor, a laser printer, and an internal modem. In software terminology, the procedures involved in preparing a program to work with the computer and its attached devices.

Shade Particular color variation produced by mixing black with a pure color; in graphic arts, also called a value; in computer graphics, also called intensity or brightness. This term also means to give added dimension to an image by including changes in appearance caused by light and shadow.

Shared Memory Memory accessed by two or more programs in a multitasking environment. Programs using this memory operate under a set of rules that prevent two programs from modifying the same addresses simultaneously. Also refers to a portion of memory used by parallel-processor computer systems to exchange information. Each processor in the machine has some local memory that only it can access, and it also has the ability to access the shared memory—a pool that each of the processors can read from or write to.

Shareware Copyrighted software distributed free of charge but usually accompanied by a request for a small payment from satisfied users to cover costs and registration for documentation and program updates.

Sheet Feeder Device that accepts a stack of paper and feeds it to the printer one page at a time, as do the paper trays in laser printers. Many dot-matrix printers and most daisy-wheel printers come with sheet feeders standard or as extra-cost options. Some sheet feeders have multiple bins, which can be loaded with paper of different sizes or quality; for example, plain "draft" paper and letterhead.

Shell Piece of software, usually a separate program, that provides

Shell

direct communication between the user and the operating system. The Macintosh Finder is a shell, as is the command interface program (COMMAND.COM) in MS-DOS. Various other shells, however, including the visual, mouse-oriented shell shipped with MS-DOS version 4, can be used to replace the keyboard-only, command-based MS-DOS shell. Similarly, a number of programs are available in UNIX systems to serve as shells.

Shift In programming, particularly in assembly language or machine language, this term means to move the bit values one position to the left or right in a register or memory location. In a shift operation, depending on the direction of the shift, one bit "falls off" the end of the register or memory location (and is permanently deleted), and a zero is added to the vacant bit position on the opposite end. For example, in a shift right operation, the rightmost bit "falls off" the right end, all other bits are shifted one position to the right, and a zero is added to the vacancy at the leftmost position.

Shift Key Key on the keyboard that, when pressed, gives an alternative meaning to another key; for example, producing an uppercase character when a letter key is pressed or producing a symbol instead of a digit when a number key in the top row of the keyboard is pressed. The Shift key is also used in various key combinations to create nonstandard characters or to perform special functions. For example, on the Macintosh, Option-Shift-hyphen produces an em-dash in most fonts; on an IBM PC or compatible, Shift plus a function key might specify a different command than would be specified by pressing the function key alone. On the original PC/XT keyboard, the shift keys are labeled with up-pointing arrows. On other IBM keyboards, they are labeled with both the arrow and the word "Shift."

Short Card Also referred to as a half-card, a printed circuit board that is half as long as a standard-size circuit board. A short card is designed to fit in the type of slot location that, on many computers, has half its space occupied by something else, such as a hard disk. Since many computer boards require only a fraction of the available board space but are designed full-length simply to comply with the standard board shape, the smaller size also gives board developers a strategic advantage because many systems have one or more half-size slots, but only a limited number of boards are available to fill them.

Sign

Sign Character used to indicate a positive or a negative number. In programming at the assembler level, the sign is indicated by a special bit, the sign bit, that accompanies the number.

Signal General term referring to any electrical quantity, such as voltage, current, or frequency, that can be used to transmit information. In a broader sense, a beep or tone from a computer speaker to signal the user, or a prompt displayed on the screen to signal the user that the computer is ready to receive a command 01-input.

Signature Sequence of data used for identification, such as an identifier appended to a message in an electronic mail message or in a fax.

Sign Bit Most significant (leftmost) bit of a number field, usually set to 1 if the number is negative. When an 8-bit value is added to a 16-bit value using signed arithmetic, the processor propagates the sign bit through the high-order half of the 16-bit register holding the 8-bit value in a process called sign extension or sign propagation.

Silicon Semiconductor material used in many devices that in its pure form is a lightweight metal resembling aluminum and having atomic number 14 and atomic weight 28. Silicon is very common in minerals, usually combined with one or more other elements. For example, common sand is composed of silicon dioxide.

Silicon Chip Integrated circuit that uses silicon as its semiconductor material.

Silicone Polymer material in which silicon and oxygen are major components. Silicone is an excellent electrical insulator and conducts heat well. It is often produced in the form of a grease and is used to facilitate heat transfer between electrical components and heat sinks.

Silicon Foundry Factory or machine used to create wafers of crystalline silicon that are used in the fabrication of transistors and integrated circuits.

Silicon Valley Nickname for the area between San Francisco and San Jose in northern California that is noted for the number and the innovative quality of the semiconductor and computer-related high-technology companies located there.

SIMM

SIMM Acronym for **Single In-line Memory Module**.

Simulation Imitation of a physical process or object by a program that causes a computer to respond to data and changing conditions as though it were the process or object itself. A simulation uses a mathematical description to construct a model of the subject and then uses more mathematics to evaluate different situations involving the subject; for example, the response of a plane to turbulence or adverse weather. Although mostly done on a scale beyond the reach of microcomputers, simulation can also be used to create models of physical objects, ranging from molecules to stars, that might otherwise be difficult or impossible to study. Simulation even enhances computer development because the design of a proposed computer or processor can be duplicated in a program and run on an existing machine that will, under the program's influence, act as if it were the one under development.

Single-Density Disk Disk certified only for use with frequency modulation (FM) recording. Single-density disks can store much less data than disks that can be recorded with modified frequency modulation encoding and run-length limited encoding, both of which place greater demands on the quality of a disk's medium. See also modified frequency modulation encoding, run-length limited encoding.

Single In-Line Memory Module Small circuit board designed to accommodate surface-mount memory chips. SIMMs use less board space and are more compact than more conventional memory-mounting hardware.

Single-Precision Type of floating-point number that has the least precision among two or more options commonly offered by a programming language. The actual precision offered in a program varies with the language and the compiler for that language and depends on whether floating-point processing is performed by a math coprocessor or by software emulation.

Single-Sided Disk Floppy disk on which data can be reliably stored on only one side. When disks are manufactured, the manufacturer tests both sides of the disk. If one side fails, the disk is sold as a single-sided disk for use in disk drives capable of reading only one side of a disk.

Single-User Computer

Single-User Computer Computer designed for use by a single individual; effectively, a personal computer.

Sink Device or part of a device that receives something from another device. For example, a data sink is the part of a terminal that receives data, and a heat sink (in electronics) is a metal radiator that collects and drains heat away from a device to prevent damage to the device.

Slave Any device, including a computer, that is under the control of another computer, referred to as the master.

Small Caps Font of capital letters smaller than the standard capital letters in that typeface.

Small Computer System Interface Usually referred to as SCSI. A standard high-speed parallel interface defined by the American National Standards Institute (ANSI). A SCSI interface is used for connecting microcomputers to peripheral devices, such as hard disks and printers, and to other computers and local area networks. Up to seven devices, not including the computer, can be attached through a single SCSI connection (port) through sequential connections called a daisy chain. Each device has an address (priority number). Only one device at a time can transmit through the port; priority is given to the device with the highest address. A SCSI port is standard on the Apple Macintosh Plus, Macintosh SE, Macintosh II, the IBM RS/GOOO, and the IBM PS/2 model 65 and higher computers. It can be installed in IBM PC and compatible computers as an expansion board.

Smooth To eliminate irregularities in statistical data by some process such as continuous averaging or by removing random (irrelevant) values.

Snapshot Making a copy of main memory or video memory at a given instant, sent to a printer or hard disk. A graphical image of the video screen can be saved by taking a snapshot of video memory, more commonly called a **screen dump**.

Snow Temporary distortion of a displayed image caused by interference, usually in a weak signal. In computer displays, a specific type of distortion, characterized by the blinking on and off of random pixels, that occurs when the microprocessor and the display hardware interfere with one another by attempting to use the computer's video memory at the same time. Such distortion can be avoided by synchronizing activities so that the microprocessor uses video memory only during the brief intervals when the hardware is writing or retracing a line on the screen.

Software Computer programs that are instructions that cause the hardware—the machines—to do work. Software can be divided into a number of categories based on the types of work done by programs. The two primary software categories are operating systems (system software), which control the workings of the computer, and application software, which addresses the multitude of tasks for which people use computers. System software thus handles such essential, but often invisible, chores as maintaining disk files and managing the screen, whereas application software performs word processing, database management, and the like. Two additional categories are network software, which enables groups of computers to communicate, and language software, which provides programmers with the tools they need to write programs.

In addition to these task-based categories, several types of software are described based on their method of distribution. These include the so-called canned programs or packaged software developed and sold primarily through retail outlets; freeware and public-domain software, which is made available without cost by its developer; shareware, which is similar to freeware but usually requests a small fee from those who like the program; and the infamous vaporware, which is software that either does not reach the market or appears much later than promised.

Software House Organization that develops and supports software for its customers.

Software Interrupt Program-generated interrupt, also called a trap, that stops current processing in order to request a service provided by an interrupt handler (a separate set of instructions designed to perform the task required). For example, a program might generate a software interrupt to refer the microprocessor to a video routine under the control of the computer's input/output system or to read input from the mouse or the keyboard.

Software Piracy Illegal copying of software with the intent to distribute it to other users.

Software Protection

Software Protection Same as copy protection.

Software Publishing Design, development, and distribution of noncustom software packages.

Sort Process that organizes data, typically a set of records, in a particular order, such as alphabetic. There are many programs and programming algorithms for sorting, which vary in performance and application. See also **bubble sort, quicksort**.

Source In information processing, a disk, file, document, or other "collection" of information from which data is taken or moved. In electronics, one of three regions (source, drain, and gate) on a MOS transistor that causes the device to be either conducting or nonconducting (to be on or off). Electric current flows from the source to the drain region when voltage is applied to the transistor via the gate. A MOS source is comparable to the emitter lead on a bipolar transistor.

Source Code Human-readable program statements written in a high-level or assembly language, as opposed to object code, which is derived from the source code and designed to be machine-readable.

Source Data Original data on which a computer application is based; for example, employee job applications and performance reports might be the source data for a company's employee database.

Source Disk Usually, the disk from which data will be read during a copy operation. Can also refer to any disk from which data will be read, as when an application is loaded from a disk into memory.

Source Document Original document from which data is taken.

Spacebar Long key occupying much of the bottom row of most keyboards that sends a space character to the computer.

Special Characters Characters that are not alphabetic, numeric, or the space character. All punctuation marks are special characters.

Specification Detailed description. In computer hardware, specifications provide information about the machine's components, capabilities, and special features. In software, especially software under development, specifications describe the

Specification

operating environment and proposed features of the new program. In information processing, specifications describe data records, programs, and procedures involved in a particular task.

Spectrum Range of frequencies of a particular type of radiation. For example, the electromagnetic spectrum is the total range of frequencies of electromagnetic radiation, and the visible spectrum is the range of frequencies of light that can be perceived by human beings.

Speech Recognition Ability of a computer to understand the spoken word for the purpose of receiving commands and data input from the speaker. Some systems have been developed that can recognize limited vocabularies, as spoken by specific individuals, but developing a system that deals with a variety of speech patterns and accents, as well as with the various ways in which a request or a statement can be made, has so far proved a daunting task for systems designers

Designers of speech recognition systems have pursued three approaches. One enables computers to recognize a small number of words spoken by a broad range of people, a method that has proven to be fairly accurate. The second method enables the recognition of a larger number of words spoken by one individual; this method is also fairly reliable provided the speaker's speech patterns are consistent. The third method enables computers to learn a speaker's speech patterns and to apply the patterns over a broad range of words. Although this last method provides the most promise for full speech-to-text conversion, it is the least accurate of the three.

Speech Synthesis Ability of a computer to produce "spoken" words. Computer speech can be produced either by "splicing" prerecorded words together or, with much more difficulty, by having the computer produce the sounds that make up spoken words. Speech synthesis is used today for interaction with the handicapped and for other special-purpose applications, but its capabilities are still too limited for general use. At its best, computer-generated speech still lacks the cadence and complexity of real speech, resulting in a somewhat "dead" sound. See also **speech recognition**.

Spelling Checker Application program that employs a disk-based dictionary to check for misspellings in documents. A sophisticated

Spelling Checker

spelling checker can have a base dictionary of well over 100,000 words and can provide the user with the ability to create special-purpose dictionaries of proper names, technical terms, and other word forms not included in the main dictionary. Some spelling checkers can be instructed to use different spelling conventions, such as those in British- instead of American-English. Some can also make certain well-defined grammatical assumptions, combining root words with suffixes or prefixes to determine if the spelling is legitimate. Spelling checkers are available either as independent packages or as part of a word processing program.

Spike Transient electrical signal of very short duration and, usually, high amplitude. Compare **surge**.

Spline In computer graphics, a curve calculated by a mathematical function that connects separate points with a high degree of smoothness. Splines are used in CAD and other graphics applications.

Split Screen Display method in which a program can divide the display area into two or more sections, each of which can contain a different file or show different parts of the same file.

Spooling Process of storing data constituting a document to be printed in memory or in a file until the printer is ready to process it.

Spreadsheet Program Application program commonly used for budgets, forecasting, and other finance-related tasks. In a spreadsheet program, data and formulas to calculate those data are entered into ledgerlike forms for analysis, tracking, planning, or "what if" evaluations of the impacts of real or proposed changes on an economic strategy. Spreadsheet programs use rows and columns of cells; each cell can hold text or numeric data or a formula that uses values in other cells to calculate a desired result. To ease computation, these programs include built-in functions that perform standard calculations. A single spreadsheet can contain anywhere from thousands to millions of cells. Some spreadsheet programs can also link one spreadsheet to another that contains related information, and can update data in linked spreadsheets automatically. Spreadsheet programs may also include macro facilities, and some can be used for creating and sorting databases. For printed output, spreadsheet programs usually provide graphing capabilities and a variety of formatting options for both printed pages and text, numeric values, and captions and legends in graphs.

Stack

Stack Region of reserved memory in which programs store status data such as procedure and function call return addresses, passed parameters, and (sometimes) local variables. The microprocessor, the program, and the operating system can all maintain one or more separate stacks. A stack is usually a data structure organized as a LIFO (last in, first out) list so that the last data item added to the structure is the first item used.

Stand-Alone Device or operation that does not require support from another device or system.

Standard Set of detailed technical guidelines used as a means of establishing uniformity in an area of hardware or software development. Computer standards have traditionally developed in either of two ways. The first, a highly informal process, occurs when a product or philosophy is developed by a single company and, through success and imitation, becomes so widely used that deviation from the norm causes compatibility problems or limits marketability. This type of de facto standard setting is typified by such products as Hayes modems and IBM PCs. The second type of standard setting is a far more formal process in which specifications are drafted by a cooperative group or committee after an intensive study of existing methods, approaches, and technological trends and developments. The proposed standards are later ratified or approved by a recognized organization and are adopted over time by consensus as products based on the standards become increasingly prevalent in the market. Standards of this more formal type are numerous, including the ASCII character set, the RS-232-C, the SCSI interface, and ANSI-standard programming languages, such as C and FORTRAN.

Startup ROM Bootstrap instructions coded into a computer's ROM (**read-only memory**) and executed at startup. The startup ROM routines enable a computer to check itself and its devices (such as the keyboard and disk drives), prepare itself for operation, and run a short program to load an operating-system loader program from disk.

Statement Smallest executable entity in a programming language. In general, each line of a program is an individual statement and is considered an individual instruction. Not all languages define a statement in the same way, but most popular ones support the concepts of assignment statements, control statements, comment statements, and so on.

State-of-the-Art

State-of-the-Art Up to date; the newest of current hardware or software technology.

Static Electricity Electrical charge accumulated in an object, called static because there is no flow of electrons in a circuit. Static charges can reach levels of 1000 volts or more but are generally harmless to people because the currents involved are low. (Damage to living tissue is caused by the combination of voltage and current, not voltage alone.) The discharge of static electricity through an electronic circuit, however, often damages the circuit because most integrated circuits are rated for maximum voltages far lower than those present in static charges.

Status Condition at a particular time of any of numerous elements of computing—a device, a communications channel, a network station, a program, a bit, a byte, and so on. Status is used in various ways to report on or to control computer operations. Application programs, for example, often use status lines to display messages for the user. Internally, programs also rely on specified bits, bytes, or registers to hold information or to record the outcome of an operation. All types of hardware use external lights, code numbers, or beeps to report on device activity or availability; for example, a light on the keyboard that is turned on when the Caps Lock key is pressed, or a number, light, beep, or message on a printer that indicates the device is on line, off line, or disabled by a paper jam.

Stop Bit In asynchronous transmission, a bit that signals the end of a character. Depending on the conventions used, the data bits composing the character can be followed by 1, 1.5, or 2 stop bits.

Storage Any physical device in or on which computer information can be kept. A microcomputer has two main types of storage. Its **random-access memory** (RAM) represents temporary storage that the microprocessor uses for programs, work in progress, and various types of internal work-control information. The computer's disk drives and other external storage media represent facilities for holding information on a more permanent basis, available but out of the way until it is needed by the microprocessor. A computer has other types of storage as well. Its **read-only memory** (ROM) is a permanent, nonerasable medium for holding necessary information, including startup instructions and input/output procedures. In addition, a computer uses various buffers—reserved areas of memory—as temporary holding areas designated for specific

Storage

information, such as characters to be sent to the printer or characters being read from the keyboard.

Storage Device Any apparatus for recording computer data in permanent or semipermanent form. A disk drive, along with the disks it records on, is a storage device. A computer is said to have primary (or main) and secondary (or auxiliary) storage device. When this distinction is made, the primary storage device is the computer's **random-access memory** (RAM)—impermanent, but a storage device nevertheless, however temporary its contents. The secondary storage includes the computer's more permanent storage devices, such as disk and tape drives.

Storage Location Position at which a particular item can be found. A storage location can be an addressed (uniquely numbered) location in memory or it can be a uniquely identified location or disk, tape, or a similar medium—for example, a particular side, track, and sector on a disk storage media, the various types of physical material on which data hits are written and stored. Common storage media for computer data are floppy disks, hard disks, tape, optical discs, and (for output purposes only) paper.

String Data structure composed of a sequence of characters, usually representing human-readable text. A string's current length (the actual sequence stored) might not be the same as its allotted maximum size; consequently, some languages provide a way of determining current length, usually by using a delimiting character at the end or by counting the number of characters.

Structure Design and composition of a program, including program flow, hierarchy, and modularity. Also, a collection of data elements.

Style Sheet File of instructions used to apply character, paragraph, and page-layout formats to a word processed document. Style sheets contain such information as margin sizes, column widths, paragraph indention, character attributes (italic, boldface, superscript, and so on), fonts, and font sizes. They are, essentially, descriptions of the different looks that can be ascribed to the characters, words, paragraphs, and pages of a document. The styles themselves are applied by relating a given style sheet to a document and linking different formats to the text with predetermined codes. Because a style sheet is maintained as a separate file, it can be

Style Sheet

attached to one document or many; it can also be detached or replaced with another and can be modified at any time. Multiple style sheets with compatible formatting instructions can be used to format or reformat documents as needed.

Stylus Pointing device used with a graphics tablet, usually attached to the tablet by a cord, although there are cordless varieties. To draw or point, the user touches the pen tip to the surface of the tablet. Selections and commands can be controlled through pressing a button on the stylus or pressing the stylus against the tablet's surface. The stylus is preferred by artists because its results most closely resemble freehand illustration and because the stylus allows a great deal of manual control.

Subdirectory Directory (logical grouping of related files) within another directory. In a hierarchical directory structure, the "parent" of all directories is the root, which can branch and rebranch like an upside-down tree into successive lower-level directories, each of which is a subdirectory of the one immediately above it. A computer's file system keeps the files in each subdirectory logically separate from all others. It locates a particular file by following a "path" of directory names from the root down through the various directory levels until it finds the appropriate subdirectory and filename.

Supercomputer Large, externally fast, and expensive computer used for complex or sophisticated calculations; typically, a machine capable of pipelining instruction execution and providing vector instructions. A supercomputer can, for example, perform the enormous number of calculations required to draw and animate a moving spaceship in a motion picture. Supercomputers are also used for weather forecasting, large-scale scientific modeling, and oil exploration.

Support The rendering of assistance; for example, the technical advice provided to customers by the manufacturer or developer of a hardware or software product. As a verb, support means to work with another program or product; for example, an application program might support file transfers from another program.

Surge Sudden increase in line voltage, which can damage data and computer equipment, especially if the surge is intense or prolonged. Devices known as surge protectors or surge suppressors can be inserted between the power source (typically a wall outlet) and the computer's power plug to eliminate or minimize changes in electrical current.

Surge Protector Also known as a surge suppressor, a device that prevents potentially damaging power surges in an electrical current from reaching a computer or other device. Surge protectors work by collecting and diffusing excess power, sometimes within a few billionths of a second.

Suspend To halt a process temporarily.

Swapping Process of exchanging one item for another, as in swapping floppy disks as needed, in and out of a single disk drive. Within a computer, swapping occurs when different segments of programs or data are moved between memory and disk storage. In a virtual memory implementation, swapping occurs after a page fault, when a program has accessed a virtual memory location that is not currently in primary storage. A page that has not been recently accessed is "swapped out" to disk and the page needed by the faulting program is "swapped in." The mapping hardware is notified of the new physical address of the page, and the instruction that caused the page fault is restarted.

Swim Condition in which images slowly move about the positions they are supposed to occupy on the display screen.

Synchronization Matching of timing between separate computers or among the components of a system so that all are coordinated. Synchronization plays a role in the internal workings of a computer, in computer communications, and in such fields as compact disc technology. Within a computer, for instance, operations are synchronized with signals of the machine's internal clock. In synchronous time-dependent communications, the individual bits composing transmissions between computers are sent and interpreted on the basis of synchronized timing. In multimedia presentations containing text, sounds, and graphics, the separate elements are synchronized so that they appear at the proper time when replayed.

Synchronous Operation Usually, any operation that proceeds under control of a clock or timing mechanism. In communications and bus operation data transfer accompanied by clock pulses either embedded in the data stream or provided simultaneously on a separate line.

Syntax Grammar of a particular language; the rules governing the structure and content of the statements.

Sysop Abbreviation for system operator, generally the overseer or operator of a multiuser computer system or a bulletin board system.

System Any collection of component elements that work together to perform a task. In computing, system is used in a variety of contexts. A computer is a hardware system consisting of a microprocessor and allied chips and circuitry, plus an input device (keyboard, mouse, disk drive), an output device (monitor, disk drive), and any peripheral devices such as a printer or modem. Within this hardware system is an operating system, often called system software, which is an essential set of programs that manage hardware and data files and work with application programs.

T

Tab Character Character used to align lines and columns on the screen and the printed page. A tab character is visually indistinguishable from a series of blank spaces entered by repeatedly pressing the spacebar, but tab characters and space characters are different to a computer. A tab is a single character and therefore can be added, deleted, or overtyped with a single keystroke. Some file-storage and transmission options allow the user to convert tab characters to equivalent numbers of spacebar spaces, which can be useful when a file created with one program is to be read and used by another. The ASCII coding scheme includes two codes for tab characters: a horizontal tab for spacing across the screen or page, and a vertical tab for spacing down the screen or page. The horizontal tab character is decimal 9 (hexadecimal 9); the vertical tab is decimal 11 (hexadecimal 08).

Tab Key Key on the keyboard, usually labeled with both left-pointing and right-pointing arrows, that is traditionally used to insert tab characters into a document, as in word processing. In other applications, however, the Tab key is often used to move the on-screen highlight from place to place. Menu-driven programs, for example, often use the Tab key to enable the user to move through the available choices. Many database and spreadsheet programs allow the user to press the Tab key to move around within a record or between cells, reserving the Enter (or Return) key for indicating that data entry is complete. In these capacities, the shifted version of the Tab key, "backtab," can be used to move back one field or cell.

Tabulate Usually, the process of performing a mathematical function on a row or column of numbers; less commonly used in reference to arranging information in table form.

Tag In programming, one or more characters containing information about a file, record type, or other structure. In certain types of data files, a key or an address that identifies a record and its storage location in another file.

Tag Image File Format Usually referred to as TIFF, a standard file format commonly used for scanning, storage, and interchange of gray-scale graphic images.

Tag Sort

Tag Sort Sort performed on one or several key fields for the purpose of establishing the order of their associated records.

Tandem Processors Multiple processors wired so that the failure of one processor transfers CPU operation to another processor. Using tandem processors is part of the strategy for implementing fault-tolerant computer systems.

Tape Thin strip of Mylar coated with magnetic material that permits the recording of data. To use a tape, a machine must have two reels between which the tape can pass, with a read/write head located somewhere between the reels. Because tape is a continuous length of data storage material and because the read/write head cannot "jump" to a desired point on the tape without the tape first being advanced to that point, a tape must be read or written sequentially, not randomly as is a floppy or a hard disk.

Tape Cartridge Module, similar in appearance to an audio cassette, that contains magnetic tape that can be written on and read from by a tape drive. Tape cartridges are primarily used to back up hard disks.

Tape Drive Device used for reading and writing tapes.

Target Term referring to the objective of a computer command or operation; for example, a computer that is to run a program translated for its use; a "foreign" language (for another computer) into which a program is to be translated; or a group of people for whom a particular product is designed. In specific usage, as often seen by users of MS-DOS, the target is the disk referred to by prompts displayed by the operating system in a copy operation (for example, "insert TARGET diskette"). In the SCSI (**Small Computer System Interface**) connection, the target is the device that receives commands; the device that issues commands is the initiator.

Target Computer Computer that receives data from a communications device, a hardware add-in, or a software package.

Target Disk Destination for a disk-copy operation. When disks are being copied, one disk is the source disk and the other is the target disk. Also refers to a disk to which data is to be written. Compare **source disk**.

Task

Task Stand-alone application or a subprogram run as an independent entity.

Task Management Operating system process of tracking the progress of and providing necessary resources for separate tasks running on a computer system, specifically in a multitasking environment.

Technology Application of science and engineering to the development of machines and procedures in order to enhance or improve human conditions, or at least to improve human efficiency in some respect.

Telecommunication Electronic transmission of information of any type, including data, television pictures, sound, facsimiles, and so on.

Telecommuting Also called electronic commuting. The practice of working in one location (often, at home) and communicating with a main office in a different location through a personal computer equipped with a modem and communications software.

Teleconferencing Use of audio, video, or computer equipment linked through a communications system to enable geographically separated individuals to participate in a meeting or discussion.

Telephony Telephone technology—the conversion of sound into electrical signals, its transmission to another location, and its reconversion to sound, with or without the use of connecting wires.

Teleprocessing Use of a terminal or computer and communications equipment to access computers and computer files located elsewhere; term originated by IBM.

Teletext All-text information sent out by a broadcast or cable television station to a subscriber's television set.

Teletype Mode Mode of operation in which a computer or an application limits its actions to those characteristic of a teletype machine. On the display, for example, teletype mode results in alphanumeric characters simply being "typed" on the screen, one letter after the other. The cursor advances to a new line when necessary, and the screen scrolls upward when necessary, but there is no provision for such features as color or the ability to move the cursor freely about the screen. A computer told to treat a printer as

Teletype Mode

if it were a teletype machine would send text to the printer in the simplest possible form, including necessary instructions such as carriage returns and linefeeds, but little else in the way of formatting.

Template Pattern or form. An application package might include a template for the keyboard, an overlay that defines special keys and key combinations. In flowcharting, a template is a form for tracing symbols and arrows. In image processing, a template is a pattern that can be used to identify or match a scanned image. In spreadsheet programs, a template is a predesigned spreadsheet that contains formulas, labels, and other elements and can be used simply by inserting information in the appropriate locations. In MS-DOS, the template refers to a small portion of memory that holds the most recently typed MS-DOS command; this command can be edited with the Fl through F5 function keys.

Temporary File Scratch file—a file created either in memory or on disk by the operating system or some other program to be used during a session and then discarded.

Temporary Storage Region in memory or on a storage device that is temporarily allocated for storing intermediate data in a computational, sorting, or transfer operation.

Terabyte Usually referred to as TB. Measurement used for high-capacity data storage. One terabyte equals 1,099,511,627,776 bytes, although it is commonly interpreted as simply one trillion bytes.

Terminal Device consisting of a video adapter, monitor, and keyboard. The adapter and monitor and sometimes the keyboard are usually combined in one unit. A terminal does little or no computer processing on its own; instead, it is connected to a computer with a communications link over a cable. Keyboard input is sent from the terminal to the computer; video output is sent from the computer to the terminal. Terminals are used primarily in multiuser systems and today are not often found on single-user personal computers.

Terminal Emulation Technique of imitating a terminal by using software that conforms to a standard such as the ANSI standard for terminal emulation. Terminal-emulation software can be used to make a microcomputer act as if it were a particular type of terminal

Terminal Emulation

while it is communicating with another computer, such as a mainframe.

Terminal Session Amount of time spent actively using a terminal.

Terminate To end a process or program. Termination can be normal or abnormal, with abnormal termination occurring in response to user intervention or because of a hardware or software error.

Terminate-and-Stay-Resident Program Usually referred to as TSR. Program running under MS-DOS that remains loaded in memory even when it is not running so that it can be quickly invoked for a specific task performed while any other application program is operating.

Test Data Set of values used to test proper functioning of a program. The reasons for choosing particular test data include verifying known output (anticipated output) and pushing the boundary conditions that might cause the program to fail.

Testing Act of promoting program correctness by trying out various sequences and input values.

Texas Instruments Graphics Architecture Video adapter architecture based on the Texas Instruments 340 x 0 graphics processor.

Text Data consisting of characters representing the words and symbols of human speech, usually coded according to the ASCII standard, which assigns numeric values to numbers, letters, and certain symbols. Text is one form in which computers can store and transmit information. Application programs might distinguish text from numeric values in a document. A spreadsheet program, for example, considers text to be alphabetic characters that are treated as symbols or labels rather than as formulas or as values to be used in calculations.

Text Editor Program used for entering or editing text. Text editors are mainly considered editors that perform simple text manipulation, such as entering new text or modifying old text, but usually do not allow special editing features such as formatting or special features such as different type faces or sizes.

Text File File composed of text characters. Also referred to as a word processing file.

Text Mode

Text Mode Mode of operation in which some computers display letters, numbers, and other text characters but no graphical images such as mouse pointers or "**What You See Is What You Get**" character formatting (italics, superscripted numbers, and so on). IBM PC and compatible computers can operate in either text mode or graphics mode.

Texture In computer graphics, the shading or other attributes added to the "surface" of a graphical image to give it the illusion of a physical substance. For example, a surface could be made to appear reflective to simulate metal or glass, or a scanned pixel image of wood grain could be applied to a shape intended to simulate an object made of wood.

Thermal Printer Nonimpact printer that uses heat to generate an image on specially treated paper. The printer uses pins to produce an image, but rather than striking the pins against a ribbon to mark the paper as does a wire-pin dot-matrix printer, it heats the pins and brings them into gentle contact with the paper. The special coating on the paper discolors when it is heated.

Thermal Wax Printer Special type of nonimpact printer that uses heat to melt colored wax onto paper to create an image. Like a standard thermal printer, it uses pins to apply the heat. Rather than making contact with coated paper, however, the pins touch a wide ribbon saturated with different-colored waxes. The wax melts under the pins and adheres to the paper, where it cools and resolidifies.

Thesaurus "Dictionary" of synonyms; in microcomputer applications, both a file of such synonyms stored on disk and the program used to search the thesaurus file for alternative words.

Thimble Type element that contains a full character set, with each character on a separate type bar. As with a daisy wheel, the spokes, or type bars, radiate out from a central hub. However, on a thimble print element each type bar is bent 90 degrees at its halfway point, so the type bars stick straight up with the type facing away from the hub. The printer spins the thimble to line up the proper character and then strikes the back of the type bar with a hammer.

Thimble Printer Printer that uses a thimble-print element, best known in a line of printers from NEC. Because these printers use fully formed characters like those on a typewriter, they generate

Thimble Printer

letter-quality output indistinguishable from that of a typewriter. This includes the slight impression created by the type hitting the paper hard through the ribbon, which distinguishes this type of printout from that of laser printers. Along with daisy-wheel printers, thimble printers were popular before the price of laser printers dropped enough to be affordable, because they offered the highest-quality computer-generated output. Now they are fading in importance as offices adopt the faster, more versatile, and far quieter laser printers.

Thin Space Amount of horizontal space in a font less than a normal space between words and equal to one-quarter the point size of the font; a thin space in a 12-point font, for example, is 3 points wide.

Third-Generation Computer Any of the computers produced from the mid-1960s to the l970s that were based on integrated circuits rather than on separately wired transistors.

Third Party Company that manufactures and sells accessories or peripherals for use with a major manufacturer's computer or peripheral, usually without any involvement from the major manufacturer. For example, a company might manufacture and sell a carrying case for the Apple Macintosh, or a company might manufacture and sell video adapters for IBM personal computers. Third-party accessories and peripherals usually represent an attempt to fill a gap in a major manufacturer's product line or to offer a similar item at a lower cost.

Thrashing State of a virtual memory system that is spending almost all its time swapping pages in and out of memory rather than executing applications.

Thread In programming, a process that is part of a larger process or program. In a tree data structure, a pointer that identifies the parent node and is used to facilitate traversal of the tree.

Threading Technique used by certain interpretive languages (such as many Forth implementations) to speed execution. The references to other support routines in each threaded support routine (such as a predefined word in Forth) are replaced by pointers to those routines; this produces a thread of execution and eliminates much of the overhead in parsing and interpretation of the references.

Three-Dimensional Model Computer simulation of a physical object in which length, width, and depth are real attributes; a model,

Three-Dimensional Model

with x-, y-, and z- axes, that can be rotated for viewing from different angles.

Throughput Measure of the data transfer rate through a complex communications system or of the data processing rate in a computer system.

Thumbwheel Wheel embedded in a case so that only a portion of the outside rim is revealed. When rolled with the thumb, the wheel can control an on-screen element such as a pointer or a cursor. Thumbwheels are used with three-dimensional joysticks and trackballs to control the depth aspect of the pointer or cursor.

Tick Regular, rapidly reoccurring signal emitted by a clocking circuit; also, the interrupt generated by this signal.

TIFF Acronym for **Tag Image File Format**.

TIGA Acronym for **Texas Instruments Graphics Architecture**.

Tiling In computer graphics programming, the process of filling adjacent blocks with a design or pattern without allowing any blocks to overlap. Tiling is used to cover defined areas of the screen with particular images. Multiple windows, for example, are tiled if they lie side by side on the screen; they are overlapped if one window partially covers another.

Time and Date Timekeeping and datekeeping functions maintained by the computer's operating system, used most visibly as a means of "stamping" files with the date and time of creation or last revision. In a computer such as an IBM PC/AT, one of the PS/2 series, or an Apple Macintosh, the time and date are kept by an internal, battery-powered, real-time clock, which continues running even when the machine is turned off. The system can check the clock to determine the correct time and calendar date when the computer is turned on.

Timer Register (high-speed memory circuit) or a special circuit, chip, or software routine contained in the computer system that is used to measure time intervals needed for such activities as speaker control, time-of-day display, and various system events. A timer is not the same as the system clock, although its pulses can be derived from the system clock frequency. Many systems, for example, include interrupt timers that interrupt the currently executing

Timer

program and give control to the operating system after a programmable period of time. This is sometimes how multitasking operating systems prevent any single application from consuming all of the processor's time.

Time-Sharing Use of a computer system by more than one individual at the same time. Time-sharing runs separate programs concurrently by interleaving portions of processing time allotted to each program (user). In this respect, it is similar to the multitasking capability that is gaining ascendancy among microcomputers. Time-sharing is generally associated with multiple users accessing larger computers and service organizations, whereas multitasking in functions related to microcomputers implies the performance of multiple tasks by a single user.

Timing Signals Any of several types of signals used to coordinate activities within a computer system; in particular, signals used to coordinate data-transfer operations.

TOF Acronym for **Top-Of-File**.

Toggle Electronic device with two states or a program option that can be turned on or off using the same action (such as a mouse click). Also refers to the ability to switch back and forth between two states; the Num Lock key on an IBM-style keyboard, for example, toggles the numeric keypad between numbers and cursor movement.

Tone In graphic arts, a particular tint of a color, also known as a shade or value. In audio, the sound or signal of a particular frequency.

Toner Powdered pigment used in office copiers and in laser, LED, and LCD printers. The toner adheres to an electrostatically charged drum; after the toner is applied to the paper in the image of the desired page, heat is applied to fuse the toner to the paper.

Toner Cartridge Disposable container that holds toner for a laser printer or other page printer. Some types of toner cartridge contain toner only; however, the most popular printer engines, such as those from Canon (used in the Hewlett-Packard LaserJet series), pack all expendables, including toner and the photosensitive drum, in a single cartridge. Cartridges that also contain the drum reduce the

Toner Cartridge

risk of accidentally touching an exposed drum and marring its surface. Toner cartridges are interchangeable among printers that use the same engine.

Top-Of-File Usually referred to as TOF. Beginning of a file; also, a symbol used by a program to mark the beginning of a file—the first character in the file or, in an indexed (ordered) database, the first indexed record. See also **beginning-of-file**.

Touch Pad Variety of graphics tablet that uses pressure sensors, rather than the electromagnetics used in more expensive high-resolution tablets, to track the position of a device on its surface. Each position on the tablet translates to a specific location on the screen; when pressure is applied to the tablet, the cursor jumps to the corresponding on-screen position. A low-resolution device, the touch pad is generally used with home computers. The best-known touch pad is the popular KoalaPad for home and educational computers.

Touch Screen Computer screen designed or modified to recognize the location of a touch on its surface. By touching the screen, the user can make a selection or move a cursor. The simplest type of touch screen is made up of a grid of sensing lines, which determine the location of a touch by matching vertical and horizontal contacts. Another, more accurate, type uses an electrically charged surface and sensors around the outer edges of the screen to detect the amount of electrical disruption and pinpoint exactly where contact has been made. A third type embeds infrared light-emitting diodes (LED) and sensors around the outer edges of the screen. These LEDs and sensors create an invisible infrared grid, which the user's finger interrupts, in front of the screen. Infrared touch screens are often used in "dirty" environments where contaminants could interfere with the operation of other types of touch screens.

The touch screen's popularity with personal-computer users has been limited because users must hold their hands in midair to point at the screen, which is prohibitively tiring over extended periods. Also, touch screens do not offer high resolution—the user is not able to touch only a specific point on the screen. Touch screens are, however, immensely popular in applications such as information kiosks and automatic teller machines because they offer pointing control without requiring any movable hardware and because touching the screen is intuitive.

Trace Ability to execute a program in such a way that the sequence of statements being executed can be observed. A simple trace can be implemented by putting numerous output statements in the program, each one writing out (to the screen, to a file, or to some other location) some identifying information and possibly some data values. Many debuggers provide a more sophisticated trace, displaying each statement as it is executed and possibly updating a list of values of variables and data structures.

Track One of numerous circular data storage areas on a floppy or hard disk, comparable to a groove on a record but concentric rather than spiral. A track is a magnetic ring slightly wider than a read/write head in a disk drive. A disk might have from 40 to 1024 or more concentric tracks on its surface. Tracks, composed of sectors, are recorded on a disk by an operating system during a disk format operation. On other storage media, such as tape, a track runs parallel to the edge of the medium.

Trackball Popular pointing device that can be roughly described as a mouse on its back. A trackball consists of a ball resting on two rollers at right angles to each other, which translate the ball's motion into vertical and horizontal movement on the screen. A trackball also typically has one or more buttons to initiate other actions. The only functional difference between a mechanical mouse and a trackball is in how the ball is moved. With a mouse, the ball is rolled by moving the entire unit over a desktop or other surface; with a trackball, the housing is stationary, and the ball is rolled with the hand. A trackball is useful for fine work because the user can exert fingertip control; a mouse is better for bold moves, such as those used in navigating within a graphical user interface. Another major advantage of a trackball is that it takes up little desktop surface.

Tracking Act of following a path. In data management, tracking means to follow the flow of information through a manual or an automated system. In data storage and retrieval, it means to follow and read from a recording channel on a disk or magnetic tape. In computer graphics, it means causing a displayed symbol, such as a pointer, to match on the screen the movements of a mouse or other pointing device.

Tractor Feed Method of feeding paper through a printer using pins mounted on rotating belts. The pins engage holes near the edges of

Tractor Feed

continuous-form paper and either push or pull the paper through. The term tractor feed is often used mistakenly as a synonym for pinfeed, which also uses small pins or sprockets.

Traffic Load carried by a communications link or channel.

Trailer Information Data that occupies several bytes at the tail end of a block (section) of transmitted data and often contains a checksum or other error-checking data useful for confirming the accuracy and status of the transmission.

Trailer Label Small block of information used in tape processing that marks the end of a file or the end of the tape and that can contain other information, such as the number of records in the file or files on the tape. Also used in reference to a label in communications data frames, or packets, that follows the data and might contain an end-of-message mark, a checksum, and some synchronization bits.

Train To teach someone to perform a particular task or job. Also used in reference to a sequence of items or events, such as a digital pulse train consisting of transmitted binary signals.

Transaction Activity within a computer system such as an entry of a customer order or an update of an inventory item. Transactions are usually associated with database management, order-entry, and other online systems. By definition, however, making a deletion or creating a file copy on a microcomputer could as easily be considered a transaction.

Transaction File File that contains the details of transactions, such as items and prices on invoices, and that is to be used to update a master database file. Transaction files are typical of transaction-based systems, such as those composed of online order-entry terminals connected to a main computer.

Transaction Processing A processional method in which transactions are executed immediately after they are received by the system.

Transceiver Device that can both transmit and receive signals; derived from transmitter/receiver. Transceivers are used for a variety of communications, among them telephones, citizens' band radio, and ship-to-shore or air-to-ground radio. On local area networks, a transceiver is the device that connects a computer to the network.

Transfer Movement of data from one location to another, or the passing of program control from one portion of code to another.

Transfer Rate Rate at which a circuit or a communications channel transfers information from source to destination, as over a network or to and from a disk drive. The transfer rate is measured in units of information per unit of time—bits per second or characters per second, for example—and can be measured either as a raw rate, which is the maximum transfer speed, or as an average rate, which includes gaps between blocks of data as part of the transmission time.

Transfer Statement Statement in a programming language that transfers the flow of execution to another location in the program.

Transfer Time Amount of time elapsed between the start of a data-transfer operation and its completion.

Transform Ability to change the appearance or format of data without altering its content, such as the ability to encode information according to predefined rules. In mathematics and computer graphics, transform means to alter the position, size, or nature of an object by moving it to another location (translation), making it larger or smaller (scaling), turning it (rotation), or changing its description from one type of coordinate system to another.

Transformer Device used to change the voltage of an alternating current signal or to change the impedance of an alternating current circuit. A transformer consists of two or more coils or windings of wire that is usually wrapped around a ferromagnetic core. The individual windings are not electrically connected to each other but are coupled by magnetic induction. As current flows (or more accurately, changes) in the input (primary) winding, a magnetic field is created. The flux lines of this field cut across the windings of the output (secondary) winding and induce a voltage there. If the secondary winding has more turns than the primary winding, the output voltage will be higher than the input voltage; if fewer, it will be less. Because a changing current is required in the primary winding to create a fluctuating magnetic field, transformers function only with alternating current.

Transistor

Transistor Solid-state circuit component, usually with three leads, that can serve many functions, including those of amplifier, switch, and oscillator. In the most common mode of operation, a relatively large current passing between two of the transistor's terminals (the emitter and the collector) is controlled by a much smaller current applied to the third terminal (the base). The current can be modulated, resulting in amplification of the waveform of the input signal. The current can also be turned on and off, providing a switching action. The transistor was invented at Bell Laboratories in the late l940s; it is a fundamental component of almost all modern electronics. References to transistors often mention bipolar transistors and field-effect transistors. In the former, the three terminals are called the base, emitter, and collector; in the later, the terminals are known as the gate, source, and drain.

Translate In programming, the ability to convert a program from one language to another; for example, to convert the source code of a program written in the C language to object code that represents the same instructions or a close approximation in machine language. Translation is performed by special programs such as compilers, assemblers, and interpreters.

In computer graphics, translate refers to the moving of an image in the "space" represented on the display, but without turning (rotating) the image.

Translator Program that translates one language or data format into another. Compilers, assemblers, and macro processors can all be thought of as translators.

Transmission Sending of information over a communications line or a circuit. Computer transmissions can take place in any of a number of ways: asynchronous (variable timing) or synchronous (exact timing); serial (bit by bit) or parallel (byte by byte; a group of bits at once); duplex or full-duplex (simultaneous two-way communication), half-duplex (two-way communication in one direction at a time), or simplex (one-way of communication only); or burst (intermittent transmission of blocks of information).

Transmitter Any circuit or electronic device designed to send electrically encoded data to another location.

Transparent Device, function, or part of a program that works so smoothly and easily that it is invisible to the user. The ability of one application to use files created by another, for example, is transparent if the user encounters no difficulty in opening, reading, or using the second program's files or doesn't even know the use is occurring.

In communications, transparent refers to a mode of transmission in which data can include any characters, including control characters, without the possibility of misinterpretation of the receiving station—such as early termination—because the data contains a character that the receiving device interprets as "end of transmission." Communications protocols allow for two methods of achieving transparency: character (byte) stuffing and bit stuffing. An extra byte bit is added to any data that could be misinterpreted as a control character; for example, a 0 (zero) might be inserted after five consecutive 1's of data.

Transpose To reverse, as in reversing the order of the letters u and o in house to correct the spelling of house, or transposing two wires in a circuit. In mathematics and spreadsheets, transpose means, in effect, to rotate a matrix (a rectangular array of numbers) about a diagonal axis.

Tree Data structure containing zero or more nodes linked together in a hierarchical fashion. The topmost node is called the root. The root can have zero or more child nodes, connected by edges (links); the root is the parent node to its children. Each child node can in turn have zero or more children of its own. Nodes sharing the same parent are called siblings. Every node in a tree has exactly one parent node (except for the root, which has none), and all nodes in the tree are descendants of the root node. These relationships ensure that there is always one and only one path from the root node to any other node in the tree.

Trigonometry Branch of mathematics dealing with arcs and angles, expressed in functions (such as sine and cosine) that show relationships; for example, between two sides of a right triangle or between two complementary angles. Trigonometric functions are used in such computer applications as spreadsheets and computer graphics programming.

Trojan Horse Destructive program disguised as a game, a utility, or an application. When run, a Trojan horse does something devious

Trojan Horse

to the computer system while appearing to do something useful. See also **virus, worm**.

Truncate To cut off the beginning or end of a series of characters or numbers; in particular, to eliminate one or more of the least significant (typically rightmost) digits. Programs such as spreadsheets often do this in order to fit a number into a smaller amount of memory or display space. Truncating as supported by a given program might or might not affect the value of a number. For example, if a spreadsheet truncates a number because a cell is too narrow to display it completely, the number probably remains intact in memory and on disk. Sometimes, however, the shortened but less precise version becomes the value used in later calculations. Note that truncation is not the same as rounding. In truncation, numbers are simply eliminated, whereas in rounding, the rightmost number remaining might be incremented to preserve accuracy.

TSR Acronym for **Terminate-and-Stay-Resident Program**.

Turnaround Time Elapsed time between submission of a job and return of the completed result. In communications, the time required to reverse the direction of transmission in half-duplex (one direction at a time) communication mode.

Turnkey System Finished system, complete with all necessary hardware and documentation and with software installed and ready to be used. Often, such a system is dedicated to a particular use; for example, a turnkey system for a dentist's office.

Tutorial Teaching aid designed to help people learn to use a product or procedure. In computer applications, a tutorial might be presented in either a book or a manual or as an interactive disk-based series of lessons provided with the program package. Lessons in any tutorial proceed from simple to complex, are usually short, and focus closely on a single topic. Disk-based tutorials use text and often striking graphics to provide on-screen explanations followed by questions and answers or hands-on practice sessions. Students progress at their own rate and can repeat lessons if desired; the tutorial might also track completed lessons so that intermittent users can take up where they left off.

Twisted-Pair Cable Cable made of two separately insulated strands of wire twisted together. One of the wires in the pair carries the sensitive signal, and the other wire is grounded. Twisted-pair cable is used to reduce signal interference introduced by a strong radio source such as a nearby cable. The grounded wire tends to absorb radio interference, thereby protecting the signal carried on the other wire.

Two-Dimensional Two measures, such as height and width; for example, a two-dimensional model drawn with reference to an x-axis and a y-axis, or a two-dimensional array of numbers placed in rows and columns.

Type Process of entering information by means of the keyboard. In programming, the nature of a variable; for example, integer, real number, text character, floating-point number, and so on. Data types in programs are declared by the programmer and determine the range of values a variable can take as well as the operations that can be performed on it.

In printing, this term is used variously to refer to the characters that make up printed text, to the design of a set of characters (typeface), or, less accurately, to the complete set of characters in a given size and style (font). See also **font, typeface**.

Type-Ahead Buffer Keyboard buffer where keystrokes are stored before being sent to the computer itself for use.

Type-Ahead Capability Ability of a computer program to gather incoming keystrokes in a temporary memory reservoir (buffer) before displaying them on the screen. This capability ensures that keystrokes are not lost if they are typed faster than the program can display them. Most application programs running on reasonably powerful computers have little difficulty keeping up with even a rapid typist. On a slow or overloaded machine, or during periods when the program is writing information on disk, however, a typist might well be a few words ahead of the display. At such times, the type-ahead capability is clearly seen as the computer plays catch-up with the keystrokes saved in the type-ahead buffer.

Typeface Specific, named design of a set of printed characters, such as Helvetica or Times Roman, that has a specified obliqueness (degree of slant) and stroke weight (thickness of line). A typeface is not the same as a font, which is a specific size of a specific typeface, such as 12-point Helvetica or 10-point Times Roman. Nor

Typeface

is a typeface the same as a typeface family, which is a group of related typefaces, such as Helvetica, Helvetica Bold, Helvetica Oblique, and Helvetica Bold Oblique.

Typematic Keyboard feature that repeats a keystroke when a key is held down longer than usual. Microcomputers register both key presses and key releases. IBM and Apple Macintosh machines are designed to wait for a short period after a key is pressed; if no "key up" signal is received (which would indicate that the key was no longer being held down), they repeat the keystroke and continue repeating at intervals until the key is released. The length of time before the first repeat and the intervals between repeat keystrokes can be controlled through the Control Panel on Macintosh systems and with the Mode command (beginning with version 4.0 of MS-DOS) on IBM and compatible computers.

Type Size Size of printed characters, usually measured in points. (A point is approximately 1/72 inch.) Thus, a line of text in 18-point type is twice the height of a line of text in 9-point type in the same typeface.

Type Style Either the obliqueness of a typeface or a reference to the overall design of a typeface or typeface family. In the first meaning, which is the correct technical usage, style specifies the degree of slant. In most typefaces, the style is either upright (normal) or slanted (italic), although backslanting is also possible. If slanted or backslanted, the style also defines the degree of slant. In the second meaning, style can refer to either the design of a specific typeface, such as Helvetica Oblique, or the design of a typeface family, such as Helvetica, Helvetica Bold, Helvetica Oblique, and Helvetica Bold Oblique. Because it is often difficult to determine which meaning is intended, the term is best avoided in this usage.

U

UART Acronym for **Universal Asynchronous Receiver-Transmitter**.

UCSD P-System Operating system and development environment developed by Kenneth Bowles at the University of California at San Diego. The system is based on a simulated, 16-bit, stack-oriented "pseudomachine" that was implemented in software. The development environment includes a text editor and compilers for several languages such as FORTRAN and Pascal. Programs written for the p-System are more portable than programs compiled to machine language.

Ultrafiche Form of microfiche with very high density. The image in ultrafiche is reduced at least 90 times from its original size.

Ultra-Large-Scale Integration Abbreviated ULSI. Density with which components (transistors and other elements) are packed onto an integrated circuit and to the fineness of the connections between them. ULSI is not precisely defined but is generally considered to apply to any integrated circuit having more than 100,000 components.

Ultralight Computer Lightweight portable computer.

Unary Mathematical operation with a single operand (object). In arithmetic, for example, the unary operator changes a positive number to a negative number.

Unary Operator Operator that takes only one operand; for example, unary minus (as in -2.5).

Unbundled Not included as part of a complete hardware/software package. A word processor is bundled if it is included in the price of a computer system and unbundled if it is purchased separately. The term unbundled particularly applies to a product that was previously bundled, as opposed to one that has always been sold separately.

Unconditional Branch Transfer of execution to another line of code that always occurs in a program because the transfer is not dependent on some condition being true or false. See also **branch**.

Undelete To restore deleted information, usually the last item deleted. An undelete is comparable to (and usually included as part

Undelete

of) an "undo" command; it is more restricted, however, in that undo reverses the last act, but undelete reverses only a deletion. Undelete usually refers only to excised text. When used in reference to file storage, undelete (or unerase) means to restore a file's storage information so that a deleted file becomes "undeleted." Because deletion typically involves nothing more than marking the file's storage space as available for new data, undeletion is generally easy, provided a good utility program for this purpose is used. If part of the file has been overwritten and replaced with new data, of course, undeletion is no longer possible.

Undercolor Separation In reference to the CMYK color model, this refers to the process of converting quantities of cyan, magenta, and yellow to equivalent gray levels, which are then printed in black ink. This produces grays that are clearer and sharper than those produced by mixing colored inks.

Underflow Condition in which a mathematical calculation produces a result too near to zero to be represented by the range of binary digits available to the computer for holding that value in the specified precision, such as the floating-point value 1.0E-9999 (1 preceded by a decimal point and 9998 zeros).

Underline Ability to format a selection of text so that the text is printed with a line slightly below it. Some word processing programs allow underlining with a single line, a double line, or a dotted line.

Underscore Underline character often used to emphasize a letter or a word; on nongraphics displays, generally used to indicate italic characters.

Undo Ability to reverse the last action; for example, to undo a deletion, thus restoring cut text to a document. Many application programs enable the user both to undo an action and to "undo" an undo.

Unerase Same as **undelete**.

Uninteruptible Power Supply Abbreviated UPS. Alternative source of power (usually a battery) that takes over the job of supplying power to a computer system when regular electrical power fails. A UPS usually supplies power only long enough to permit the orderly shutdown of the computer.

Union

Union In set theory, the smallest combination of two sets that contains all elements of both sets; for example, if set A contains 1, 2, 3, and 4 and set B contains 2, 4, 6, and 8, the union of both sets is 1, 2, 3, 4, 6, and 8. In logic, it refers to an inclusive OR operation. This means the result of any union of A and B is true (1) except when A and B are both false (0). In programming, union refers to a structure that can be used by different variables, which might or might not be of the same type (such as integer, character, or Boolean). In C, a union can reserve an area of memory that can legitimately hold any of several types of data representing different variables defined as "members" of the union; for example, the union might receive integer values from variable A and character values from variable B. Similarly, in Pascal, a union is a record that can have different components, each representing a different data type; for example, a record named "size" might have letter values (S,M,L) for a variant named "eggs" and numeric values (8, 16, 32) for variants named "meat." When used in reference to database management, this refers to a relational operator. Given two relations (tables), A and B, that are union-compatible (contain the same number of fields, with corresponding fields containing the same types of values), A UNION B builds a new relation containing those tuples (records) that appear either in A or B or in both.

Union Compatibility In database management, term implying that two relations (tables) are of the same order (have the same number of attributes) and that corresponding attributes are based on the same domain (set of acceptable values).

Unipolar Having one state. In electronics, this refers to a unipolar device or signal is one in which the same voltage polarity (positive or negative) is used to represent binary states—on/off or true/false. For example, 0 volts might represent false and -5 volts might represent true.

Unit Position "1's place" in a multiple-digit number; for example, the 3 in the number 123.

UNIVAC I First commercially available electronic computer, designed by J. Presper Eckert and John Mauchly, also the inventors of ENIAC (generally considered the first fully electronic computer). UNIVAC I was the first computer to handle both numeric and textual information. Control of their corporation, the Eckert-

UNIVAC I

Mauchly Computer Corporation, passed in 1951 to Remington Rand, who delivered the first machine to the U.S. Bureau of the Census in March 1951.

Universal Asynchronous Receiver-Transmitter Abbreviated UART. Module, usually composed of a single integrated circuit, that contains both the receiving and transmitting circuits required for asynchronous serial communication. Two computers, each equipped with a UART, can communicate over a simple wire connection. Since the operations of the sending and receiving units are not synchronized by a common clock signal, the data stream itself must contain information as to when packets of information (usually bytes) begin and end; such information is provided by the start and stop bits in the data stream. A UART is the most common type of circuit used in personal computer modems. Compare **Universal Synchronous Receiver-Transmitter**.

Universal Synchronous Receiver-Transmitter A module, usually composed of a single integrated circuit, that contains both the receiving and transmitting circuits required for synchronous serial communication. Synchronous serial communication differs from asynchronous communication in that the operations of the sending and receiving units are synchronized by a common clock line. Because of this synchrony. the receiving unit "knows" when the sending unit starts and stops a data packet; thus, start and stop information need not be encoded in the data stream. Synchronous communication requires two communication channels between sender and receiver. Compare **Universal Asynchronous Receiver-Transmitter**.

UNIX Multiuser, multitasking operating system originally developed by Ken Thompson and Dennis Ritchie at AT&T Bell Laboratories in 1969 for use on minicomputers. UNIX exists in various forms and implementations; among these are versions developed at the University of California at Berkeley (known as BSD releases) and versions released by AT&T, the most recent being AT&T System V. UNIX is considered a powerful operating system which, because it is written in the C language, is more portable and less machine-specific than other operating systems. UNIX is available in several related forms, including AIX, a version of UNIX adapted by IBM (to run on RISC-based

UNIX

workstations), A/UX (a graphical version for the Apple Macintosh), and Mach (a rewritten but essentially UNIX-compatible operating system for the NeXT computer).

Unmount To remove a disk or tape from active use. This term originated with the practice of mounting and unmounting reels of magnetic tape used for information storage with large computers.

Unpack To restore packed data to its original format.

Unpopulated Board Circuit board whose sockets are empty of memory and add-on boards.

Unset Making the value of a bit position equal to zero; the opposite of set, which means to make the value of a bit position equal to 1.

Up Functioning or ready for use; applied to computers, printers, communications lines on networks, and other such hardware.

Update To change a system or a data file to make it more current. Also refers to a new release of an existing software product. A software update usually adds relatively minor new features to a product or corrects errors (bugs) found after the program was released. Updates are generally indicated by small changes in software version numbers, as in incrementing version 4.01 to 4.02. Compare **release**.

Upgrade To change to a newer, usually more powerful version; for example, to upgrade a computer system with a faster and larger hard disk or to upgrade to a newer or more sophisticated version of a software product. Also refers to the new or enhanced version of a product. With hardware, especially in the case of one or more pieces intended to replace or supplement existing pieces, an upgrade is generally called an upgrade kit.

Uplink Transmission link from an earth station to a communications satellite.

Upload In communications, the process of transferring a copy of a file from a local computer to a remote computer by means of a modem or network. With a modem-based communications link, the process generally involves instructing the remote computer to prepare to receive the file on its disk and then wait for the transmission to begin.

Uppercase

Uppercase Capital letters, such as X, Y, Z, derived from the old typesetting practice of placing capitalized letters in the top (upper) case of a pair of type cases. Opposite of **lowercase**.

UPS Acronym for Uninterruptible Power Supply.

Uptime Amount or percentage of time a computer system or associated hardware is functioning and available for use. Opposite of **downtime**.

Upward Compatibility Computer products, especially software, designed to perform adequately with other products that are expected to become widely used in the foreseeable future. The use of standards and conventions makes upward compatibility easier to achieve.

Usability Ease and adaptability with which a product can be applied to the performance of the work for which it is designed. A high degree of usability implies ease of learning, flexibility, freedom from bugs, and good design that does not involve unnecessarily complicated procedures.

USENET Worldwide network of UNIX systems, with decentralized administration, used for electronic mail and transmission by special-interest discussion groups. It was originally implemented using UUCP (UNIX-to-UNIX Copy) software and telephone connections; that method of communication remains important, although more modern methods are also used.

User-Defined Data Type Data type defined in a program. User-defined data types are usually combinations of data types defined by the programming language being used and are often used to create data structures.

User-Defined Function Key Keyboard enhancer, programmable function key.

User-Friendly Easy to learn and easy to use.

User Group Group of people drawn together by interest in the same computer system or software. User groups, some of which are large and influential organizations, provide support for newcomers and a forum where members can exchange ideas and information.

User Interface

User Interface Portion of a program with which a user interacts. If the user enters commands at the keyboard and the program responds by operating in a specific manner, the program has a command-line interface. If commands to the program are typically given via menu selections, the program is said to have a menu-driven interface. Programs that graphically display information and require a pointing device for user interaction have graphical user interfaces.

User Name Name by which a person is known and addressed on a communications network.

User Profile Computer-based record maintained about an authorized user of a multiuser computer system. A user profile is needed for security and other reasons; it can contain such information as the person's access restrictions, mailbox location, type of terminal, and so on.

User State The least privileged of the modes in which a Motorola 60 x O microprocessor can operate. This is the mode in which application programs are run.

USRT Acronym for **Universal Synchronous Receiver-Transmitter**.

Utility Program, such as an editor or a debugger, designed to perform a particular function. Usually refers to software that solves narrowly focused problems or those related to computer system management.

Utility Program Program designed to perform maintenance work on the system or on system components; for example, a storage backup program, a disk and file recovery program, or a resource editor.

V

V2O, V30 Microprocessors from NEC that are slightly improved versions of the Intel 8088 and 8086, respectively. They use the same command sets as their Intel counterparts but use different microcodes (low-level instructions).

VAC Acronym for **Volts Alternating Current**.

Vacuum Tube Glass tube containing metal electrodes and grids designed to control electron flow, from which essentially all gas has been removed, creating a vacuum. Before the advent of semiconductors in the 1950s, vacuum tubes performed amplification and switching functions in electronic circuits. They are still used today in certain applications, such as those requiring very high power levels, and in cathode-ray tubes.

Validation Suite Set of tests designed to measure compliance to a standard, especially a standard definition of a programming language. For example, for a compiler to be an Ada compiler, it must successfully and correctly compile and run all the source-code programs in the Ada validation suite created by the U.S. Department of Defense.

Validity Checking Process of analyzing data to determine whether it conforms to certain predefined parameters of completeness and consistency. For example, a utility program could do a validity check on a disk to determine whether it contains any bad sectors, or a database program could perform a validity check on new records to be added to a database to ensure that each record has been encoded in a way compatible with the database.

Value In programming and applications, a quantity assigned to a variable, symbol, label, or other such element. For example, a value can be numeric, as in TOTAL = 3755, or it can be a text string, as in SHAPE = triangle.

Value-Added Reseller Company that acquires hardware and software in complete form and resells it to the public, adding value through user support, service, and so on.

Vaporware Sarcastic term for promised software that misses its announced release date, usually by a considerable length of time.

Variable In programming, a named storage location capable of

Variable

containing a certain type of data that can be modified during program execution. Most programming languages support the concept of variables.

Variable Expression Any expression containing at least one variable; hence, an expression that must be evaluated during program execution.

Variable-Length Field In reference to a record, a field whose length can vary depending on the data it contains.

Variable-Length Record Type of record that can vary in length because it contains fields of variable length, because it contains certain fields only under certain conditions, or for both reasons.

VDM Acronym for **Video Display Metafile**.

VDT Acronym for Video Display Tube; same as **Cathode-Ray Tube** (CRT).

VDU Acronym for Video Display Unit; a monitor.

Vector In mathematics and physics, a variable that has both distance and direction. In computer graphics, this refers to a line drawn in a certain direction from a starting point to an ending point, both of which are coordinates in a rectangular grid with horizontal (x) and vertical (y) axes. Vectors are used in drawing programs and similar applications that create graphical images as sets of lines, rather than as sets of dots (pixels) on the screen and on paper. In computer data structures, vector refers to a one-dimensional array—a set of items arranged in a single column or row.

Vector Display Cathode-Ray Tube (CRT) that allows the electron beam to be arbitrarily deflected based on x-coordinate and y-coordinate signals. For example, to draw a line on a vector display, the video adapter sends signals to the X and Y yokes electromagnets that control the direction of the electron beam in the two dimensions to move the electron beam over the path of the line; there is no background composed of scan lines, so the line drawn on the screen is not constructed of pixels. Vector displays are commonly used in oscilloscopes and DVST (direct view storage tube) displays. Compare **raster display**.

Vector Font Font in which the characters are drawn in arrangements of line segments rather than arrangements of curves

Vector Font

or bits. Vector fonts are used in CAD programs and other applications that are optimized for output to plotters rather than to printers that print in patterns of dots.

Vector Graphics Method of generating images that uses mathematical descriptions to determine the position, length, and direction in which lines are to be drawn. In vector graphics, objects are created as collections of lines, rather than as patterns of individual dots (pixels), as is the case with raster graphics.

Venn Diagram In mathematics, a diagram used to express the result of operations on sets (groups of objects). In a Venn diagram, all objects are considered to exist in a universe represented by a rectangle. Within this universe, individual sets are represented by circles. Relationships between sets are indicated by the positions of the circles: A circle within a circle means that all items in one set are contained within another, and overlapping circles mean that the items in the overlap belong to both sets.

Verify To ascertain either that a result is correct or that a procedure or sequence of operations has been performed.

Version Number Number assigned by a software developer to identify a particular program at a particular stage. Version numbers are used both before and after public release of a program, but the prerelease numbers have meaning only to those involved in development and testing. Usually version numbers include a decimal fraction. Successive public releases of a program, marking changes, updates, and bug fixes, have increasingly higher version numbers. Major changes in a program are usually marked by a significant change in version number, as from version .3 to version 4.0. Less significant changes, such as bug fixes, are indicated by smaller changes in the version number, as from 4.0 to 4.01 or 4.1.

Verso Left-hand page, always an even-numbered page.

Vertical Redundancy Check Error-checking method used to verify the accuracy of transmitted data. VRC generates an extra bit (parity bit) for each character transmitted. The parity bit determines whether the character (byte) contains an odd (for odd parity) or an even (for even parity) number of 1 bits. If its value does not correspond with the type of parity being used, the character is assumed to be incorrect.

VT-52, VT-100, VT-200

VT-52, VT-100, VT-200 Popular sets of control codes used in terminals originally manufactured by Digital Equipment Corporation. Appropriate software can enable a microcomputer to use these control codes to emulate such terminals in computer communications.

Vertical Retrace In raster-scan displays, the movement of the electron beam from the bottom right corner back to the top left corner of the screen after the beam has completed one sweep of the screen. The time required for the electron beam to move is called the vertical blanking interval because the beam is turned off as it moves from the bottom to the top of the screen.

Vertical Scrolling Movement up or down in a displayed document to bring other parts into view.

Vertical Sync Signal Part of a video signal to a raster display that denotes the end of the last scan line at the bottom of the display. The vertical sync signal moves the electron beam of the CRT to the beginning of the first scan line at the top of the display.

Very-High-Speed Integrated Circuit Abbreviated as VHSIC. An integrated circuit that performs operations, usually logic operations, at a very high rate of speed. The higher the speed of logic circuits, the greater the amount of information that can be processed in a specific amount of time.

Very-Large-Scale Integration Abbreviated as VLSI. Density with which components (transistors and other elements) are packed onto an integrated circuit; also refers to the fineness of the connections between them. VLSI is not precisely defined but is generally considered to range from 5000 to 50,000 components.

Vesicular Film Coating for optical-disc platters that permits the raising of small bumps on the surface instead of the pits used in standard CD-ROM discs for recording data. Bumps, unlike pits, can be flattened out to make an optical disc erasable and thus rewritable.

VGA Acronym for **Video Graphics Array**.

Video Visual (rather than the audio) component of a television signal. In computer use, video refers to the technology used to render text and graphical images on displays.

Video Adapter

Video Adapter Also referred to as a video controller. Electronic components required to generate a video signal that is sent to the video display through a cable. The video adapter is usually located either on the computer's main system board or on an expansion board, but it can also be part of a terminal.

Video Board Same as **video adapter**.

Video Buffer Memory on a video adapter used to store the data waiting to be shown on the video display. When the video adapter is in a character mode, this data takes the form of ASCII character codes and attribute codes. (The video buffer might also be used for storing character font definitions.) When the video adapter is in a graphics mode, one or more bits of data define each pixel. The number of bits used for each pixel determines the number of colors that can be simultaneously displayed.

Video Controller Another name for a video adapter.

Video Digitizer Device used in computer graphics that employs a video camera, rather than a scan head, to capture a video image, such as one from television or videotape, and store it in memory with the aid of a special-purpose circuit board. Video digitizers function like display adapters in reverse. A display adapter moves an image from memory to the display; a video digitizer records a displayed image and stores the information in memory in digital (bit) form. Most video digitizers can be attached to any video equipment that produces an RGB (red-green-blue) signal—the standard for video monitors, or an NTSC (National Television Standards Committee) signal—the standard for American television.

Videodisc Optical disc used to store video images and associated audio information.

Video Display Any device that is capable of showing text or graphics output from a computer but is not a hard-copy device (such as a printer).

Video Display Board Video adapter implemented on an expansion board rather than on the computer's main system board.

Video Display Card Same as a video display board.

Video Display Metafile Abbreviated VDM. Standard graphics

Video Display Metafile

format, now largely superseded by Computer Graphics Metafile (CCM), for exchanging bit-mapped images.

Video Display Page Portion of a computer's video buffer (memory reserved for the display) that holds one complete screen image. If the buffer is designed to hold more than one page, or frame, screen updates can be rapid because a program can be filling one unseen page at the same time it is displaying the contents of another. Switching from one page to another, known as page flipping, is a technique sometimes used by programmers to create animation sequences.

Video Display Tube Same as **Cathode-Ray Tube** (CRT).

Video Display Unit Computer monitor.

Video Graphics Array Seen mostly in its abbreviated form as VGA, a video adapter introduced by IBM in 1987. The VGA duplicates all the video modes of the EGA (Enhanced Graphics Adapter) and adds several modes, the most popular of which are two graphics modes: One supports 640 horizontal pixels by 480 pixels with 2 or 16 simultaneous colors from a table of 262,144 colors; the other supports 320 horizontal pixels by 200 vertical pixels with 256 colors chosen from a table of 262,144 colors.

Video Graphics Board Video adapter capable of generating appropriate video signals for displaying graphical images on a video screen.

Video Memory Memory located in the video card or video subsystem, from which the display image is created. In some cases, the video memory can be accessed only by the display hardware. Often, however, both the video processor and the central processing unit (CPU) have access to video memory, and images are produced as a result of the CPU modifying video memory. The video circuitry normally has priority over the processor when both attempt to read or write to a video memory location. As a result of this, updating video memory is often slower than accessing main memory.

Video Mode Manner in which a computer's display adapter and monitor present on-screen images. The most commonly encountered video modes, particularly on IBM PC and compatible computers, are text (character) mode and graphics mode. In text

Video Mode

mode, displayed characters include letters, numbers, and certain symbols but no graphical images created as dot-by-dot on-screen "drawings." In contrast, graphics mode produces all screen images—letters, numbers, icons, drawings, and so on—as patterns of pixels (dots) that are drawn one pixel at a time. Other video modes are also possible and are defined by number of colors, resolution, or a combination of the two. A number of such modes are defined for display adapters used on IBM PC and compatible computers. Among them are 40-column text mode, 80-column text mode, and various screen resolutions (such as 640 by 200 pixels) offering combinations of from 2 through 256 colors in graphics mode or text mode.

Video RAM Generally referred to as VRAM. Special type of dynamic RAM (DRAM) used in high-speed video applications. With conventional DRAM, both the processor and the video circuitry must access RAM by sharing the same control pins on the RAM chips. VRAM provides separate pins for the processor and the video circuitry. The processor accesses the VRAM in a manner almost identical to that for DRAM, but the video circuitry is provided with a special "back door" to the VRAM. This back door lets the video circuitry access the memory bit by bit (serially), which is more appropriate for transferring pixels to the screen than is the parallel access provided by conventional DRAM.

Video Signal Signal sent from a video adapter or another video source to a raster display to control the image on the display. The video signal may include horizontal and vertical synchronization signals as well as display (image) information.

View Ability to display information on a computer screen, as in "to view a file." Also refers to the display of data or a graphical image from a given perspective. When used in reference to relational database management systems, this refers to a logical table created through the specification of one or more relational operations (select, project, join, union, intersect, difference, divide) on one or more tables. In many systems, a view can be cataloged and subsequently manipulated as though it were a physical table. A view is equivalent to a divided relation in the relational model. In CAD programs, this refers to an image of a three-dimensional graphics model as it would be seen from a particular location or viewpoint.

Viewport

Viewport In computer graphics, a view into a document or a graphical image similar to the view seen through a window but usually differs in clipping (cutting off) portions of the document or image that lie outside the range of the viewport. A viewport is controlled by an application program and can cover all of the screen or only a portion.

Virtual Device or service perceived to be what it is not in actuality. The way in which a virtual device is actually presented or implemented is much different from the device or service the user experiences. For example, a computer user can treat a virtual disk as if it were a physical disk, but a virtual disk is actually a portion of the computer's memory that is used as if it were a disk. Another example is virtual memory, which is simulated by paging, caching, and disk storage.

Virtual Address In reference to a virtual memory system, the address the application uses to reference memory. The memory management unit (MMU) translates this address into a physical address before the memory is actually read or written.

Virtual Circuit Communications link that appears to be a direct connection between sender and receiver, although physically (as on a packet-switching network) the link can involve routing through more circuitous paths. A virtual circuit is conceptual rather than physical. The virtual circuit connects caller A with receiver B, but the physical circuit through which they actually communicate can run from A through stations D, E, and F before reaching B.

Virtual Device Device that can be referenced but that does not physically exist. A virtual memory-addressing scheme, for example, uses magnetic disk storage to simulate memory larger than that physically available.

Virtual Disk More commonly known as a RAM disk. **Random-Access Memory** (RAM) used as a disk drive. Since the computer does not need to wait for the hardware to respond, reading and writing to such a "disk" can vastly improve performance. However, because a virtual disk exists only in memory, its contents must be copied to a physical disk or the data will be lost. The exception is a virtual disk on battery-backed RAM; when the power to the computer is turned off, that battery ensures that the contents of RAM are left intact. Ultralight laptops often use battery-backed

Virtual Disk

RAM as a virtual disk because such storage consumes less power than a hard disk.

Virtual Image In computer graphics, an image that has been copied into a computer's memory but that is too large to be displayed all at one time on the screen. Because it exists in memory, a virtual image could theoretically be displayed if the screen were large enough. In actuality, however, methods such as scrolling and panning are used to bring unseen portions of a virtual image into view.

Virtual Machine Software that mimics the performance of a hardware device. For example, a software program that allows applications written for an Intel processor to be run on a Motorola chip interprets the Intel machine instructions, becoming a virtual Intel machine.

Virtual Memory Technique that allows an application to see the system as providing a large uniform primary memory, which in reality is smaller, more fragmented, and/or partially simulated by secondary storage such as a hard disk. Applications access memory through virtual addresses, which are translated (mapped) by special hardware onto physical addresses. Paging and segmentation are two common implementations of virtual memory.

Virtual Peripheral Peripheral that can be referenced but that does not physically exist. For example, an application might treat a serial port through which data is being transmitted as a printer, but the device receiving the data might be another computer instead.

Virtual Real Mode Feature of the Intel 80386 (SX and DX) and i486 microprocessors that allows them to emulate several 8086 environments (real-mode environments) simultaneously. The microprocessor provides a set of virtual registers and virtual memory space to each virtual 8086 environment. Controlling software, usually an operating system or operating environment, is required for the microprocessor to run in virtual real mode. The software controls the external interface—input and output, exception handling, and interrupts—to each virtual 8086 environment. An application program running in a virtual 8086 environment on the 8086 or i486 microprocessor is completely protected from other virtual 8086 environments in the system and behaves as if it had control of the entire system.

Virus Program that "infects" computer files by inserting in those files copies of itself. This is usually done in such a manner that the copies will be executed when the file is loaded into memory, allowing them to infect still other files, and so on. Viruses often have damaging side effects, sometimes intentionally, sometimes not. See also **Trojan horse**, **worm**.

Visible Page In computer graphics, the image that is being displayed on the screen; called a page because screen images are written into a computer's display memory in sections called pages, each of which contains one screen display.

Visual Interface Same as graphical user interface.

VLSI Acronym for **Very-Large-Scale Integration**

Voice Answer Back Abbreviated as VAB. Use of recorded messages by a computer in responding to commands or queries.

Voice Coil Wire coil device that moves a disk-drive actuator arm by acting like an electromagnet, the amount of movement depending on the amount of current. The device is so named because it is the same type used in a loudspeaker to vibrate the speaker cone, producing sound. Voice coils can move a read/write head more quickly than can a stepper motor.

Voice-Grade Channel Communications channel suited for carrying speech. On telephone lines, a voice-grade line carries frequencies in the range of about 300 through 3100 hertz, or cycles per second. Voice-grade channels are also used for the transmission of facsimile, analog, and digital information and can reliably transfer information at rates up to about 9600 bits per second.

Voice Input Vocal instructions translated by a computer into executable commands or that are input into documents via the use of a microphone and speech recognition technology.

Voice Output Speech synthesis.

Voice Recognition Speech recognition voice synthesis.

Volatile Memory Memory that loses its data when power is disconnected from the system. Random-access memory (RAM) is volatile; core memory is not. The term can also refer to memory used by a program that can change independently of the program.

Volatile Memory

For example, the memory might be shared by another program or by an interrupt service routine.

Volt Unit used to measure potential difference or electromotive force. One volt is defined as the potential across which 1 coulomb of charge will do 1 joule of work. However, it is more useful to think of 1 volt as the potential generated by 1 ampere of current flowing through 1 ohm of resistance. Voltage can be thought of as analogous to water pressure in a pipe.

Voltage Regulator Circuit or circuit component that maintains a constant output voltage despite variations in input voltage.

Volts Alternating Current Measure of the peak-to-peak voltage swing of an electrical signal. By its very nature, alternating current does not have constant voltage, as does direct current. A signal that altern.ates between +10 and -10 volts would measure as 20 VAC.

Volume Another name for a disk or tape that stores computer data. Each separate disk or tape is a volume, with a unique volume name or number. In some instances, a large hard disk can be divided into separate volumes, each of which is treated as a separate disk, even though all volumes reside physically in the same drive volume label. Also called volume name, a name for a disk or tape, usually assigned by the user when the disk or tape is formatted (initialized). The name can consist of letters, numbers, certain symbols, or a combination of these. MS-DOS systems, which seldom use disk names except in directory listings, refer to the names as volume labels. Apple Macintosh systems, which often refer to disks by name, refer to volume names rather than volume labels. Volume labels enable a system to identify a particular disk, using a unique identifier volume name volume serial number. The optional identifying volume number of a disk or tape MS-DOS (version 4 and higher) assigns a volume serial number (displayed at the beginning of a directory listing) to each disk it formats. The Apple Macintosh operating system assigns a similar type of identifying label, called a volume reference number, which programs can use in referring to disks. The volume serial (or reference) number is not the same as a volume label in MS-DOS or a volume name on the Macintosh.

Von Neumann Architecture Approach to computer design characteristic of most commonly used computers, including

Von Neumann Architecture

microcomputers, attributed to the work of Hungarian-born mathematician John von Neumann. The von Neumann architecture is synonymous with the concept of a stored program—one that can be permanently stored in a computer and, because of the way it is coded, can be manipulated or made self-modifying through machine-based instructions. The familiar concept of sequential processing, a one-instruction-at-a-time approach to operations, is characteristic of von Neumann architecture. Parallel architectures have evolved to bypass this sequential-instruction encumbrance, which has come to be known as the "von Neumann bottleneck."

VRC Acronym for **Vertical Redundancy Check**.

Wafer Thin, flat piece of semiconductor crystal used in the fabrication of integrated circuits. Various etching, doping, and layering techniques are used to create the circuit components on the surface of the wafer. Usually, multiple identical integrated circuits are formed on the surface of a single wafer, which is then cut into individual sections. Each integrated circuit then has leads attached and is packaged in a plastic, metal, or ceramic holder.

Wafer-Scale Integration Fabrication of integrated circuits (ICs) with such a large number of components that only a single IC can be fabricated from one wafer. Normally, multiple ICs are formed on a single wafer of semiconductor material, which is then cut apart. See also **wafer**.

Wait State Pause of one or more clock cycles during which a microprocessor waits for data from an input/output device or from memory. Wait states are most often used to control the speed at which the microprocessor receives data from random-access memory (RAM). A wait state is not noticeable to a human because it is based on the computer's internal clock, which runs at millions of cycles per second. Given the speed at which a computer operates, however, wait states are, like the speed of the clock itself, a factor that can slow system performance. In terms of system memory, "zero wait states" means that the microprocessor does not have to idle for one or more clock cycles while waiting for data from random-access memory.

Wand Any pen-shaped object, including a graphics tablet's stylus, but generally the pen-shaped scanning mechanism used with many bar code readers. The user passes the tip of the bar code wand, which contains optical scanning equipment, over a bar code to read it. Compare **stylus**; see also **optical scanner**.

Warm Boot System restart that does not involve turning on the power and waiting for the computer to check itself and its devices. A warm boot typically means loading or reloading the computer's operating system. On IBM and compatible personal computers, a warm boot is accomplished by using the Ctrl-Alt-Del key sequence. On Apple Macintosh computers, a warm boot can be requested with the Restart command on the special menu.

Warm Start Same as warm boot.

Watt Unit of electrical power equal to the expenditure of 1 joule of energy in 1 second. The power of a circuit is a function of the potential across the circuit and the current flowing through the circuit. A mall flashlight uses 1-2 watts, a car radio has an output of roughly 5 watts, and a toaster uses approximately 1200 watts. For low-power circuits, power is often measured in microwatts (0.000001 watt) or milliwatts (0.001 watt). In high-power circuits, units of kilowatts (1000 watts) or megawatts (1,000,000 watts) are often used.

Wave Any disturbance or change that has an oscillatory, periodic nature such as light or sound waves. In electronics, wave (or waveform) is used to refer to the time-amplitude profile of an electrical signal.

Waveform General term used to refer to the manner in which a wave's amplitude changes with time.

Wavelength Distance between successive peaks or troughs in a periodic signal that is propagated through space. Wavelength is symbolized by the Greek letter lambda. Wavelength is directly related to the frequency of the signal and the speed of propagation, and it can be calculated as speed divided by frequency. For electromagnetic radiation, wavelength in meters equals 300,000,000 meters per second divided by frequency in hertz. For sound traveling through air, wavelength in meters equals 335 meters per second divided by frequency in hertz.

Weak Typing Characteristic of a programming language, such as C, that allows the program to change the data type of a variable during program execution.

Weighted Code Data representation code in which each bit position has a specified inherent value, which might or might not be included in the interpretation of the data, depending on whether the bit is on or off.

Well-Behaved Program that performs properly, even when given extreme or erroneous input values. A program that obeys the rules of a particular programming environment can also be described as well-behaved. Operating-system vendors often promise that well-behaved programs will be upwardly compatible with future enhancements of the operating system.

"What-If" Evaluation

"What-If" Evaluation Kind of spreadsheet evaluation in which certain values in a spreadsheet are changed in order to reveal the effects of those changes; for example, trying different mortgage rates and terms to see the effect on monthly payments and on total interest paid over the life of the loan. Spreadsheet programs allow values in an existing model to be changed and recalculated with little effort, so these programs are considered ideal for the otherwise tedious task of preparing and comparing financial alternatives.

What You See Is What You Get Usually referred to as WSYWIG (pronounced "Wizzywig"). Display method that shows documents and graphic characters on the screen as they will appear when printed. WSYWIG attempts to duplicate print output as closely as possible but is not always exact. Some programs, for example, can display italics, boldface, and graphic characters on the screen, but only in a predetermined type size. Other programs, particularly on computers such as the Apple Macintosh, can display fonts, font sizes, and graphical images that closely approximate those in the printed version. Regardless of a program's capabilities, however, WYSIWYG requires display hardware capable of operating in graphics mode rather than in text mode.

Wheel Printer Same as **Daisy-Wheel Printer**.

Whetstone Benchmark test that attempts to measure the speed and efficiency with which a computer carries out floating-point operations. The result of the test is given in units called whetstones. The whetstone benchmark has fallen out of favor because it produces inconsistent results compared to other benchmarks such as the Dhrystone and the sieve of Eratosthenes.

White Noise Noise that contains components at all frequencies, at least within the frequency hand of interest. It is called "white" by analogy to white light, which contains light at all the visible frequencies. In the audible spectrum, white noise is a hiss or a roar, as when a television set is tuned to a channel over which no station is broadcasting.

Whole Number A number without a fractional component-error, such as an integer.

Wide Area Network Communications network that connects geographically separated areas.

Wildcard Character

Wildcard Character Keyboard character that can be used to represent one or many characters; usually encountered with operating systems as a means of specifying more than one file by name. In MS-DOS, for example, the question mark (?) wildcard character can be used to represent any single character; and the asterisk (*) can be used to represent any number of characters. Thus, ?OOK.DOC would refer to BOOK.DOC, COOK.DOC, LOOK.DOC, and so on; *.DOC would refer to any filename ending in the extension .DOC; and *.* could refer to any filename and any extension; in other words, to all files on the specified disk or in a specified directory.

Winchester Disk Early IBM name for a hard disk, derived from IBM's internal code name for the first hard disk that stored 30 megabytes (MB) and had a 30-millisecond access time, reminding its inventors of a Winchester .30-caliber rifle known as a "30-30."

Window In applications and graphical interfaces, a portion of the screen that can contain its own document or message. In window-based programs, the screen can be divided into several windows, each of which has its own boundaries and can contain a different document (or another view into the same document). Each window might also contain its own menu or other controls, and the user might be able to enlarge and shrink individual windows at will. In some programs, windows are opened side by side on the screen; in others, open windows can overlap one another.

In computer graphics, this refers to a software tool for scaling (sizing) an image to fit within certain boundaries on the display screen. In this sense, a window not only provides a working area for a program and a view into a particular portion of a document or graphical image but can also be used as a reference area for translating an image based on three-dimensional coordinates (points on x-, y-, and z- axes) into an appropriately scaled pattern of pixels (dots) on the screen.

Windowing Environment Operating system or shell that presents the user with specially delineated areas of the screen called windows. Each window can act independently, as if it were a virtual display device. Windowing environments typically allow windows to be resized and moved around on the display. The Apple Macintosh Finder, Microsoft Windows, and the OS/2 Presentation Manager are all examples of windowing environments.

Windowing Software

Windowing Software Programs such as Microsoft Windows that enable users to work with multiple on-screen windows. Windowing software acts as an intermediary between an operating system, such as MS-DOS, and application programs designed to work within a windowing environment.

Windows Common or "street" name for Microsoft Windows, a multitasking graphical user interface environment that runs on MS-DOS-based computers. Windows provides a standard interface based on drop-down menus, screen windows, and a pointing device such as a mouse. Programs must be specially designed to take advantage of these features.

Wire-Frame Model In computer graphics applications such as CAD programs, a display of a three-dimensional object composed of separate lines that resemble strands of wire joined to create a model.

Wire-Pin Printer Same as **Dot-Matrix Printer**.

Wire-Wrapped Circuits Circuits constructed on perforated boards using wire instead of the metal traces found on printed circuit boards. The bare ends of insulated wires are wrapped around the long pins of special wire-wrapped integrated circuit sockets. Wire-wrapped circuits are generally handmade one-of-a-kind devices used for prototyping and research in electrical engineering. Their advantage is that the wires are easily unwrapped and the pin-to-pin connections changed, permitting circuit designers to experiment with a circuit's design without having to lay out and etch a new printed circuit board. Compare **printed circuit board**.

Wizard An outstanding and creative programmer or a power user, someone adept at making computers perform their "magic."

Word Native unit of storage on a particular machine. Depending on the microprocessor, a word can be an 8-bit, a 16-bit, or a 32-bit quantity.

Word-Addressable Processor Processor that cannot access an individual byte of memory but can access only a larger unit. In order to perform operations on an individual byte, the processor must read and write memory in the larger unit. For example, a word-addressable processor might read a word (two bytes) from memory at one time, add a value to only one of the bytes, and then write the word back to memory.

Word Length

Word Length Standard data unit (8-bit, 16-bit, and 32-bit words are by far the most common) in a particular computer, representing both the largest amount of data that can be handled by the microprocessor in one operation and also, as a rule, the width of the main data bus (the hardware pathway that carries information from place to place within the computer).

Word Processing Procedure of entering text and editing with a word processor.

Word Processor Application program for manipulating text-based documents; the electronic equivalent of paper, pen, typewriter, eraser, and, most likely, dictionary and thesaurus. Word processors run the gamut from simple through complex, but all ease the tasks associated with editing documents (deleting, inserting, rewording, and so on). Depending on the program and the equipment in use, word processors can display documents either in text mode, using highlighting, underlining, or color to represent italics, boldfacing, and other such formatting, or in graphics mode, wherein formatting and, sometimes, a variety of fonts appear on the screen as they will on the printed page. All word processors offer at least limited facilities for document formatting, such as font changes, page layout, paragraph indention, and the like. Some word processors can also check spelling and find synonyms, incorporate graphics created with another program, correctly align mathematical formulas, create and print form letters, perform calculations, display documents in multiple on-screen windows, and enable users to record macros that simplify difficult or repetitive operations.

Wordwrap Ability of a word processing program to break lines of text automatically to stay within the page margins of a document. Line breaks created by wordwrap are known as soft returns.

Worksheet Data file created by and used with an electronic spreadsheet program. Also, an alternative name for a spreadsheet.

Workstation Combination of input, output, and computing hardware that can be used for work by an individual. More often, however, the term refers to a powerful stand-alone computer of the sort used in computer-aided design and other applications requiring a high-end, usually expensive, machine ($10,000 to $100,000) with considerable calculating or graphics capability. Sometimes,

Workstation

workstation also refers to a microcomputer or terminal connected to a network.

Worm Program that propagates itself across computers, usually by spawning copies of itself in each computer's memory. A worm might duplicate itself in one computer so often that it causes the computer to crash. Sometimes written in separate "segments," a worm is introduced surreptitiously into a host system either for "fun" or with intent to damage or destroy information. The term comes from a science-fiction novel and has generally been superseded by the term virus.

WORM Acronym for **Write Once, Read Many**.

Wrap Around Ability to continue movement, as with the cursor or a search operation, to the beginning or to a new starting point rather than stopping when the end of a series is reached. For example, the screen cursor normally wraps around to the first column of the next line rather than stopping when it reaches the last column of the current line. Likewise, a program starting a search or replace operation in the middle of a document might be instructed to wrap around to the beginning rather than stop when it reaches the end of the document.

Write Pertaining to the transfer of information either to a storage device, such as a disk, or to an output device, such as the monitor or a printer. Writing is the means by which a computer provides the results of processing. Writing is almost synonymous with outputting, except that writing implies outputting to a medium such as a disk drive. The opposite is reading or the gathering of information from storage or an input device such as the keyboard. Write is used as either a noun or a verb. For example, a disk write means that information is transferred from memory to storage on disk. A computer can also be said to write to the screen when it displays information on the monitor.

Write Error Error encountered while a computer is in the process of transferring information from memory to storage or to another output device. In contrast, a read error is a problem in correctly gathering information from storage or an input device.

Write Mode In computer operations, the state in which a program can write (record) information in a file. In write mode, the program

Write Mode

is permitted to make changes to existing information. In contrast, read-only mode allows the program (and thereby the user) to read but not to change an existing file. In computer graphics, write mode refers to the method by which pixel values are set for display on the screen.

WORM Acronym for Write Once, Read Many, a type of optical disc that can be read and reread but cannot be altered after it has been recorded. Because they are high-capacity storage devices that cannot be erased and rerecorded, WORMs are suited to storing archives and other large bodies of unchanging information.

Write Protect Ability to prevent the writing (recording) of information, usually on a disk. Write protection can be applied either to a floppy disk or to an individual file on a floppy or hard disk. Covering the write-protect notch on a 5.25-inch floppy disk enables programs to read, but not record on, the disk. Moving the slide to open the "notch" on a 3.5-inch disk provides the same protection. Individual files can also be made "read-only" through software commands; read-only files, like protected disks, can be read but not written to.

Write-Protect Notch Small opening in the jacket of a floppy or microfloppy disk that can be used to make the disk unwritable. On a 5.25-inch floppy disk, the write-protect notch is a rectangular hole on the edge of the disk. When this notch is covered (usually with one of the sticky write-protect tabs included with boxes of disks), a computer can read from the disk but cannot record new information on it. On the 3.5-inch microfloppy disks enclosed in plastic shells, the write-protect "notch" (also called a write-protect tab) is an opening in a corner. When the sliding tab in this opening is moved to uncover a small hole, the disk is "locked" and cannot be written to. The disk drive will refuse any requests by the computer to write on the microfloppy-disk until the user covers the write-protect notch.

WYSIWYG Acronym for **What You See Is What You Get**.

X.25 Recommendation published by the CCITT international communications standards organization that defines the connection between a terminal and a packet-switching network. A packet-switching network routes information in units (packets) whose contents and format are controlled by standards such as those defined in the X.25 recommendation. X.25 incorporates three definitions: the electrical connection between the terminal and the network, the transmission or link-access protocol, and the implementation of virtual circuits between network users. Taken together, these definitions specify a synchronous, full-duplex terminal-to-network connection. Packets transmitted in such a network can contain either data or control commands. Packet format, error control, and other features are equivalent to portions of the HDLC (High-level Data Link Control) protocol defined by the International Organization for Standardization (ISO). X.25 standards are related to the lowest three levels: the physical, data-link, and network layers of the ISO/OSI (Open Systems Interconnection) model.

X-Axis Horizontal reference line on a grid, chart, or graph that has horizontal and vertical dimensions.

XCMD Abbreviation for External Command. An external code resource used in HyperCard, a hypermedia program developed for the Apple Macintosh system. Developers can program XCMDs to perform a task not available in HyperCard, thus extending the features of the product.

XENIX Version of the UNIX system that was originally adapted by Microsoft for Intel-based personal computers. Although it has been sold by many vendors, including Microsoft, Intel, and the Santa Cruz Operation (SCO), it has become principally identified with SCO.

Xerox PARC Acronym for Xerox Palo Alto Research Center, the site of significant research in computer-related areas from the 1970s to the present. Among the concepts pioneered at Xerox PARC were the mouse and windows, both aspects of a graphical interface, and Smalltalk, an early object-oriented programming language.

XFCN Abbreviation referring to external function. An XFCN is an external code resource that returns a value after it has completed executing. XFCNs are used in HyperCard, a hypermedia program developed for the Apple Macintosh system. Developers can program XFCNs to perform tasks not available in HyperCard, thus extending the features of the product.

X-Height In typography, the height of the lowercase letter x in a particular font. The x-height thus represents the height of the body of a lowercase letter, excluding ascenders (such as the top of the letter b) and descenders (such as the tail on the letter g).

Xmodem File-transfer protocol used in asynchronous communications. Developed in 1977 by Ward Christensen, Xmodem is widely available as public-domain software and in numerous communications programs. Xmodem transfers information in blocks of 128 bytes. It assigns each transmitted frame a sequential block number, which is used to report errors or duplications in transmission. A 1-byte checksum (sum of the data bytes) is included in each block to check for errors in transmitted data.

Xmodem 1K Version of the Xmodem file-transfer protocol designed for larger, longer-distance file transfers. Xmodem 1K transmits information in 1-kilobyte (1024-byte) blocks and uses a more reliable form of error checking.

Xmodem-CRC Enhanced version of the Xmodem file-transfer protocol that incorporates a 2-byte cyclical redundancy check to detect transmission errors.

XMS Acronym for Extended Memory Specification.

XON/XOFF Asynchronous communications protocol in which the receiving device or computer uses special characters to control the flow of data from the transmitting device or computer. When the receiving computer cannot continue to receive data, as when its buffer is full, it transmits an XOFF control character that tells the sender to stop transmitting; when transmission can resume, the computer signals the sender with an XON character. This protocol is also referred to as software handshaking.

XT Keyboard Keyboard used on PC/XT computer systems.

X Windows Standardized set of display-handling routines, developed at MIT for UNIX workstations, that allow the creation of hardware-independent graphical user interfaces.

X-Y Matrix

X-Y Matrix Arrangement of rows and columns with a horizontal (x) axis and a vertical (y) axis.

X-Y-Z Coordinate System Three-dimensional system of Cartesian coordinates that includes a third (z) axis running perpendicular to the horizontal (x) and vertical (y) axes. The x-y-z coordinate system is used in computer graphics for creating models with length, breadth, and depth and for moving models in three-dimensional space.

Y-Axis Vertical reference line on a grid, chart, or graph that has horizontal and vertical dimensions.

Ymodem Variation of the Xmodem file-transfer protocol that includes the following enhancements: the ability to transfer information in 1-kilobyte (1024-byte) blocks; the ability to send multiple files (batch-file transmission); cyclical redundancy checking; and the ability to abort transfer by transmitting two CAN (cancel) characters in a row.

Yoke Also known as deflection coils, the part of a CRT (cathode-ray tube) that deflects the electron beam, causing it to strike a specific area on the screen.

Z

Z80 8-bit microprocessor from Zilog, a company founded by former Intel engineers. The Z80 has a 16-bit address bus, yielding 64 kilobytes of addressable memory, and an 8-bit data bus. A descendant of the Intel 8080, it was the favorite processor in the days of the CP/M operating system. One of the most popular computers of the day, the Radio Shack TRS-80, is based on this chip.

Z8000 16-bit microprocessor from Zilog, descended from the popular Z80.

Zap To erase permanently; for example, to remove a file without hope of retrieval. Also, to damage a device, usually by discharging static electricity through it.

Z-Axis Third axis in a three-dimensional coordinate system, used in computer graphics to represent depth.

Zero Arithmetical symbol (0) representing no magnitude. Also refers to the process of filling or replacing with zeros; for example, to zero a specified portion of memory, a field, or some other limited structure.

Zero Divide Division operation in which the divisor is zero. In mathematics, division by zero produces an indeterminate result, impossible to calculate. Consequently, division by zero is not allowed in a program and is considered a bug.

Zero Flag Flag (bit) in a microprocessor that is set (turned on), typically in a flag register, when the result of an operation is zero.

Zero Out Ability to set a variable value or series of bits to zero.

Zero suppression Elimination of leading (nonsignificant) zeros in a number. For example, zero suppression would truncate 000123.456 to 123.456.

Zero Wait State Fast enough to respond to the processor without requiring wait states; applied to RAM memory. Occasionally a system is advertised as "90 percent zero wait state" or something similar; this means that a technique such as caching or interleaving has been used and that zero wait state accesses occur some percentage of the time but not always.

Zmodem

Zmodem Enhancement of the Xmodem file-transfer protocol that handles larger data transfers with fewer errors. Zmodem includes a feature called checkpoint restart, which resumes transmission at the point of interruption, rather than at the beginning, if the communications link is broken during data transfer.

Zone In a **local area network**, such as AppleTalk, a subgroup of users within a larger group of interconnected networks. In Apple Macintosh programming, used in reference to the heap—the portion of memory allocated and reallocated by the Memory Manager program as memory is requested and released by applications and by other parts of the operating system

Zooming Enlarging a selected window or portion of a graphic image to fill the screen. Zooming is a feature of drawing programs that allow the user to select a small part of a graphic, zoom the image, and make changes to the enlarged portion at a finer level of detail.

SYMBOLS

* Asterisk, used as wildcard.

. "Star-dot-star," a wildcard that includes everything in a directory.

? Question mark, used as a wildcard.

3-D Graphic Any graphical image that depicts one or more objects in three dimensions—height, width, and depth. A 3-D graphic is rendered on a two-dimensional medium; the third dimension, depth, is indicated by means of perspective and by techniques such as shading or gradient use of color.

7-Track Tape storage scheme that places data on seven separate parallel tracks on 1/2-inch reel-to-reel magnetic tape. This is an old recording format used with computers that transfer data G bits at a time. Data is recorded as G data bits and 1 parity bit. Some personal computers now use the 9-track tape storage scheme.

8-Bit, 16-Bit, 32-Bit Designation that describes some new microcomputer channel designs, such as the IBM Micro Channel Architecture, which includes one or more 32-bit data buses with additional 16-bit and 8-bit data lines.

8-Bit Machine Computer that works with information in groups of 8 bits (binary digits) at a time. A description of a computer as an 8-bit machine can refer either to the word size (basic working unit) of its microprocessor or, more commonly, to the number of bits transferred along the computer's data bus (path along which information travels to and from the microprocessor) at a time. An 8-bit microprocessor thus has a word size of 8 bits, or 1 byte; an 8-bit data bus has 8 data lines, so it ferries information through the system in sets of 8 bits at a time. The Apple IIe is an 8-bit machine in terms of both the word size of its microprocessor and the size of the data bus. The IBM PC, PC/XT, and similar computers based on the Intel 8088 microprocessor work with a 16-bit word size but use an 8-bit data bus. For this reason, they are sometimes considered one step above 8-bit machines and one step below 16-bit machines. However, such machines are generally called 8-bit machines because the size of the data bus limits the machine's overall speed.

9-Track Tape storage scheme that places data on nine separate parallel tracks on 1/2-inch reel-to-reel magnetic tape. This format records in parallel the 8 data bits of a byte and 1 parity bit.

16-Bit Machine Computer that works with information in groups of 16 bits (binary digits) at a time. A description of a computer as a 16-bit machine can refer either to the word size (basic working unit) of its microprocessor or, more commonly, to the number of bits transferred along the computer's data bus (data path along which information travels to and from the microprocessor) at a time. A 16-bit microprocessor thus has a word size of 16 bits, or 2 bytes; a 16-bit data bus has 16 data lines, allowing it to ferry information through the system in sets of 16 bits at a time. The IBM PC/AT and similar models based on the Intel 80286 microprocessor are 16-bit machines, in terms of both the word size of the microprocessor and the size of the data bus. The Apple Macintosh Plus and Macintosh SE have a 32-bit microprocessor (the Motorola CG8000) but a 16-bit data bus and are generally considered 16-bit machines.

32-Bit Machine Computer that works with information in groups of 32 bits (binary digits) at a time. A description of a computer as a 32-bit machine can refer either to the word size (basic working unit) of its microprocessor or, more commonly, to the number of bits transferred along the computer's data bus (data path along which information travels to and from the microprocessor) at a time. A 32-bit microprocessor thus has a word size of 32 bits, or 4 bytes; a 32-bit data bus has 32 data lines, so it ferries information through the system in sets of 32 bits at a time. The Apple Macintosh II is a 32-bit machine, in terms of both the word size of its microprocessor and the size of the data bus, as are the IBM PS/2 Model 80 and similar models based on the Intel 80386 microprocessor.

101-Key Keyboard Enhanced keyboard.

8080 Intel microprocessor with 8-bit addressing and an 8-bit data bus, introduced in 1974. One of the first chips suitable to serve as the base of a personal computer, the 8080 influenced the design of the Z80, the favorite microprocessor in the era of the CP/M operating system. It was also an ancestor of the entire 80x86 line of microprocessors that has so far been the backbone of the IBM-compatible world.

8086 Intel microprocessor introduced in 1978, a direct descendant of the 8080, but with 16-bit registers and 20-bit addressing,

8086

allowing control over a full megabyte of memory. It is available in speeds of 4.77 MHz, 8 MHz, and 10 MHz. An 8-MHz 8086 is used in the IBM PS/2 models 25 and 30.

8087 Math, or floating-point, coprocessor from Intel for use with the 8086/8088 and 80186/80188 microprocessors. Available in speeds of 5 MHz, 8 MHz, and 10 MHz, the 8087, if supported by the application software, can dramatically improve system performance by offering arithmetic, trigonometric., exponential, and logarithmic instructions not offered in the 8086/8088 and 80l86/80188 instruction sets. If used, these additional instructions are carried out by the 8087, freeing the main microprocessor to perform other tasks. The 8087 is capable of working with 16-, 32-, and 64-bit integers; 32-, 64-, and 80-bit floating-point numbers; and 18-digit BCD (binary coded decimal) operands It conforms to the proposed IEEE 754 standard for binary floating-point arithmetic.

8088 Microprocessor released by Intel Corporation in 1978; used in computers such as the IBM PC, PC/XT: Portable PC, PCjr, and compatible models. It is available in speeds of 4.77 MHz and 8 MHz. A 14-bit microprocessor, the 8088 is capable of manipulating 16 bits of data at a time and can access 1 megabyte of memory. In these respects, it is identical to the 8086 used in IBM PS/2 Models 25 and 30 and in IBM compatibles. The only difference between the two microprocessors is that the 8088 transfers information 8 bits at a time (through an 8-bit data bus), whereas the 8086 does so 16 bits at a time (through a 16-bit data bus).

80286 Also referred to as a 286, a 16-bit microprocessor from Intel, introduced in 1982 and included in the IBM PC/AT and compatible computers in 1984. The 80286 has 16-bit registers, transfers information over the data bus 16 bits at a time, and uses 24 bits of address memory locations. The 80286 operates in two modes, real (which is compatible with MS-DOS and the limits of the 8086 and 8088 chips) and protected (which increases the microprocessor's functionality). Real mode limits the amount of memory the microprocessor can address to 1 megabyte; in protected mode, however, the 80286 can directly access 16 megabytes of memory. In addition, an 80286 in protected mode protects the operating system from ill-behaved applications that normally could halt (or "crash") a system with a nonprotected microprocessor, such as the 80286 in real mode or the 8088.

80287 Math, or floating-point, coprocessor from Intel for use with the 80286 family of microprocessors. Available in speeds of 6 MHz, 8 MHz, 10 MHz, and 12 MHz, the 80287, if supported by the application software, can dramatically improve system performance by offering arithmetic, trigonometric, exponential, and logarithmic instructions not offered in the 80286 instruction set. If used, these additional instructions are carried out by the 80287, freeing the 80286 to perform other tasks. The 80287 is capable of working with 32- and 24-bit integers; 32-, 64-, and 80-bit floating-point numbers and 18-digit BCD (binary-coded decimal) operands. It conforms to the proposed IEEE 754 standard for binary floating-point arithmetic. Because the 80287 conforms to the 80286 memory management and protection schemes, it can be used in both the real and protected modes of the 80286. Also, if the computer manufacturer implemented support for it in the motherboard design, the 80287 can be used in a system with an 8086 microprocessor.

80386DX Also referred to as the 80386, 386, and 386DX, a 32-bit microprocessor from Intel, introduced in 1985 and used in IBM and compatible microcomputers such as the PS/2 Model 80. The 80386 is a full 32-bit microprocessor, meaning that it has 32-bit registers, it can transfer information over its data bus 32 bits at a time, and it can use 32 bits in addressing memory. Like the earlier 80286, the 80386 operates in two modes; real (which is compatible with MS-DOS and the limits of the 8086 and 8088 chips) and protected (which increases the microprocessor's functionality and protects the operating system from halting because of an inadvertent application program error. Real mode limits the amount of memory the microprocessor can address to 1 megabyte; in protected mode, however, the total amount of memory that the 80386 can address directly is 4 gigabytes (roughly 4 billion bytes). The 80386 also includes a virtual 8086 mode, which allows operating systems to effectively divide the 80386DX into several 8086 microprocessors each having its own 1-megabyte space, allowing each 8086 to run its own program.

80386SX Also referred to as the 386SX, a microprocessor from Intel, introduced in1988 as a low-cost alternative to the 80386DX. The 80386SX is basically an 80386DX processor limited by a 16-bit data bus. That 16-bit design allows 80386SX systems to be configured from less expensive AT-class parts, resulting in a much lower total system price. The 80386SX offers improved

80386SX

performance over the 80286 and access to software designed for the 8038DX. The 8086SX also offers 80386DX features such as multitasking and virtual 8086 mode.

ABBREVIATIONS

AC Alternating Current

ACK Acknowledge

ADC Analog-to-Digital Converter

ADP Automatic Data Processing

AI Artificial Intelligence

ALGOL Algorithmic Language

AM Amplitude Modulation

ANSI American National Standards Institute

API Application Program Interface

APL A Programming Language

APPC Advanced Program-to-Program Communication

ASCII American Standard Code for Information Interchange

AUX Auxiliary

B Byte

BAK Backup file

BAT Batch

BIOS Advanced Basic Input/Output System

CAD Computer-Aided Design

CAE Computer-Aided Engineering

CAL Computer-Assisted Learning

CAM Computer-Aided Manufacturing

CAT Computer-Aided Testing

CBL Computer-Based Learning

CCD Charge-Coupled Device

CCITT

CCITT Comité Consultatif Interationale de Telegraphie et Telephonie (Swiss Organization)

CD Carrier Detect; Compact Disc (CD-ROM)

CGA Computer Graphics Adapter

CGI Computer Graphics Interface

CGM Computer Graphics Metafile

CIM Computer-Integrated Manufacturing

COM Communications

CON Console

CPM Critical Path Method

CPS Characters Per Second

CPU Central Processing Unit

CR Carriage Return

CRC Cyclical Redundancy Check

CRT Cathode-Ray Tube

CTL Control

CTRL Control

DAC Digital-to-Analog Converter

DAT Digital Audio Tape

dB Decibel

DB Database

DC Direct Current

DCD Data Carrier Detect

DCE Data Communications Equipment

DDE Dynamic Data Exchange

DDL Data Definition Language

DIA Document Interchange Architecture

DIP Dual In-line Package

DMA Direct Memory Access

DOS Disk Operating System

DP Data Processing

DPI Dots Per Inch

DRAM Dynamic Random-Access Memory

DSP Digital Signal Processor

DSR Data Set Ready

DTE Data Terminal Equipment

DXF Drawing Interchange Format

EAROM Electrically Alterable Read-Only Memory

EBCDIC Extended Binary Coded Decimal Interchange Code

EDI Electronic Data Interchange

EDP Electronic Data Processing

EEMS Enhanced Expanded Memory Specification

EEPROM Electrically Erasable Programmable Read-Only Memory

EGA Enhanced Graphics Adapter

E-Mail Electronic Mail

EMM Expanded Memory Manager

EMS Extended Memory Specification

EOF End Of File

EOT End Of Transmission

EPROM Erasable Programmable Read-Only Memory

EPS Encapsulated PostScript

ESC

ESC Escape

ESDI Enhanced Small Device Interface

E-Time Execution Time

.EXE Executable

FAT File-Allocation Table

FAX Facsimile

FCB File Control Block

FCC Federal Communications Commission

FEP Front-End Processor

FF Form Feed

FLOP Floating Point Operation

FM Frequency Modulation

FPD Full-Page Display

FTAM File Transfer Access and Management

Gig Gigabyte

GPIB General-Purpose Interface Bus

GUI Graphical User Interface

HGC Hercules Graphics Card

Hi-Res High Resolution

HLS Hue, Lightness, Saturation

HPFS High-Performance File System

HPGL Hewlett-Packard Graphics Language

HPIB Hewlett-Packard Interface Bus

HSB Hue, Saturation, Brightness

HSV Hue, Saturation, Value

IBM International Business Machines

IC Integrated Circuit

IDE Integrated Device Electronics

IEEE Institute of Electrical and Electronics Engineers

IFIP International Federation of Information Processing

INS Key Insert Key

I/O Input/Output

IPL Initial Program Load

ISA Industry Standard Architecture

ISAM Indexed Sequential Access Method

ISO International Organization for Standardization

I-Time Instruction Time

K Kilobyte

KB Kilobyte

kHZ Kilohertz

KWIC Key Word In Context

LCC Leaderless Chip Carrier

LCD Liquid Crystal Display

LED Light-Emitting Diode

LF Line Feed

LLC Logical Link Control

LRC Longitudinal Redundancy Check

LSB Least Significant Bit

LSD Least Significant Digit

LSI Large-Scale Integration

MAC Media Access Control

Meg Megabyte

MFM

MFM Modified Frequency Modulation

MHz Megahertz

MIDI Musical Instrument Digital Interface

MIPS Millions of Instructions Per Second

MIS Management Information Service

MMU Memory Management Unit

MOS Metal-Oxide Semiconductor

ms Millisecond

MSB Most Significant Bit

MSD Most Significant Digit

MTBF Mean Time Between Failures

NAK Negative Acknowledge

NDR Nondestructive Readout

NL New Line

NLQ Near-Letter-Quality

NOP No Operation Instruction

NRZ Nonreturn to Zero

ns Nanosecond

NTSC National Television System Committee

NUM Number

OCR Optical Character Recognition

OEM Original Equipment Manufacturer

OOP Object-Oriented Program

OS Operating System

PAM Pulse Amplitude Modulation

PC Personal Computer

PCB Printed Circuit Board

PCL Printer Control Language

PCM Pulse Code Modulation

PDL Page Description Language

PGA Pin Grid Array

PgDn Page Down

PgUp Page Up

PLA Programmable Logic Array

PLCC Plastic Leaderless Chip Carrier

PMS Pantone Matching System

POS Point Of Sale

POST Power On Self-Test

POT Potentiometer

PPM Pages Per Minute

PRN Printer

PROM Programmable Read-Only Memory

psec Picosecond

QAM Quadrature Amplitude Modulation

QBE Query By Example

RAM Random-Access memory

REM Remark

RF Radio Frequency

RGB Red-Green-Blue

RIP Raster Image Processor

RISC Reduced Instruction Set Computing

RLL Run-Length Limited Encoding

RO

RO Read Only

RTF Rich Text Format

RTS Request To Send

R/W Read/Write

RXD Receive Data

RZ Return to Zero

SAA Systems Application Architecture

SCR Silicon-Controlled Rectifier

SCSI Small Computer System Interface

SDLC Synchronous Data Link Control

SIP Single In-line Package

SLSI Super-Large-Scale Integration

SMT Surface-Mount Technology

SNA Systems Network Architecture

SNOBOL String-Oriented Symbolic Language

SYN Synchronizing

TB Terabyte

TCM Trellis-Coded Modulation

TIFF Tag Image File Format

TIGA Texas Instruments Graphics Architecture

TSR Terminate-and-Stay-Resident

TTL Transistor-Transistor Logic

TTY Teletypewriter

TXD Transmit Data

UART Universal Asynchronous Receiver-Transmitter

ULSI Ultra-Large-Scale Integration

UPS Uninteruptible Power Supply

VAC Volts Alternating Current

VAN Value-Added Network

VAR Value-Added Reseller

VDM Video Display Metafile

VDT Video Display Terminal

VDU Video Display Unit

VGA Video Graphics Array

VHSIC Very High Speed Integrated Circuit

VRAM Video Random-Access Memory

VRC Vertical Redundancy Check

WAN Wide-Area Network

WP Word Processing

WYSIWYG What You See Is What You Get

XCMD External Command

XMS Extended Memory Specxification

XMT Transmit

NOTES

NOTES

NOTES

NOTES

NOTES

NOTES

NOTES

NOTES

NOTES

NOTES

NOTES

NOTES

NOTES

NOTES

NOTES

NOTES

NOTES

NOTES

NOTES